Absolute Beginner's Guide to Databases

que®

201 West 103rd Street,
Indianapolis, Indiana 46290

Absolute Beginner's Guide to Databases

International Standard Book Number: 0-7897-2569-X

Library of Congress Catalog Card Number: 2001098154

Printed in the United States of America

First Printing: March 2002

05   04   03   02   4   3   2

Trademarks

All terms mentioned in this book that are known to be trademarks or service marks have been appropriately capitalized. Que cannot attest to the accuracy of this information. Use of a term in this book should not be regarded as affecting the validity of any trademark or service mark.

Warning and Disclaimer

Every effort has been made to make this book as complete and as accurate as possible, but no warranty or fitness is implied. The information provided is on an "as is" basis. The author and the publisher shall have neither liability nor responsibility to any person or entity with respect to any loss or damages arising from the information contained in this book.

Associate Publisher
Dean Miller

Acquisitions Editor
Jenny Watson

Development Editor
Maureen A. McDaniel

Technical Editor
Jim Booth

Managing Editor
Thomas F. Hayes

Project Editor
Tricia Liebig

Production Editor
Maribeth Echard

Indexer
Ken Johnson

Proofreaders
Juli Cook
Bob LaRoche

Team Coordinator
Cindy Teeters

Interior Designer
Kevin Spear

Cover Designer
Trina Wurst

Page Layout
Michelle Mitchell

Contents at a Glance

Table of Contents

About the Author

John V. Petersen is president and founder of Main Line Software, Inc., a Philadelphia, Pennsylvania–based software application and database design firm. MLSI development platforms include Visual FoxPro, Visual Basic, Access, SQL Server, and Microsoft's newest development platform Visual Studio .NET.

John earned an MBA from the Haub School of Business at St. Joseph's University in 1993. John is currently a 2L at the Rutgers University School of Law. John has presented at many industry events including Microsoft Developer Days and Microsoft Tech-Ed. John's writing projects have included *Visual FoxPro 6 Enterprise Development* and *Hands-On Visual Basic 6 Web Development* from Prima Publishing, *ADO Jumpstart MSDN Whitepaper*, and numerous feature articles on application development and database design issues. John has been an annual recipient of Microsoft's Most Valuable Professional award since 1996.

Dedication

To my sons Karl and Keith. You both make me proud in all that you do. I know you both will accomplish great things. I love you both very much.

To my wife Evelyn. Thank you again for all of the love and support you have given me over the years, especially now in light of my "starting over" in a new career in law.

Acknowledgments

I want to first thank Jenny Watson for presenting this project to me. Initially, the project had lots of starts and stops due to my hectic work schedule. Jenny believed in two things: the project and my doing the project. Thank you, Jenny, for your patience and support!

An author is very lucky when he has a great development editor like Maureen McDaniel. Whenever I have had a question or concern, Maureen was always right there, ready with an answer and guidance. Thank you, Maureen, for making this a fun and rewarding project.

I have had the fortune of Jim Booth's friendship and guidance for many years now. I was very happy that he accepted the technical editing assignment for this project. Jim is one of the smartest people I know and this project has benefited from his expertise, wisdom, and guidance.

Writing a book is a big deal. It takes a lot of time, and to some degree, other things suffer. While writing this book, in addition to trying to keep up with two active sons, seeing my wife every now and then, and supporting a software consulting business, I have been using what little spare time I have to study law at Rutgers University School of Law—Camden. To keep up with that endeavor, I have to give big thanks to two people. First, to my classmate Stephanie Meade for constantly nudging me to keep up on schoolwork. Second, to professor Beth Hillman—for breathing life into the Constitution and opening my eyes to what this country and the law are supposed to stand for. Your encouragement made coming home from school at 10:30 at night a lot more bearable. Third, I would like to thank my legal writing professor, Brian Foley. Thank you for making me a better writer. Finally, I want to thank my best friend Rod Paddock. Words here cannot adequately express just how much his friendship and guidance have meant to me over the years. Keeping with our philosophy of "less is more," this is all that has to be said.

Tell Us What You Think!

As the reader of this book, *you* are our most important critic and commentator. We value your opinion and want to know what we're doing right, what we could do better, what areas you'd like to see us publish in, and any other words of wisdom you're willing to pass our way.

As an Associate Publisher for Que, I welcome your comments. You can fax, e-mail, or write me directly to let me know what you did or didn't like about this book— as well as what we can do to make our books stronger.

Please note that I cannot help you with technical problems related to the topic of this book, and that due to the high volume of mail I receive, I might not be able to reply to every message.

When you write, please be sure to include this book's title and author as well as your name and phone or fax number. I will carefully review your comments and share them with the author and editors who worked on the book.

Fax: 317-581-4666

E-mail: feedback@quepublishing.com

Mail: Associate Publisher
          Que
          201 West 103rd Street
          Indianapolis, IN 46290 USA

INTRODUCTION

Believe it or not, the market is barren for the person who wants a basic and simple-to-read book on databases. When I was approached with this book project, I said to myself, "There must be a ton of books on the market that explains fundamental database concepts for the beginner." To my amazement and astonishment, I found very few resources. At that moment, it became clear that this project needed to see the light of day.

The hardest part in any task is getting started. After you get on the path, and perhaps most importantly the right path, the rest is easy. The goal of this book is to point you in the right direction as you begin your journey through the world of database technology.

The goal of this book is to be "specific-database-product" agnostic. Although the samples in this book use Access, the database concepts presented apply to any relational database. Why did I choose Access as a platform for presenting the database concepts in this book? There are two reasons. First, Access is by far the simplest personal database system to use and learn. Second, chances are very good that you have Microsoft Office. As a consequence, you probably already own a version of Microsoft Access. Although Access 2000 was used in writing this book, other versions (Access 97 or the newest version of Access: Access XP) should work just fine.

Whom This Book Is For

This book is for the person who has heard of databases but does not know what they really are, what they contain, or how to build them. This book is written from the perspective of helping a person who is tasked with his/her first database project. The task may be imposed by an employer or self-imposed with the goal of learning a new skill. However you have come to embark on your database journey; if you are a beginner who must start at step 0, this book is for you!

How This Book Is Organized

This book is divided into five parts. The division of the parts takes you through the evolution of database concepts, analysis, design, building, and eventual implementation of a database.

Part I—Database Basics

You need to crawl before you walk! What is a database? What are the different kinds of databases and how are they used in business today? These questions and many more are explored in Part I.

Part II—Designing and Building Your First Database

Having covered the theoretical aspects of what databases are, it is time to get to work. The first step in building a database involves the analysis of some business problem and the design of a database to solve that problem. Part II takes you through the steps of conceptual design to the actual construction of a database.

Part III—Maintaining Your Database—An Introduction to Database Integrity

After your database has been built, it must be maintained. What keeps a database in good working order? A database is only as good as the data it contains. Part III covers the concepts of making sure only valid data is stored in the database.

Part IV—Using Your Database to Provide Information—An Introduction to SQL

At this point, you know what a database is, how to design and build a database, and how to maintain a database. Part IV turns to topics of putting the database to work. It all starts with understanding how to extract information from the database. This part explores the language of databases: SQL (Structured Query Language).

Part V—Putting Your Database to Work—Building a Simple Access Database Application

Part V wraps things up by showing you how to expose your database to end users. At some point, people have to interact with your database. This part covers topics such as data entry forms and reports in the context of a simple Access database application.

Conventions Used in This Book

The layout of this book is designed to help you digest and absorb the material as quickly as possible. At the beginning of each chapter, you will find an overview, in bullet format, of the topics covered in that chapter.

In addition, you will find several icons used throughout the book. These icons direct your attention to more detailed information, a clue to help make your work more productive, or a warning to help you steer clear of potential problems. The icons are as follows:

Notes provide additional information about the subject matter covered in a particular section. You can safely skip these items and still learn the core concepts presented.

Clues give you a sense of "what's going on here." By learning some of the background information on a given task, you will derive a better understanding of the concept being presented. Clues also offer important tips that will help make your development efforts easier and more efficient.

Warnings are here to save you grief! In any development environment, there are 1,000 things that can go wrong. Where it is particularly easy to lose work and get off track, you will find a warning to help you stay on the right path.

PART

I

DATABASE
BASICS

AN INTRODUCTION TO DATABASES

CHAPTER HIGHLIGHTS:

- What Is a Database?
- How Databases Are Used
- Typical Database Management Systems Used Today
- Key Database Terminology
- The Relational Database Model: An Overview
- Database-Related Careers
- What You Have Learned

"A journey of 1,000 miles begins with 1 step."

—Ancient Chinese proverb

This chapter covers the basics of what relational databases are, how they are used, and key database terminology. Several types of databases, such as network, hierarchical, and object-oriented, exist. Of interest in this book is the relational database that is, by far, the most popular type of database in use today. The specifics of what a relational database is are discussed later in this chapter.

As you begin your study of databases, you might find that although technology has made databases more powerful than ever, at their core, databases have been around a lot longer than computers. This might surprise you, but after you understand the fundamentals of what databases are, you will understand why this is so. Because you chose this book, I can assume the study of databases is new and the territory is unfamiliar. The best advice that can be offered at this point is to buckle your seat belt, take a deep breath, have fun, and be prepared to learn a lot of new and useful information!

What Is a Database?

The best definitions are those that require as few words as possible. In the case of databases, the most concise definition can be broken down to one word: *collection*. A *database* is a collection of related data elements. The three basic elements of a database are as follows:

- Tables
- Columns
- Rows

Tables, also referred to as *entities*, represent the basic elements of information you are interested in tracking. For example, a typical business services customers, fills orders, and produces invoices. It follows, therefore, that a typical database representing a business would have customers, orders, and invoices tables.

Columns, also referred to as *fields*, represent the attributes of a table. Consider the customers table of a business. How would one describe a customer entity? Attributes such as first name, last name, address, city, state, ZIP Code, phone number, and so on would be appropriate to store.

Rows, also referred to as *records*, represent the actual data. Whereas fields describe what data is stored, the rows of a table are where the actual data is stored.

Modern database management systems manage the system of tables, rows, and columns. Does the word *modern* in the previous sentence imply that nonmodern databases exist or existed? The answer is yes. Consider the filing cabinets of invoices in your company's accounts payable department. The filing cabinet can be thought of as a table, whereas the fields of data on the typical invoice can be considered the columns. Finally, each individual invoice can be considered a row. Also consider the old card-catalog systems libraries used to use. Each card in the catalog contains the same data elements: book title, author, year of publication, publisher, and so on. It is easy to see that the entire card catalog was the table; the elements each card contained were the columns; and each card was a row of data.

The main difference between modern databases and their old paper-based ancestors deals with the ability to retrieve data. In a modern system, finding all the books published in the year 2000 is as simple as typing a query and asking the computer a question. Chances are, you will get your answer back in subsecond speed. In an old paper-based system, the task might take several minutes, several hours, or perhaps even several days.

In a nutshell, tables, columns, and rows are the basic building blocks of a relational database. When constructing a database, the theme of tables, rows, and columns is carried throughout. A typical business-related database can have as many as 100 tables or more. Each table can have as few as 1 or as many as 100 fields. The optimal number of each is determined through good design practices that are discussed later in this book. Even though the subject of databases is interesting, how databases are used is perhaps more interesting.

How Databases Are Used

If you are like most people today, you receive your fair share of junk mail. It seems as soon as you provide somebody with information about yourself, you start getting mail—either the traditional or electronic kind. If you buy something from company X, you then get information from company Y that has related products and services. The question you might have is, "How did they know to send me this information?" Or, "How did they know I made that purchase?"

The answer is twofold. First, there is data out in the world about you that you provided either directly or indirectly. Second, companies have assimilated the data into databases. Whenever you make a purchase with a credit card, you are providing somebody with information about both you and people like you. Every month, you receive a statement that details all the prior month's purchases. Data regarding your purchases, as well as those of the millions of other individuals who use credit cards, is stored in a database.

It can be said that the construction of databases entails the process of turning disparate pieces of data into information. In the world of business today, and marketing in particular, the goal and purpose of these databases are also twofold. First, companies want to know as much about you as possible. Second, by knowing as much as they can about you, companies know what you want. This gets back to the previous credit card illustration. In the process, companies can target their marketing efforts. What is the end result? As a consumer, you are more likely to buy what they are selling. And what do the companies have to thank for their increased sales? A database, of course!

Have you ever purchased anything from Amazon.com? In the beginning, data was used marginally on the Amazon site. However, with the addition of time, more data, and experience, data is an integral part of Amazon. Today, when you go to the site—assuming, of course, you have registered with Amazon—all sorts of product suggestions are offered to you. Based on data produced from purchases you make, Amazon stores this data in a database and in turn uses that data to predict which other products you might be interested in purchasing.

The predictive value of data is perhaps the most important benefit of storing data in a database. Companies use financial data to learn about how the business performed and how it is likely to perform in the future. By analyzing the data, the company can take corrective action should problems be discovered.

The preceding by no means is an exhaustive list of ways a database can be used. Only a fraction of the tip of the iceberg has been revealed. Every day, new uses for data are discovered. Through modern technology, databases make millions of bytes of data available as information instantaneously. If data had to be compiled manually, the task could take hours, days, weeks, months, or perhaps even years! This benefit is extremely important because after data reaches a certain age, its value immediately drops to zero.

Many popular database management systems are in use today. The next section describes the most popular systems.

Typical Database Management Systems Used Today

Many popular database management systems (DBMSs) are in use today. Among the most popular are these:

- Microsoft Access
- Microsoft SQL Server

- MSDE (Microsoft Data Engine)
- Oracle
- IBM DB2

Microsoft Access is one of two primary database offerings from Microsoft. Access is a network/desktop-based database. Although feature rich, Access is limited by both the amount of data it can store and the number of users it can service simultaneously. Currently, the maximum size an Access database can be is 2 billion bytes (2 gigabytes). The chief benefit of Access is that it is easy to use. For this reason, Access was chosen to be the database of choice to illustrate the examples in the book.

On the other end of the database scale are products such as Microsoft SQL Server, Oracle, and DB2. These types of database management systems are capable of trillions of bytes (terabytes) of data. Furthermore, these types of systems are capable of hosting thousands of users simultaneously. The world's biggest Web sites and database applications use products like these. Because this is an introductory book on the subject, products such as SQL Server and Oracle are beyond this book's scope. Please see Appendix E, "Web-Based Resources," for information on more advanced resources.

It is important to note that although this book is using Microsoft Access to illustrate how databases work, you as the reader are not being shortchanged with respect to features. The focus of this book is to teach you what databases are and how to use them. At their core, all databases operate under the same general theory. After you have mastered the fundamentals illustrated in this book, you will find transferring that knowledge to the more advanced platforms of SQL Server, Oracle, or DB2 relatively easy.

Up to now, the systems have been described as database management systems (DBMSs). More accurately, they are relational database management systems. All the databases mentioned so far are built on the relational model. Understanding what databases are has two important steps: knowing some key database terminology and understanding the basics of the relational database model. These steps are the focus of the next two sections.

Key Database Terminology

A complete glossary of database terminology can be found in Appendix C, "Glossary." At the expense of being redundant, it is beneficial at this time to acquaint you with the most common and essential terms you will encounter not only in this book, but in all the database-related work you perform.

Database

Early in this chapter, a database was described as a collection of related data elements. More precisely, a database is a collection of related data tables or entities. For example, a typical database for an organization would consist of a customer, an order, and order line-item tables. All these tables are related to one another in some way. In this example, customers have orders and orders have line items. Even though each table exists on its own, collectively the tables comprise a database.

Tables and Entities

A table represents a "thing" about an organization. Tables also are referred to as entities. If you want to track or store information about something, chances are it is a good candidate for being defined as a table. One of the first steps in building a database involves defining the tables that constitute that database.

Fields, Columns, and Attributes

Just as a database is composed of tables, tables are composed of fields. Fields are also known as *columns* and *attributes*. Depending on the text you read, one or more of these terms will be used. Don't get thrown off track by the use of multiple terminologies because field, column, and attribute all mean the same thing. A good way to think of fields is to think of them as descriptors of tables. For example, how would you describe a customer entity? Good examples of fields include first name, last name, city, state, ZIP Code, phone number, and so on.

Normalization

When creating a database, defining tables and fields is not enough. The optimal number of tables and the optimal construction of tables are determined through a process called *normalization*. The process of normalization entails creating numerous smaller tables as opposed to a smaller number of monolithic tables. One of the primary goals of normalization is to reduce data redundancy. The topic of normalization is discussed in Chapter 4, "Database Design Continued: An Introduction to Normalization."

Rows and Records

Each table in a database contains zero or more rows. Rows are also referred to as *records*. For example, say every customer for a company has a distinct record in the table that holds customer data. Therefore, each order for a specific customer comprises one record in the table that holds order data.

Primary Key

An expression that uniquely identifies a record from all other records is called a *primary key*. The topic of keys and indexes is discussed in Chapter 3, "An Introduction to Database Design."

The Relational Database Model: An Overview

In 1970, IBM researcher Dr. E. F. Codd published a paper titled "A Relational Model of Data for Large Shared Data Banks." In this paper, Dr. Codd proposed a new theory of representing data structures that was primarily mathematical in nature. The theory also proposed new mathematical models for accessing and manipulating a database. In recognizing some of the limitations that could be encountered, Dr. Codd formulated rules for normalizing a database. The rules of data normalization are discussed in detail in Chapter 4.

The previous section discussed several "relational" database systems available on the market today. The use of the word *relational* in this context troubled Dr. Codd. His concern was that confusion existed between the ideas that data could be represented in related tables and his relational database theory. Therefore, in 1988, Dr. Codd created his famous 12 rules for relational databases. The 12 rules are contained in the following list: both the actual wording of the rules and a brief note as to what practical meaning the specific rule has. Some concepts might be introduced in the following rules and explanations of the rules with which you are not familiar. Where that possibility exists, the explanation points out the location in the book where that topic is explained in further detail. The rules are as follows:

1. All information in a relational database is represented explicitly at the logical level and in exactly one way—by values in tables.

All data in a database is contained in tables. The values in tables are represented as columns (fields).

2. Each and every datum (atomic value) in a relational database is guaranteed to be logically accessible by resorting to a combination of table name, primary key, and column name.

Data in a table does not exist as one continuous string of data. Rather, you can access a data element by referencing its column name. For example, you can reference the order number of the orders table as orders.ordernumber. In other words, you don't need to search through a string of characters to locate the order number.

3. Null values (distinct from the empty character string or a string of blank characters and distinct from zero or any other number) are supported in a fully relational DBMS for representing missing information and inapplicable information in a systematic way, independent of data type.

Nulls, initially, can be a difficult concept to understand. Consider an empty field for a customer record. Is the field really blank, or is the real value of the field unknown? Nulls indicate a situation in which the value is unknown, as opposed to being empty. Think of the value NULL as "I don't know."

4. The database description is represented at the logical level in the same way as ordinary data, so that authorized users can apply the same relational language to determine data structures as they apply to the regular data.

In the process of building a database, you define elements such as tables, fields, indexes, and so on. The names of tables, fields, indexes, and so on are data that describes the data the database contains. Because it is literally data that describes other data, it is known as *metadata*. In the database world, metadata is also known as a *data dictionary*. The data dictionary for a truly relational database is stored in data tables that are similar to the data tables you define. Further, the same language you use to extract data from the tables you design can be used against the tables the system defines for storing the data dictionary.

5. A relational system can support several languages and various modes of terminal use. However, there must be at least one language whose statements are expressible, per some well-defined syntax, as character strings and that is comprehensive in supporting all the following items:

- Data definition
- View definition
- Data manipulation
- Integrity constraints
- Authorization

This rule is about a database's capability to support some language that allows you to work with, view, manipulate, control access to, and protect data. Although not specifically stated, the most popular language used for these tasks today is SQL (Structured Query Language). The details on what SQL is and how to implement SQL are the focus of Part IV, "Using Your Database to Provide Information—An Introduction to SQL."

6. All views that are theoretically updatable are also updatable by the system.

This rule means that a fully relational DBMS has the intelligence built in to modify data. In products such as SQL Server and Oracle, jobs can be established to run data update and maintenance tasks at specified intervals.

7. The capability of handling a base relation or a derived relation as a single operand applies not only to the retrieval of data but also to the insertion, updating, and deletion of data.

A *view* can be thought of as a window through which data can be looked at and worked with. A view can consist of columns from one table or several tables. Because a view is a single entity composed of one or more tables, only one operation is required to fetch, insert, update, or delete data in one or more tables simultaneously.

8. Application programs and terminal activities remain logically unimpaired whenever any changes are made in either storage representations or access methods.

The user should not have to have special knowledge about where the data is physically stored or the platform on which the data is stored. In other words, the user does not need to know whether data is stored on a Unix box or a Windows 2000 Server box. With regard to where the data is stored, a user needs to know only the name of the server. As far as location is concerned, the server could be in the next room or 2,000 miles away. It is up to the network to resolve this issue, not the user or the database.

9. Application programs and terminal activities remain logically unimpaired when information-preserving changes of any kind that theoretically permit unimpairment are made to base tables.

Application programs should not be required to know of changes made to data structures. For example, if new columns are added to a table, the application program that affects that table should be capable of operating unimpaired.

10. Integrity constraints specific to a particular relational database must be definable in the relational sublanguage and storable in the catalog, not in the application programs.

Maintaining data integrity is perhaps one of the most important features of a relational database. To be relational, a database system must be capable of providing these services. Therefore, a database can't rely on disparate application programs to maintain data integrity. If a field can accept only certain values, or if data in a table can't be deleted if other data exists, this must be definable in the database. Part III, "Maintaining Your Database—An Introduction to Database Integrity," focuses on the topic of maintaining data integrity in a database.

11. A relational DBMS has distribution independence.

A database that conforms to the relational model can be split, or partitioned, across multiple physical locations. So, a database can be hosted by numerous machines in a clustered server environment. Regardless of whether a database is contained on one server or multiple servers, application programs or the end user should not have to be aware of the difference.

12. If a relational system has a low-level language, that low-level language cannot be used to subvert or bypass the integrity rules and constraints expressed in the higher-level relational language.

Low-level languages tend to work on one record at a time, whereas higher-level languages are set based (they work on multiple records at the same time). Rule 12 basically states that low-level languages and higher-level languages must respect the same rules.

Ironically, no database system exists that adheres to all 12 rules. Therefore, by definition, a database system that calls itself a relational database system is not relational! You might be saying to yourself, "So what? It is an argument over semantics." This would be a good observation. Understanding the capabilities of and how to work with a relational database is far more important than understanding all the intricacies of the relational theory. Although the focus of this book is on the practical aspects of databases, some understanding of the orgins of the relational database model is helpful. That is why the preceding coverage of Codd's 12 rules was offered. Resources on where to find more information and learn about the relational theory can be found in Appendix E for information on advanced resources.

Database-Related Careers

You might be asking yourself, "With this knowledge of databases I am gaining, what type of job can I get?" Because you have chosen to read this book, one of two assumptions is likely to be true:

- Your study of databases is career related.
- Your study of databases is motivated by personal reasons.

Regardless of whether your interest in databases is personal or professional, this book will get you started on the right path. Perhaps you are trying to qualify for a new job. Even if you are not looking for a new job now, after reading this book, your curiosity about a job in the database field might be piqued. What follows are a list and brief descriptions of database-related jobs.

Database Administrator

A database administrator (DBA) is often the gatekeeper of data in an organization. Normally, all requests for data structure changes, new stored procedures, and so on are filtered through a DBA. The DBA ensures that an organization's databases are properly maintained and perform optimally. Through time, as a database matures and grows, a database's current implementation often must be reanalyzed. A DBA plays a central role in this process.

When a new application for an organization is being developed, the developer of that application consults the DBA to learn about the technical details of a database. Although an applications developer might want to make a change to a database, other applications probably use the same database. It is up to the DBA to ensure that a requested change by a specific application is compatible with other applications. If it is not, the DBA needs to be able to suggest viable alternatives.

Database Applications Programmer

Perhaps you are an experienced programmer who has not worked with data before. With the addition of database skills to your arsenal, you will be ready to tackle the world of developing database applications. Unlike other types of software applications, database applications directly impact the operations of a business.

To develop a database application for a business, you must first understand the business. This is wholly different from developing a utility that can deal with a specific aspect of a business. Database applications tend to deal with an entire business or an entire segment of a business. If you are experienced at developing utility-based applications, database applications will initially pose some new challenges. These new challenges exist because the requirements are different. A question you might have at this point is, "How are the requirements different?" Consider the following: Utility-based programs that do one thing tend to be finite. How they do things today is how they will do things tomorrow. Databases, on the other hand, grow as a business grows. Furthermore, as the business environment changes, the requirements of a database application change as well. The need to track new information, new report requests, and so on (all to one degree or another) requires changes to the underlying database. It has been said that a database application is never finished because a business never stops changing.

Database Analyst

Perhaps you do not develop programs. Rather, you are somebody who understands the business and the data related to a business. A key position in the mix is that of a database analyst. Database analysts are key players in the design of a database. It is important to note that the disciplines of developing applications and designing databases differ. The first, and most important, step in developing a database application is designing the database. Nothing else can occur until this first step is complete.

What You Have Learned

In this chapter, you have been introduced to the basics of what databases are. To recap, a database is a collection of related entities. These entities, also known as tables, are composed of fields, which are also known as attributes. Within a table are zero or more rows of data.

What databases technically are is not nearly as interesting as what databases are capable of performing. Data is the lifeblood of business. Anything a business is interested in tracking can be traced to data. To understand a business first requires understanding its data. Whether it is in support of a marketing campaign or customer service, data plays an important role.

Today, the most popular database used in business is built on the relational model developed by Dr. E. F. Codd. Even though the term *relational database management system* is pervasive, no database management system on the market today adheres to all 12 of Codd's rules. The distinction might be semantic, but it is still helpful to have an understanding of the foundation on which relational databases are built.

Because databases are the lifeblood of business, many interesting careers are associated with databases. Three such careers—database administrator, database applications programmer, and database analyst—were briefly described in this chapter.

With a basic understanding of what a database is, you are now ready for the next step of getting your hands dirty in designing and building your first database.

THE ANATOMY OF A REAL DATABASE

CHAPTER HIGHLIGHTS:

- An Introduction to Microsoft Access
- The Sample Northwind Traders Database
- What You Have Learned

2

Chapter 1, "An Introduction to Databases," was devoted to the theoretical aspects of what a database is. This chapter, and most of the remaining parts of this book, are devoted to the practical aspects of what databases are. Databases are tangible entities that you can get your hands around and work with. Although the theory is important and helpful, no better method of learning exists than to examine a real database, inspect its contents, and understand how it was constructed.

This chapter examines the Northwind Traders Database that ships with Microsoft Access. To get the most out of this chapter and the rest of this book, you need to have Access installed on your computer. Please refer to the software requirements section of the introduction for details on how to obtain and install Access.

This chapter is not meant to be an all-encompassing review of the entire Access feature-set. Rather, the chapter's purpose is to serve as a quick how-to on getting Access up and running and being productive in the Access environment. Many fine resources are available today that teach you the ins and outs of Microsoft Access.

Before moving on to the rest of the book, you should make sure you have a solid understanding of the material covered in this chapter.

Popular resources for Microsoft Access include the following:

- The official Microsoft Access Web site at
  `http://www.microsoft.com/office.access`
- The official Microsoft Support newsgroups at
  `http://communities.microsoft.com/newsgroups/default.asp?icp=gss&slcid=us`
- The official Microsoft Knowledge Base at `http://www.microsoft.com/KB/`
- *Easy Microsoft Access 2000* (Que Publishing)
- *Using Microsoft Access 2000* (Que Publishing)
- *Microsoft Office Pro Magazine* (Informant Communications)

An Introduction to Microsoft Access

Access, part of Microsoft's Office suite, is a full-featured desktop database product. In addition to being full featured, Access is very easy to use. The first step in the process is to start Access. Figure 2.1 illustrates the menu options for Microsoft Access.

After Access starts, you will see a dialog box prompting you to create a blank Access database, start an Access wizard, or open an existing Access database (see Figure 2.2).

FIGURE 2.1

Access is started
by selecting
Start, Programs,
Microsoft Access
from the main
menu.

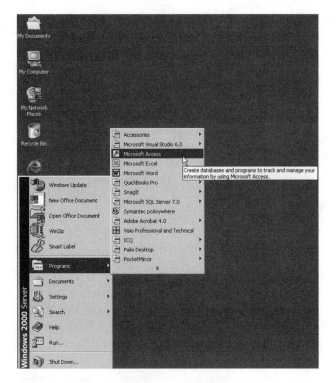

FIGURE 2.2

When Access is
started, the
startup dialog
box appears,
allowing you to
create or open
an existing
Access database.

In this case, you should choose to open an existing file by clicking that option and
then clicking OK. Then, open the \Program Files\Microsoft Access\Office\Samples\
Northwind.mdb database file. The default file extension for an Access database file
is MDB.

After the Northwind Traders Database is open, the main database form—providing access to all components of the database—is displayed (see Figure 2.3).

FIGURE 2.3

The main database dialog box provides access to all database components, including tables, queries, forms, and reports.

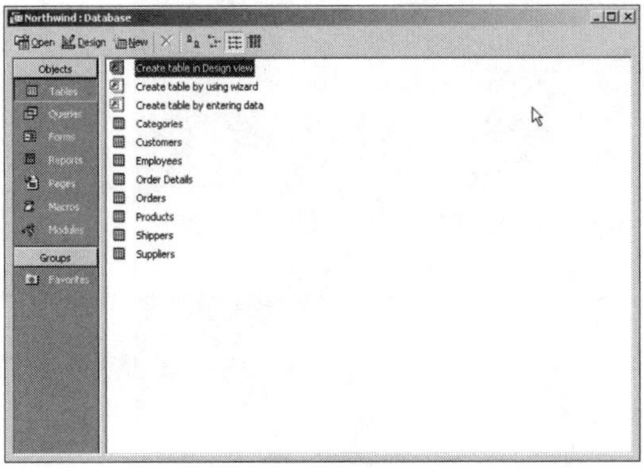

Note

Access also provides the ability to write Web pages, macros, and module code. Although you will see references to these items in various illustrations, they are beyond the scope of this book. For more information on these items, refer to the Note at the beginning of this chapter regarding popular Access resources.

Clue

Here's a recap on starting Microsoft Access:

1. Select Start, Programs, Microsoft Access.
2. From the startup dialog box, choose to create or select an existing database.

The Sample Northwind Traders Database

Figure 2.3 illustrates the main database form for an Access database. From this form, you can view the various objects in the database, as well as the data in the database.

The Database's Relationships

To get a sense of the database's purpose, you need to see the relationships among the various database entities. Figure 2.4 illustrates the relationship view for a database. In order to access the relationship view, you need to click the Relationship View button (also shown in Figure 2.4).

FIGURE 2.4

The relationship view enables you to view all the tables in a database as well as how the tables are related.

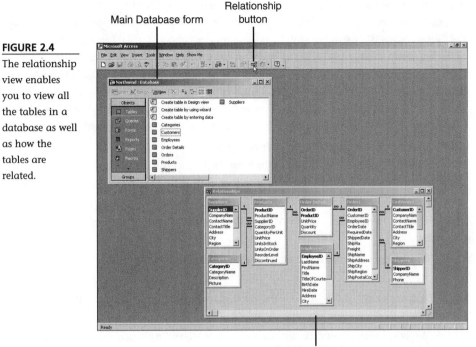

Relationship view

In reviewing the database diagram illustrated in Figure 2.4, the purpose of the Northwind Traders Database becomes clear. Working from the right side of the diagram, the Customers table is connected to the Orders table. Next to the Customers table is the number 1. Next to the Orders table is the infinity symbol, which looks like the number 8 lying on its side. This relationship is known as a *one-to-many relationship*. In other words, a customer can have 0 or more orders. Looking at the relationship in reverse, an order can have only one customer. In this case, the Customers table is referred to as the *parent*, and the Orders table is referred to as the *child*.

The three types of relationships you will encounter as you work with databases are as follows:

- **One-to-One**—A record in the parent table is related to one and only one record in the child table.

- **One-to-Many**—A record in the parent table is related to zero or more records in the child table.

- **Many-to-Many**—Multiple records in the parent table are related to multiple records in the child table. These types of relationships are actually broken down into multiple one-to-many relationships. This type of relationship is explained in further detail in the next Note.

Relationships work in a very simple way. Referring to each of the tables in Figure 2.4, you can see that some fields appear in boldface type. The combination of these fields makes up the primary key. In reviewing concepts discussed in Chapter 1, a *primary key* is the unique identifier of a row for a table. In the case of the Customers table, the primary key or unique identifier is the CustomerID field. If you look ahead to Figure 2.7, you can see that each customer row has a different value for CustomerID. That same CustomerID value is carried in the Orders table. This is how a database knows which child records belong to a given parent record.

Continuing to move from right to left in Figure 2.4, you can see the Orders table is both a child and a parent. It is a child with respect to the Customers table and a parent with respect to the Order Details table. From the perspective of the Customers table, the Order Details table is a grandchild.

The following summarizes the relationships contained in the Northwind Traders Database:

- A customer can have zero or more orders, and an order belongs to one customer.
- A shipper can have zero or more orders, and an order can be shipped by only one shipper.
- An employee can book zero or more orders, and an order can be booked by only one employee.

Consider the relationship between the Orders table and the Employee table. As it is currently designed, only one employee can book an order. What if multiple employees could book an order? Perhaps the organization uses teams of employees to book orders. If this is the case, the current database design could not meet this requirement. Enter the concept of the many-to-many relationship.

Suppose, hypothetically, that more than one employee needs to book an order. Looking at the current relationships, the Employee table is the parent and the Orders table is the child. You already know that an EmployeeID field exists in the Orders table and that only one EmployeeID value can be stored in the field. How can you accomplish this task? The answer is to add an additional table called EmployeeOrders. Figure 2.5 illustrates a modified version of the Northwind Traders Database. To accomplish this task, because there is no way in the relational model to directly support a many-to-many relationship, the relationship is indirectly supported through two one-to-many relationships. The intermediate table is called a *junction* table.

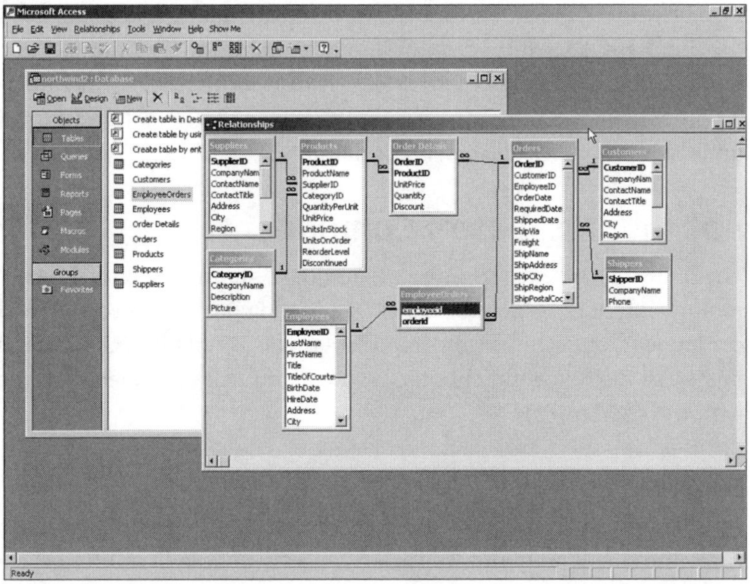

FIGURE 2.5

Many-to-many relationships are supported through the creation of an intermediary table called a *junction* table.

To continue the illustration, assume that for a given order, two employees are involved in the booking of that order. In this case, two records would appear in the junction table. From the perspective of the order, you could view the employees associated with the order. From the perspective of the employee, you could view all the orders that employee has participated in. In this scenario, the same order can be associated with multiple employees.

In a nutshell, the following make up the essence of the many-to-many relationship:

■ An order can have one or more order details, and an order detail can be part of only one order.

■ A product can be in zero or more order details, and an order detail can have only one product.

■ A supplier can supply zero or more products, and a product can be supplied by only one supplier.

■ Categories can be composed of zero or more products, and a product can be a member of only one category.

Note

How about a product that can be a member of more than one category? If you are thinking that a many-to-many relationship needs to be crafted with a junction table, you are on the right track! You are catching on!

In reviewing the relationships of Northwind Traders, it is clear that the purpose of the database is to support an order-entry operation. In addition to order entry, a basic inventory management system is also supported. As mentioned in Chapter 1, if you understand the data and its structure, you can get an immediate initial understanding of what a business does.

Overview of the Database's Components

The following sections describe the major components of an Access Database. The major components include Tables, Queries, Reports, and Forms. Within each major component are various subcomponents. This is only an introduction to these elements. In the following chapters, more detail will be presented as you begin working with the components.

Tables

For example, let's assume you want to view the contents of the Customers table. How would you go about this task? It is very simple if you follow these steps (see Figure 2.6):

1. Select the Customers table with a single click of the mouse.

2. After it's selected, click the Open button on the toolbar.

Open button

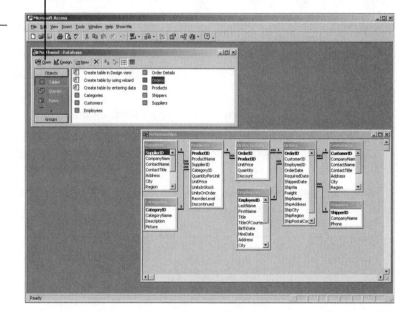

FIGURE 2.6

The data content of a table can be viewed by opening the table.

Figure 2.7 illustrates the contents of the Customers table. This view is known as the Datasheet View. It is aptly named because the view resembles an Excel spreadsheet of data.

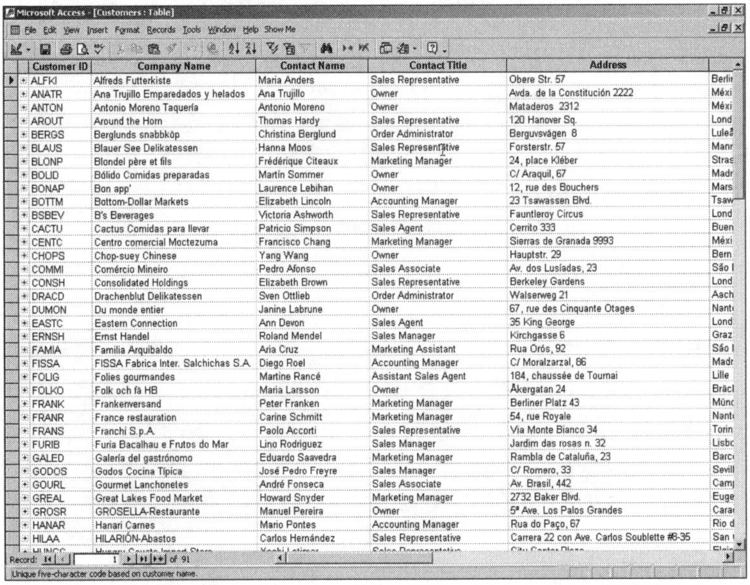

Customer ID	Company Name	Contact Name	Contact Title	Address	
ALFKI	Alfreds Futterkiste	Maria Anders	Sales Representative	Obere Str. 57	Berlii
ANATR	Ana Trujillo Emparedados y helados	Ana Trujillo	Owner	Avda. de la Constitución 2222	Méxi
ANTON	Antonio Moreno Taquería	Antonio Moreno	Owner	Mataderos 2312	Méxi
AROUT	Around the Horn	Thomas Hardy	Sales Representative	120 Hanover Sq.	Lond
BERGS	Berglunds snabbköp	Christina Berglund	Order Administrator	Berguvsvägen 8	Luleå
BLAUS	Blauer See Delikatessen	Hanna Moos	Sales Representative	Forsterstr. 57	Manr
BLONP	Blondel père et fils	Frédérique Citeaux	Marketing Manager	24, place Kléber	Stras
BOLID	Bólido Comidas preparadas	Martín Sommer	Owner	C/ Araquil, 67	Madr
BONAP	Bon app'	Laurence Lebihan	Owner	12, rue des Bouchers	Mars
BOTTM	Bottom-Dollar Markets	Elizabeth Lincoln	Accounting Manager	23 Tsawassen Blvd.	Tsaw
BSBEV	B's Beverages	Victoria Ashworth	Sales Representative	Fauntleroy Circus	Lond
CACTU	Cactus Comidas para llevar	Patricio Simpson	Sales Agent	Cerrito 333	Buen
CENTC	Centro comercial Moctezuma	Francisco Chang	Marketing Manager	Sierras de Granada 9993	Méxi
CHOPS	Chop-suey Chinese	Yang Wang	Owner	Hauptstr. 29	Bern
COMMI	Comércio Mineiro	Pedro Afonso	Sales Associate	Av. dos Lusíadas, 23	São I
CONSH	Consolidated Holdings	Elizabeth Brown	Sales Representative	Berkeley Gardens	Lond
DRACD	Drachenblut Delikatessen	Sven Ottlieb	Order Administrator	Walserweg 21	Aach
DUMON	Du monde entier	Janine Labrune	Owner	67, rue des Cinquante Otages	Nant
EASTC	Eastern Connection	Ann Devon	Sales Agent	35 King George	Lond
ERNSH	Ernst Handel	Roland Mendel	Sales Manager	Kirchgasse 6	Graz
FAMIA	Familia Arquibaldo	Aria Cruz	Marketing Assistant	Rua Orós, 92	São I
FISSA	FISSA Fabrica Inter. Salchichas S.A.	Diego Roel	Accounting Manager	C/ Moralzarzal, 86	Madr
FOLIG	Folies gourmandes	Martine Rancé	Assistant Sales Agent	184, chaussée de Tournai	Lille
FOLKO	Folk och fä HB	Maria Larsson	Owner	Åkergatan 24	Bräcl
FRANK	Frankenversand	Peter Franken	Marketing Manager	Berliner Platz 43	Münc
FRANR	France restauration	Carine Schmitt	Marketing Manager	54, rue Royale	Nant
FRANS	Franchi S.p.A.	Paolo Accorti	Sales Representative	Via Monte Bianco 34	Torin
FURIB	Furia Bacalhau e Frutos do Mar	Lino Rodriguez	Sales Manager	Jardim das rosas n. 32	Lisbc
GALED	Galería del gastrónomo	Eduardo Saavedra	Marketing Manager	Rambla de Cataluña, 23	Barc
GODOS	Godos Cocina Típica	José Pedro Freyre	Sales Manager	C/ Romero, 33	Sevill
GOURL	Gourmet Lanchonetes	André Fonseca	Sales Associate	Av. Brasil, 442	Camp
GREAL	Great Lakes Food Market	Howard Snyder	Marketing Manager	2732 Baker Blvd.	Euge
GROSR	GROSELLA-Restaurante	Manuel Pereira	Owner	5ª Ave. Los Palos Grandes	Cara
HANAR	Hanari Carnes	Mario Pontes	Accounting Manager	Rua do Paço, 67	Rio d
HILAA	HILARIÓN-Abastos	Carlos Hernández	Sales Representative	Carrera 22 con Ave. Carlos Soublette #8-35	San

FIGURE 2.7
From the Datasheet View, data can be viewed, modified, and deleted.

Caution When viewing data in the Datasheet View, it is important to note that the view is a live view of the data. This means that data can be modified or deleted. Remember, be careful as to which buttons on the keyboard you are pressing when viewing data.

What about the structure of the table? Remember the discussion from Chapter 1 about tables? Tables are composed of one or more columns. How do you view the structure of a table in Access? Figure 2.7 and the following steps illustrate how to view the structure of an Access table:

1. Locate the View button, which is the leftmost button on the toolbar (see Figure 2.8).
2. Click the View button. This toggles to the Design View.
3. Click the View button again; this toggles to the Datalist View. The Datalist View is an alternative way of designing a table. It is not as useful as the Design View.

FIGURE 2.8

Clicking the
View button
enables the user
to toggle
between the
Design View and
Datalist View of
a table. Column
details, such as
column name,
data type, and
description, can
be viewed in the
Design View.

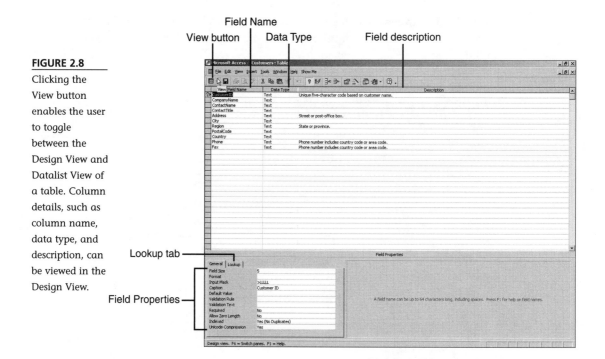

View button   Field Name   Data Type   Field description

Lookup tab

Field Properties

It is important to take great care when viewing the structure of a table. As you scroll up
and down the list of fields, it can be easy to disrupt the attributes of the field.
Remember—be careful as to which buttons on the keyboard you are pressing when
viewing the table structure!

The purpose and use of the Lookup tab are discussed in further detail in the section
"Forms," later in this chapter. Lookups provide a user-friendly way of associating data in
related tables.

Properties

From the Design View, by scrolling up and down the field list, you can view
extended properties for a field. In addition to the name, data type, and description,
more field attributes—such as size, format, input mask, and caption—can be viewed.
These extended attributes can be viewed in the lower-left portion of Figure 2.7.

FieldName The `FieldName` property specifies the name of the field within a table. A field name can be up to 64 characters long and can contain any combination of letters, numbers, spaces, and special characters. Invalid characters include the period, exclamation point, accent, and brackets. Believe it or not, double quotation marks are valid characters in a field name. It is doubtful whether anybody would find this feature useful. As a rule, you will want to stick with the letters of the alphabet, the numbers 0 through 9, and the underscore character.

Although you can have embedded spaces in your field names, they can be more trouble than they are worth. For example, consider the Company Name field in the Northwind Customers table. If an embedded space were used, you would have to refer to the field as `[customers.company name]`. Alternatively, if no embedded spaces were used, the field could simply be referred to as follows: `customers.companyname`. The use of spaces tends to complicate rather than simplify. So, avoid the use of spaces in field names.

DataType The `DataType` property specifies the type of data stored in the field. The standard data types are listed in Table 2.1.

Table 2.1 Standard Data Types Supported by Access

Data Type	Description	Maximum Size
Text	Character data	255 bytes
Memo	Character data	64K
Number	Numeric data	8 bytes
Date/Time	Date and time data	8 bytes
Currency	Monetary data	8 bytes
Autonumber	Autoincrementing numeric data	4 bytes
Yes/No	True/False logical data	1 bit

Access supports additional data types, including OLE Object and Hyperlink. For more information on these data types, consult the Access documentation.

Description The Description property enables you to provide descriptive information about the field. A description can be up to 255 characters long.

Field Size The Field Size property enables you to specify the maximum size of data stored in the field. Refer to Table 2.1 for the maximum field size values.

Format The Format property controls how data appears when displayed. This property enables you to customize how numbers, currency, text, and date-time data appear.

Input Mask The Input Mask property provides a mechanism for making data entry easier. For example, with a telephone number, an input mask of (____) - ____ - ____ makes entering the various components of a phone number easier. Access provides a wizard to create values for this property.

Caption The Caption property specifies the contents of the descriptive label that is used on a form or report in which the field is used. The Caption property also specifies the contents of the column header for a field in the Datalist View. (Refer to Figure 2.7 for an illustration of the Datalist View.)

Default Value The Default Value property specifies the value that is automatically entered into the field when a new record is created. For example, a number type field might have a default value of 0, and a date-time type field might have a default value of the current date-time value.

Validation Rule The Validation Rule property specifies a condition that an entered value must satisfy. For example, a number type value must be >= 0. Validation rules help preserve data integrity.

Validation Text The Validation Text property specifies the message text displayed to the user when the validation rule fails. The maximum size of a validation text property is 255 characters.

Required The Required property specifies whether a data value is required for the field.

Allow Zero Length The Allow Zero Length property specifies whether a zero-length string is a valid entry. This property applies only to text, memo, and hyperlink fields.

Indexed The Indexed property specifies whether an index is created for the field. Two types of indexes can be created. One allows duplicate field entries, and the other type does not allow duplicates.

Unicode Compression

Access supports Unicode character representation, which means characters are represented by two bytes instead of one. With two bytes, multiple language code pages can be supported. With one byte, on the other hand, a single code page is supported and a smaller disk storage requirement exists.

Queries

Queries provide a view to data. Most of the time, you will need to use and interact with data in a manner different from the way the data is stored. Figure 2.9 shows the query definitions for the Northwind Traders Database.

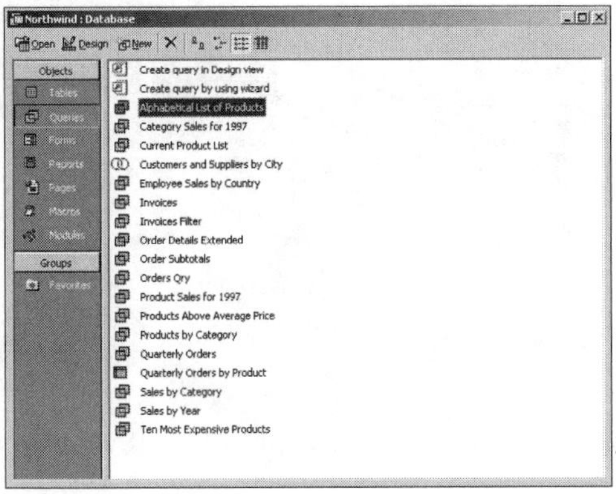

FIGURE 2.9

A wide variety of queries are defined in the Northwind Traders Database.

The best way to illustrate queries is with a simple example. The requirement is a simple alphabetical product listing for active products. In a query such as this, you need only two pieces of information: the product ID and the product name. The Current Product List query fulfills these requirements. The steps to viewing the contents of a query are exactly the same as viewing the contents of a table:

1. Select the Current Product List query by clicking it.
2. After it's selected, click the Open button on the toolbar.

Figure 2.10 illustrates the results of running the Current Product List query.

One question you might have is, "What is the structure of a query?" The structure of a query is derived from the structure of the tables from which the query gets its information. The steps to view the structure of a query are just like viewing the structure of a table:

1. Click the View button. This toggles to the Design View.
2. Click the View button again; this toggles to the Datalist View.

The structure of the Current Product List query is shown in Figure 2.11.

View button

The Current
Product List
query provides
an alphabetical
list of active
products.

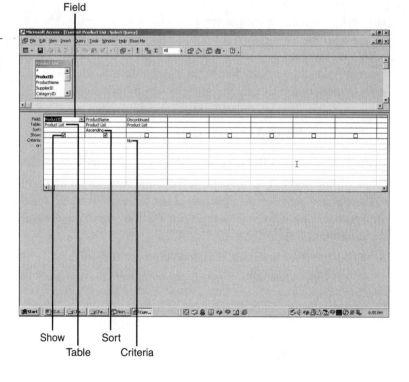

Field

The structure of
a query specifies
the tables and
columns used,
the sort order,
and the selec-
tion criteria.

Show

Table

Sort

Criteria

In the Current Product List query, three fields are used, but only two fields are displayed in the resultset. The third field, Discontinued, is used only for purposes of establishing criteria. In this case, only records with a discontinued value of no are selected.

Of the two fields displayed, the Product Name field is both displayed and used as the basis of the sort order. In this case, the resultset is ordered by product name in ascending order.

Queries involving multiple tables are not materially different from queries involving only one table. A simple illustration is the Alphabetical List of Products query. In that query, data from the products and categories are combined to form a single resultset (see Figure 2.12).

FIGURE 2.12

Tables in multi-table queries are automatically related based on the relationships defined in the database.

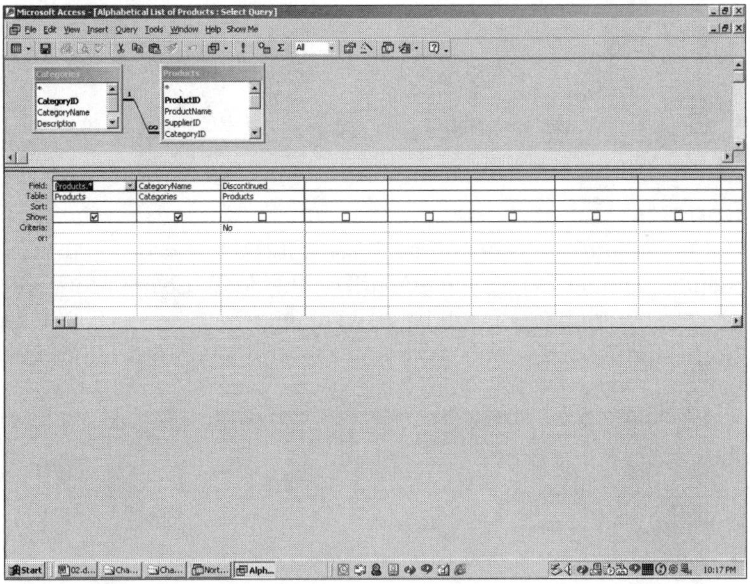

The resultset of the Alphabetical List of Products query is shown in Figure 2.13.

FIGURE 2.13

The output in a
multitable query
appears as one
logical table.

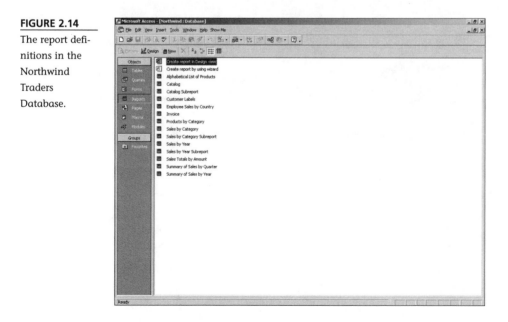

Reports

Data in a database is not of much use if it can't be accessed and used in a user-
friendly manner. When you embark on the database application development
process, invariably, you will be asked about which reports can be generated. The
Northwind Traders Database contains several report definitions (see Figure 2.14).

FIGURE 2.14

The report defi-
nitions in the
Northwind
Traders
Database.

To illustrate how the reports work, consider the Products by Category query. This query is similar to the queries examined in the previous section and is illustrated in Figure 2.15.

The Products by Category query displays the information shown in Table 2.2.

Table 2.2 Structure of the Products by Category Query

Field Name	Table	Sort/Criteria
Category Name	Categories	Ascending
Product Name	Products	Ascending
Quantity per Unit	Products	
Units in Stock	Products	
Discontinued	Products	<> Yes

The output of the Products by Category query is shown in Figure 2.16.

FIGURE 2.15

The Products by Category query in Design View.

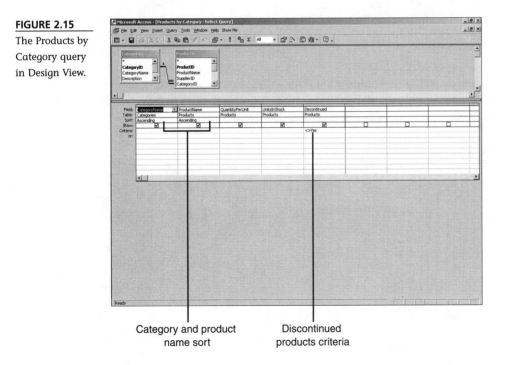

Category and product name sort

Discontinued products criteria

FIGURE 2.16
The Products by Category query in Datalist View.

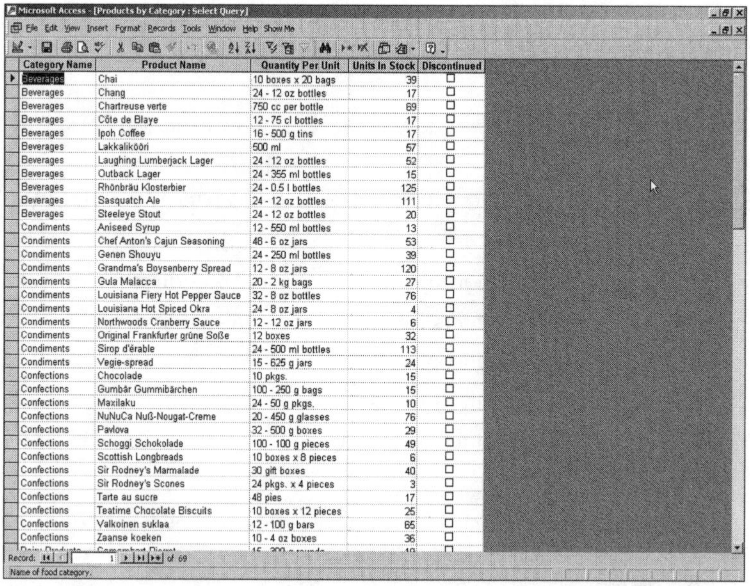

Category Name	Product Name	Quantity Per Unit	Units In Stock	Discontinued
Beverages	Chai	10 boxes x 20 bags	39	☐
Beverages	Chang	24 - 12 oz bottles	17	☐
Beverages	Chartreuse verte	750 cc per bottle	69	☐
Beverages	Côte de Blaye	12 - 75 cl bottles	17	☐
Beverages	Ipoh Coffee	16 - 500 g tins	17	☐
Beverages	Lakkalikööri	500 ml	57	☐
Beverages	Laughing Lumberjack Lager	24 - 12 oz bottles	52	☐
Beverages	Outback Lager	24 - 355 ml bottles	15	☐
Beverages	Rhönbräu Klosterbier	24 - 0.5 l bottles	125	☐
Beverages	Sasquatch Ale	24 - 12 oz bottles	111	☐
Beverages	Steeleye Stout	24 - 12 oz bottles	20	☐
Condiments	Aniseed Syrup	12 - 550 ml bottles	13	☐
Condiments	Chef Anton's Cajun Seasoning	48 - 6 oz jars	53	☐
Condiments	Genen Shouyu	24 - 250 ml bottles	39	☐
Condiments	Grandma's Boysenberry Spread	12 - 8 oz jars	120	☐
Condiments	Gula Malacca	20 - 2 kg bags	27	☐
Condiments	Louisiana Fiery Hot Pepper Sauce	32 - 8 oz bottles	76	☐
Condiments	Louisiana Hot Spiced Okra	24 - 8 oz jars	4	☐
Condiments	Northwoods Cranberry Sauce	12 - 12 oz jars	6	☐
Condiments	Original Frankfurter grüne Soße	12 boxes	32	☐
Condiments	Sirop d'érable	24 - 500 ml bottles	113	☐
Condiments	Vegie-spread	15 - 625 g jars	24	☐
Confections	Chocolade	10 pkgs.	15	☐
Confections	Gumbär Gummibärchen	100 - 250 g bags	15	☐
Confections	Maxilaku	24 - 50 g pkgs.	10	☐
Confections	NuNuCa Nuß-Nougat-Creme	20 - 450 g glasses	76	☐
Confections	Pavlova	32 - 500 g boxes	29	☐
Confections	Schoggi Schokolade	100 - 100 g pieces	49	☐
Confections	Scottish Longbreads	10 boxes x 8 pieces	6	☐
Confections	Sir Rodney's Marmalade	30 gift boxes	40	☐
Confections	Sir Rodney's Scones	24 pkgs. x 4 pieces	3	☐
Confections	Tarte au sucre	48 pies	17	☐
Confections	Teatime Chocolate Biscuits	10 boxes x 12 pieces	25	☐
Confections	Valkoinen suklaa	12 - 100 g bars	65	☐
Confections	Zaanse koeken	10 - 4 oz boxes	36	☐

It should be clear to you how useful queries can be. The Datalist View, however, is not very useful to an end user. This is where reports come in. With a report, you can build a layout that makes the data easier to view and is more useful to the end user. Queries gather data together from one or more tables, and reports provide a useful format for viewing the data. Figure 2.17 demonstrates how a report brings a query to life.

FIGURE 2.17
The Products by Category report in Print Preview View.

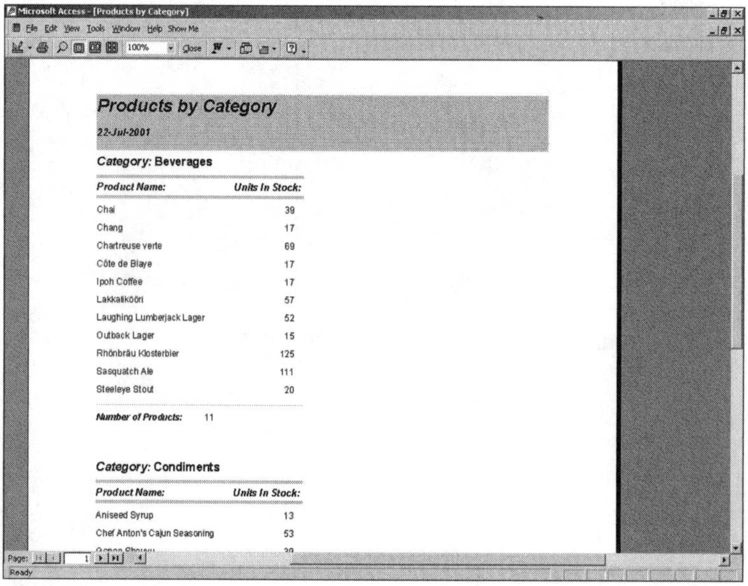

The structure of a report is a bit more complicated than the structure of tables and queries. Figure 2.18 shows the Products by Category report in Design View.

The details on how to construct reports are discussed in Chapter 12, "Providing Useful Output: An Introduction to Creating and Designing Reports."

Forms

The final Access database objects to examine in this quick overview are forms. You have seen where data is stored (tables), how data can be combined in a useful format (queries), and how data can be presented in a useful format (reports). But how can you get data into the database? Data can be entered into tables in two ways:

- Via the Table Datalist View (refer to Figure 2.6)
- Via data entry forms

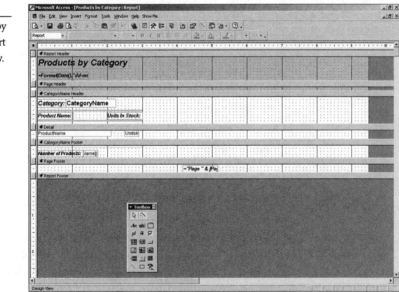

FIGURE 2.18

The Products by Category report in Design View.

Although you can enter, modify, and delete data in the Datalist View, it is not terribly useful. Data entry forms provide a user-friendly way of interacting with data. Like reports, the structure of forms can be quite complex. Although the high points are covered in this chapter, the details on how to construct forms are covered in Chapter 11, "Building the User Interface Components."

Figure 2.19 shows the form definitions in the Northwind Traders Database.

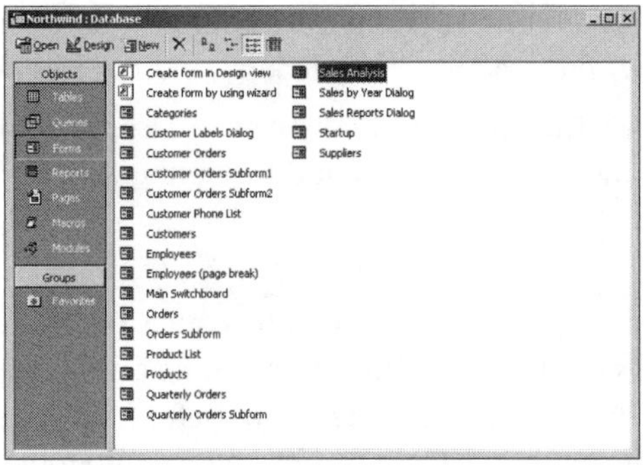

FIGURE 2.19

The form defini-
tions in the
Northwind
Traders
Database.

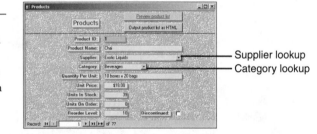

In several contexts, the Products table has been discussed. The Products form provides a good illustration of both how forms work and the benefit forms provide (see
Figure 2.20). To review, consider the following relationships involving the Products
table:

- A product belongs to one category.
- A product is supplied by one supplier.

FIGURE 2.20

The Products
form provides a
user-friendly
way of entering
data for a given
product.

Because the Products table is involved in two relationships, two lookups exist for the
Products table. The lookups involve the SupplierID and CategoryID fields. If you
recall from the beginning of this chapter, these foreign key fields point to the
Supplier and Category tables, respectively. Information supporting how this infor-
mation will be displayed in a form can be found in the Lookup tab of the Table
Designer. The Lookup tab of the SupplierID field of the Products table is shown in
Figure 2.21.

FIGURE 2.21

The Lookup tab provides the information and user interface components used to support form construction.

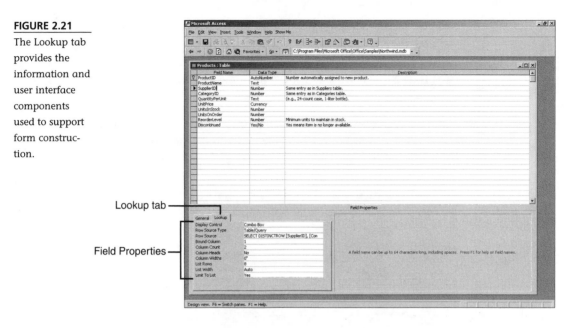

Lookups are easier for users to work with because users can work with descriptions instead of the meaningless numerical key values.

Using the SupplierID field as an illustration, the following outlines the information the Lookup tab provides:

- **Display Control**—The user-interface element (combo box, list box, or text box) that is used to display the lookup.

- **Row Source Type**—A lookup can pull its data from a query, static values, or fields from another table. In this case, the SupplierID and companyname fields are queried from the supplier table as the source of the lookup.

- **Row Source**—The actual query, static list, or field list used to populate the lookup.

- **Bound Column**—The column value that is written to the field. In this case, the SupplierID value from the Supplier table is written to the SupplierID field of the Products table. The SupplierID field is the first field in the query; hence, the bound column for the lookup is set to 1.

- **Column Count**—The column count specifies the number of columns to display.

- **Column Heads**—Specifies whether column headings should be used.

- **Column Widths**—Specifies the width of each column. In this case, the first column, SupplierID, has a width of 0 and thus is not displayed. The only displayed column is column 2, Company Name.

- **List Rows**—Specifies the maximum number of rows to display.
- **List Width**—Specifies the width of the list portion of a combo box and list box.
- **Limit To List**—If set to yes, only values that appear in the list can be entered.

Toggling between views for forms is similar to toggling views for tables, queries, and reports: Click the View button to toggle between the Design and Form views.

Figure 2.22 shows the structure of the Products form.

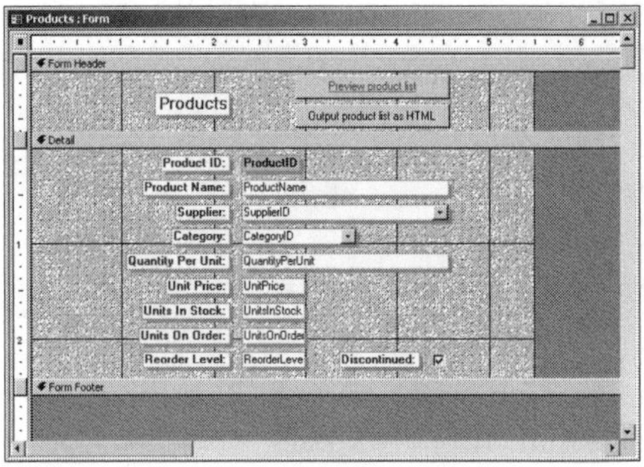

FIGURE 2.22

The Products form in Design View.

What You Have Learned

In a nutshell, you have seen the most important elements in an Access database, which are as follows:

- Tables
- Relationships
- Queries
- Reports
- Forms

Data is stored in tables, and relationships define how various tables are associated. Queries combine the tables and relationships to make data useful, whereas reports bring the data to life. Finally, forms enable users to interact with the data.

By examining a sample Access database, you get to see the finished product and, hopefully, a glimpse of how it all fits together. This chapter gives you a view of the forest by taking a quick look at the trees. If you understand the big picture, you will have an easier time understanding the details that will come in the remaining chapters.

Now that you have an understanding of what a database is and how databases are implemented in Access, it is time to apply this knowledge in creating your own database. The next three chapters focus on how to design and build a time-entry and billing database. As you are taken through the process of designing and building the Time Entry and Billing Database, keep the Northwind Traders example in mind because the same concepts apply—the only difference is the problem being solved.

PART II

DESIGNING AND BUILDING YOUR FIRST DATABASE

AN INTRODUCTION TO DATABASE DESIGN

*C*HAPTER HIGHLIGHTS:

Part I, "Database Basics," focused on giving you a foundation of what a database is and an understanding of how an actual database is implemented in Microsoft Access. In Part II, "Designing and Building Your First Database," and beginning with this chapter, the focus will be on applying what you've learned in Part I. Before you can build a database, you have to design the database. Before you can design the database, you have to understand the business problem you are tasked with solving. Sometimes the process of designing and building a database is simple; sometimes the process can be quite challenging and complex. The factors that can determine how difficult your task will be include the following:

- Your degree of understanding of the business
- Your analytical skills
- The number of databases you've previously developed
- The amount of patience you possess

Of all the skills, patience is perhaps the most important and most difficult to acquire. With time, you can learn the business, hone your analytical skills, and build databases. Databases are never fully developed in the first pass. By the end of the second pass, you will just about be there. With luck, the third pass might be the charm. More than likely, though, it will take four iterations of the design to complete a solid initial design. Only by having the patience to see each iteration through can you achieve the goal of a solid database design.

The topic of database design can be a slippery slope into a world of complex theories. Not that the design theories in the database world are useless—they aren't. In a beginning book on databases, however, about two-thirds of the theory is useless. This chapter and Part II are a recipe consisting of one-third cup theory and two-thirds cup hard work.

By doing, you will learn. Let's get to work!

Your Project: A Time Entry and Billing Database

You have been hired by the law firm of Dewey, Cheatem, and Howe to construct a time entry and billing system. Other than a few bad lawyer jokes (such as "Why don't sharks eat lawyers? Professional courtesy."), you don't know much about the inner workings of a law firm. Based on the name of the system, though, you know two things for certain:

- The system needs to collect and keep time.
- The system needs to create bills.

This might sound overly simplistic, but sometimes that might be all you initially have to go on. As you will learn, knowing one piece of information can lead to learning one, two, or more additional pieces of information. And so the process repeats. Perhaps the most important elements of information you can possess at the beginning of a project are how and where to find the required information to build a database. This topic is the focus of the next section.

Determine the Requirements of the Database

How do you go about making decisions regarding database requirements? The key to making decisions lies in knowing where to find information. In spite of the varied nature of different companies and departments, the sources of information are common. As you develop different database systems, you will find the process of requirements gathering to be very repeatable. Among the many sources of information regarding database requirements, the most common include interviews, business forms, and existing systems.

Interviews

For all the computing power companies use today, people still make the decisions and make things happen in a business. Don't underestimate the power of talking and—perhaps more important—listening to the employees of a firm. These people might not be able to speak in technical database terms, but then again, that is why you are on the scene—to be the gatherer and translator of information.

Through interviews, you will be able to learn how information passes through an organization. You will also be able to learn which specific pieces of data individuals rely on and the decisions they make based on that data.

You are putting together a puzzle.

When conducting interviews, don't limit yourself to just the management personnel and the frontline staff. Each level of an organization has a piece of the puzzle to contribute. Each is equally important because without all the pieces of a puzzle, you can never have a complete picture. As a result, without all the pieces, you can never have a complete understanding of the business and the requirements of the database you are being tasked with building.

UNDERSTANDING STRATEGIC VERSUS TACTICAL NEEDS

The decisions a company makes fall into one of two categories:

- Strategic
- Tactical

Strategic decisions are decisions regarding things such as whether to go into a certain line of business, whether to start or end a specific product line, and whether to alter head count. Strategic decisions affect a company as a whole. As far as timing is concerned, the strategic planning horizon is usually more than six months and can extend for time periods as long as five years. You might be familiar with your company's rolling three-, four-, or five-year plan. If you are tasked with designing a database for your company, you must have an understanding of your company's strategic plan. Your database might very well have to support those plans by providing information for decision making.

Whereas strategic decisions are long range in nature, *tactical* decisions are short range and much more detailed in nature. Strategic decisions focus on what a company wants to do; in contrast, tactical decisions focus on how those things get done. For example, a strategic decision might be to increase operations over the next two years. To fuel the growth, cash-flow requirements for the business would have to increase by 10%. Tactical decisions to support this strategy might include the following:

- Increasing time to pay accounts payable from 30 to 60 days
- Requiring payment of invoices in 10 days instead of 30 days
- Finding new sources of bank financing

You might be asking what this has to do with database development. The answer is everything! Data is the lifeblood of a business. Without data, a company can't make decisions. To make the tactical decisions previously listed, a database must provide the required information in a usable format. Through interviews, you can learn much about what a company hopes to achieve, and in the process, learn what the requirements of the database need to be.

Business Forms and Documents

Interviews can provide both high-level and detail-oriented information. Examining and analyzing business forms is where you start to get into the nitty-gritty details. The following are examples of business forms:

- Invoices
- Reports
- Shipping documents

- Timesheets
- Customer service surveys
- Any other piece of paper somebody in the business uses

In an interview, you might discover that it is critical the database stores information about customers. Through the analysis and examination of business forms and documents, you discover the specific pieces of customer information that must be captured. Another example is tracking time. In your current project, the Time Entry and Billing database, you know you will have to keep track of time at some level of detail. A typical timesheet might contain some or all of the following information:

- Employee name
- Date of work
- Start time
- End time
- Task performed
- Project
- Client

In looking at this example involving a timesheet, it becomes clearer as to what information the database must store. Chapter 4, "Database Design Continued: An Introduction to Normalization," focuses on how the information is organized. At this point, what is important is where to find the information.

 Time to stop and catch your breath here. It is important to illustrate how interviews and business forms work together. It is all a seamless web. Interviews provide the big picture of what information the database stores. To some extent, interviews also can provide information on the details. However, an analysis of the business forms and documents a company uses provides the bulk of the detail information.

Existing Systems

It might very well be the case that your project's purpose is to replace an existing system. Perhaps the company has outgrown the capabilities of the existing system. Perhaps the existing database design simply does not meet the growing needs of the company. To understand the requirements of your database design, you must understand the current system. Most importantly, you must understand the shortcomings that might exist. If you don't know and understand issues regarding an existing system, the possibility of perpetuating database design flaws into the new system increases dramatically.

In many respects, the user-interface components of an existing system can be regarded as business documents and forms. For example, a physical piece of paper that represents a timesheet might not exist. Rather, employees might enter their time online via a time-entry screen. As a database developer, you will need to be aware that the line between disparate sources of information is not black and white. Further, there is no set order in which the different elements are reviewed. Finally, it might very well be the case that the same sources of information will need to be revisited. For example, after you have analyzed a business document, you might have to return to the process of employee interviews to get further clarification of the database requirements.

Remember the mantra of patience? The process of requirements gathering might seem like a never-ending process. Some believe that systems and databases are never "complete" because the business environment constantly evolves and changes. At some point, you will acquire enough information to establish an initial database design. Just because you create that first design does not mean the requirements-gathering process is complete. Remember, you might have to repeat the process two, three, or perhaps four or more times to achieve that first database design. As you gain experience, the process will become more familiar to you.

At this point, you have an understanding of where sources of information can be found for requirements gathering. The question now is how do you put an initial design together. The answer is in the form of a database model. The process of creating your first database model is the focus of the next section.

Introduction to Database Modeling

It is said that a picture is worth a thousand words. Nowhere can that saying be truer than in the world of database modeling. As you have seen, databases are much more than groupings of tables. Databases are groupings of related business entities. Ask yourself the question of which is easier to convey: a static list of table names or a diagram that illustrates the tables and the relationships between the tables? Whether the person is technical or nontechnical, diagrams are much easier to work with. Diagrams enable people to more easily comprehend difficult problems and concepts.

Consider the blueprint of a building. Looking at a blueprint, you immediately get a sense of the building's purpose and structure. The blueprint accomplishes much more than words could ever hope to accomplish. In a sense, a database model is a blueprint of a database. The focus of this section is to get you on the path to creating your first database model.

What Does a Database Model Look Like?

In Chapter 2, "The Anatomy of a Real Database," you were introduced to your first database model. To review, Figure 3.1 illustrates the database model for the sample Northwind Traders Database that ships with Access.

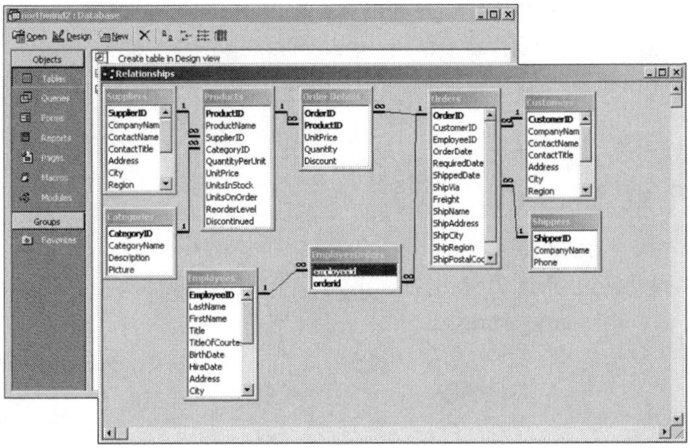

FIGURE 3.1

The Relationships View enables you to view all the tables in a database as well as how the tables are related.

In reviewing Figure 3.1, you get an immediate sense of the database's purpose. Chapter 2 delved into the purpose of the database by examining the model. Now, you will be introduced to the components of a database model.

A FEW WORDS ABOUT DATABASE DESIGN TOOLS

Database design tools can be as simple as a pen and paper. Database design tools can also be quite feature rich and complex. You can spend as little as a few hundred dollars or as much as several thousand dollars. Sam Snead, one of the greatest golfers in history, discussed how he shot a 76 with a swamp-maple sapling and a wedge in his book, *The Game I Love*. The lesson, of course, is that it is not the tool you use, but rather, how effectively you use that tool. A drawing on a piece of paper can be just as effective as a diagram produced with a tool costing thousands of dollars. Okay, maybe that is a bit of a stretch. Still, you don't have to take out a second mortgage to afford a good design tool. Two very affordable tools are on the market today:

- **Microsoft Visio**—Since the Microsoft acquisition, Visio has shipped as part of the Microsoft Office Suite. For more information, go to the Microsoft Visio Web site at http://www.microsoft.com/office/visio/.

- **Resolution xCase**—This is a full-featured database design tool that works with SQL Server, Access, Sybase, Informix, DB2, and many other databases on the market today. For more information, go to the Resolution xCase site at http://www.xcase.com.

Of course, if higher-end tools are what you need, you might be interested in the following tools:

- **Computer Associates ErWin**—Find this at
  `http://ca.com/products/alm/erwin.htm`.

- **Visible Analyst DB Engineer**—Find this at
  `http://www.visible.com/dataapp/dappprods/vadbe.htm`.

For purposes of illustrating database modeling and related notation, this book uses Microsoft Visio.

Creating Your First Model

Let's take a step back and start with a fleshed-out design to get you familiar with how to create a graphical database model. In this hypothetical situation, you have identified the following entities:

- Customers

- Orders

- Order Line Items

 Note All the concepts in this section can be employed with tools as simple as a piece of paper and a pencil. Graphical and automated design tools do make some jobs easier, such as ensuring foreign keys are created in child tables and deciphering whether a one-to-one or one-to-many relationship is involved. Some automated tools can even generate scripts that automatically create database definitions based on the model. Further, some tools are smart enough to keep the model and database in sync whenever changes are made to the model. All these features are nice. However, none of them is crucial when it comes to employing database modeling concepts and learning the notation.

Remember, it is the fiddler, not the fiddle!

When you start Visio, you are greeted with a dialog box prompting you for the proper drawing template to use (see Figure 3.2).

After you select the Database folder, you see five templates (see Figure 3.3). For this sample model, select the Crow's Foot ERD.VST template. Recalling the beginning of the chapter, the acronym ERD stands for Entity Relationship Diagram.

After you have opened the template, you can immediately use the Visio Design Surface. The Visio Designer is shown in Figure 3.4.

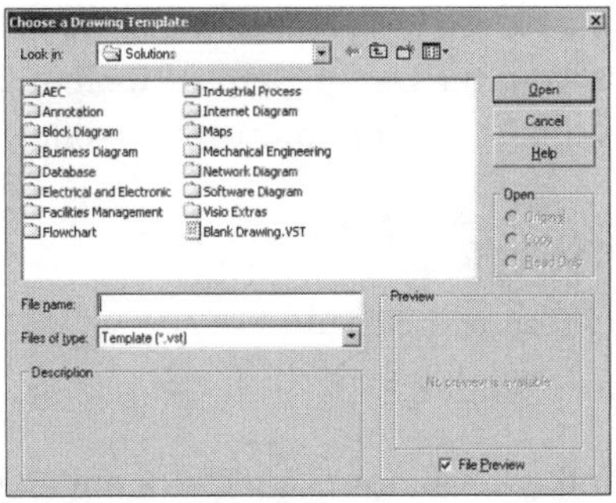

FIGURE 3.2

Visio is capable of creating many types of technical drawings, including database model diagrams.

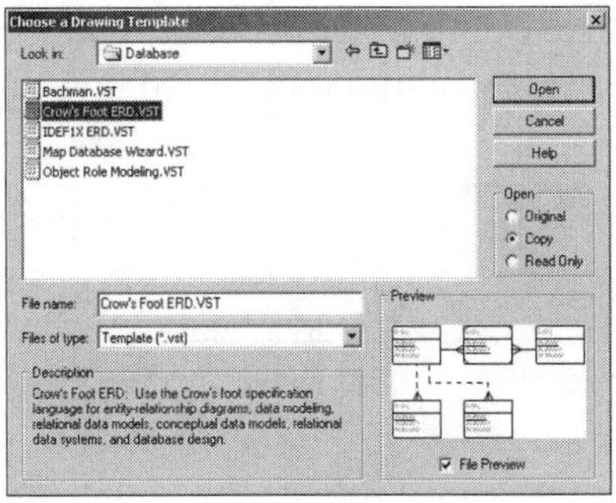

FIGURE 3.3

Visio ships with five database design templates. The most common modeling template is the Crow's Foot ERD.

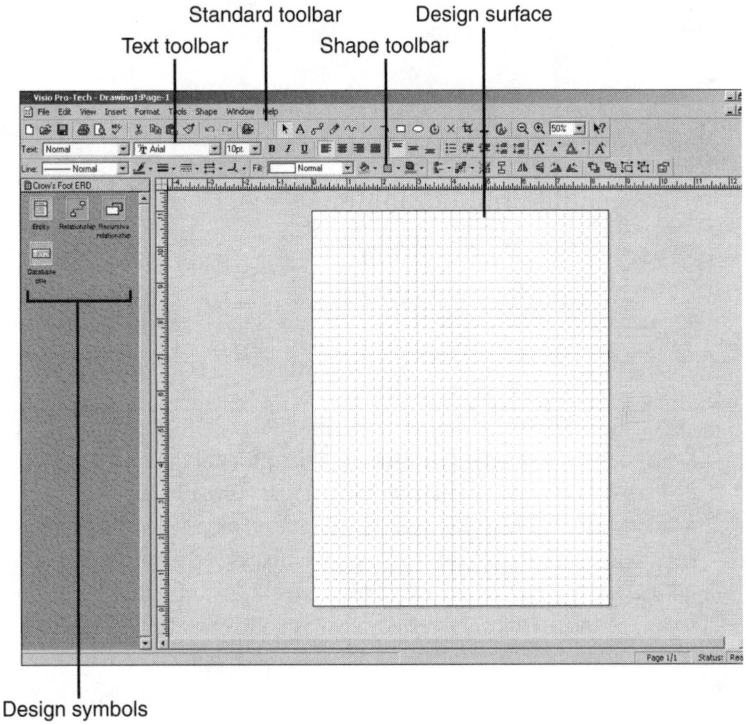

Standard toolbar   Design surface

Text toolbar   Shape toolbar

FIGURE 3.4

The Visio Design Surface starts like a blank piece of paper. Many toolbars with design tools are available to create just about any type of shape and to control just about any attribute.

Design symbols

With an empty design surface, you are ready to create your first chart. The process involves dragging design symbols from the Design Symbol toolbox and dragging the items to the design surface. Looking at the entire process, the following steps are performed in this order:

1. Place an entity on the design surface.

2. Add attributes to the entity (name, fields, and keys).

3. Specify relationships between entities.

To get a sense of how steps one and two will turn out, check out Figure 3.5. Figure 3.5 shows the Customer entity with one field defined. The field, CustomerID, is set as the primary key for the entity. There will be other fields, of course. However, the topic of which fields to include in which entities is discussed in Chapter 4.

FIGURE 3.5

The Customer consists of two attributes: the name of the entity and one primary key field.

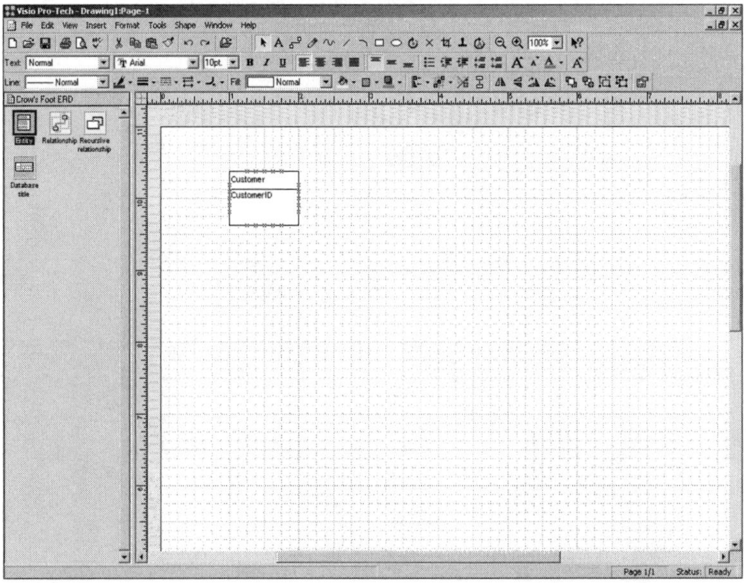

Let's take a moment to review some important concepts. Although the topic of which fields to include in an entity is being deferred until the next chapter, some fields have to be added to the entities early in the process. These fields exist to support the various relationships that exist between the entities. These fields are primary keys and foreign keys. The concepts of primary and foreign keys were introduced in Chapter 1, "An Introduction to Databases," and were illustrated in Chapter 2. If you need a quick review of these concepts, take a few moments now to do so before continuing.

Now that you know what an entity looks like in Visio, let's take a few moments to examine the notation of an entity (refer to Figure 3.5).

The type of diagram being created is called an *Entity Relationship Diagram (ERD)*. An entity in an ERD consists of a rectangle, the name of the entity, and a listing of fields. As you can see, you don't need a special design tool to create diagrams. As you will see very shortly, however, design tools make the job a lot easier.

Creating entities in Visio is very simple. The following steps guide you through the process of creating entities for the Orders and Order Line Items entities:

1. Select the entity symbol from the Design Symbol toolbox.

2. While holding the left mouse key down, drag the symbol to the design surface.

3. After it's positioned over the design surface, release the left mouse key. A new entity on the design surface will be created.

4. Select the newly created entity in the design surface, and press Ctrl+C, copying the entity to the Windows Clipboard.

5. Press Ctrl+V to paste a new entity onto the design surface. The design surface should look similar to Figure 3.6 after you have arranged the entities.

FIGURE 3.6

The two empty entities in the design surface represent the Orders and Order Line Items entities, respectively.

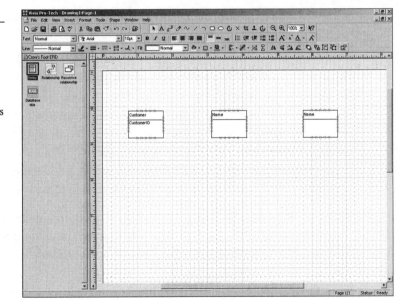

6. Select the middle entity, right-click, and select Add Attributes from the pop-up menu. Name the entity Orders, and click the OK button. Figure 3.7 shows the first tab of the Define Entity dialog box.

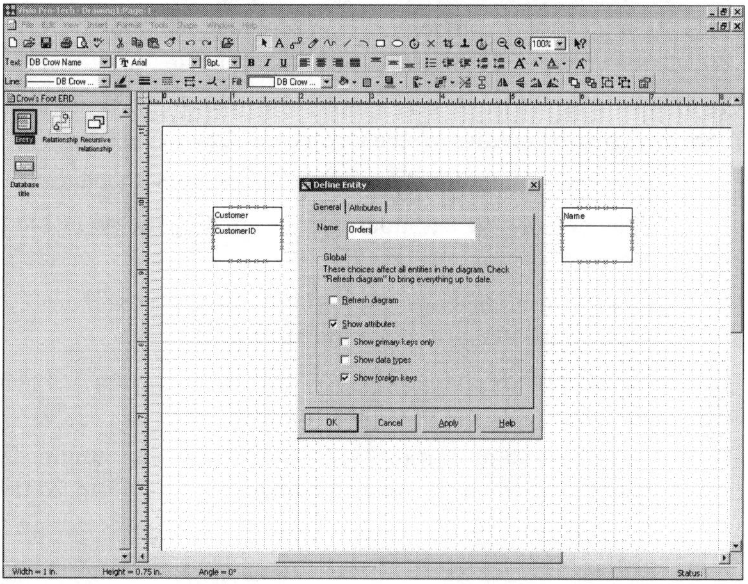

FIGURE 3.7

The General tab of the Define Entity dialog box enables you to specify the name of the entity, as well as various display attributes of the entity in the diagram.

7. Repeat step 6 for the entity, naming the entity OrderLineItems.

8. Going back to the Orders entity, repeat step 6, selecting the Attributes tab of the Define Entity dialog box.

9. Click the New button to create a new field. Name the new field OrderID, specify that the field is the primary key, and specify the data type as Integer. Figure 3.8 shows how the dialog box should look.

10. Repeat step 9 for the OrderLineItem entity, adding a field called OrderLineItemID. Your diagram should look similar to Figure 3.9.

Here is where the fun really begins and the power of an automated design tool becomes truly apparent. With the entities and their associated primary keys in place, the relationships between the entities can be created. Creating relationships, like entities, is a simple process if you follow these steps:

1. Select the relationship symbol from the Design Symbol toolbox.

2. Drag the relationship symbol to the design surface. After it's over the design surface, you will see the relationship line. Before dropping the line, be sure the left end of the line touches one of the blue markers on the Customers entity. If you did the operation correctly, the left end of the relationship line should appear in red when the relationship line is selected (see Figure 3.10).

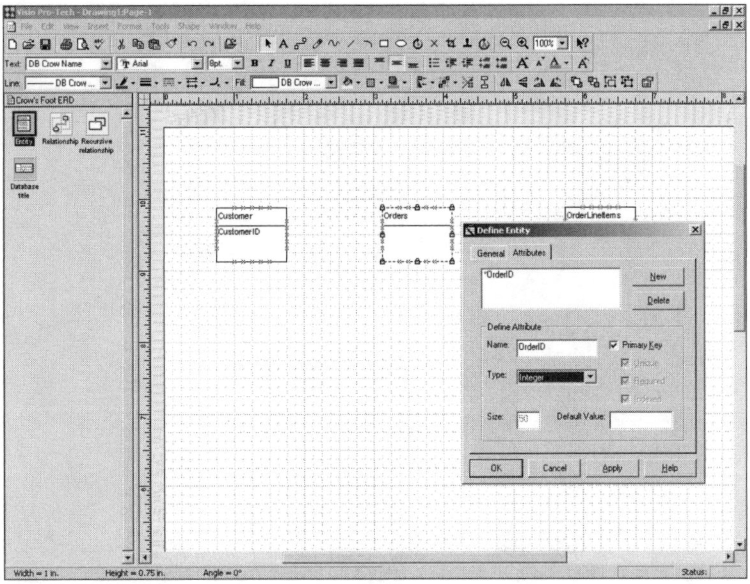

FIGURE 3.8

The Attributes
tab of the Define
Entity dialog
box enables you
to specify the
fields and their
respective attrib-
utes for an
entity.

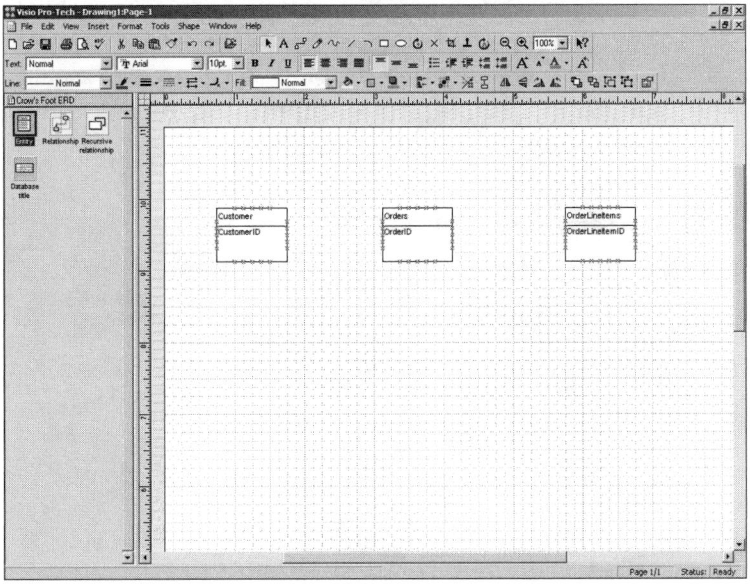

FIGURE 3.9

The sample ERD
with three enti-
ties, each with a
primary key
defined.

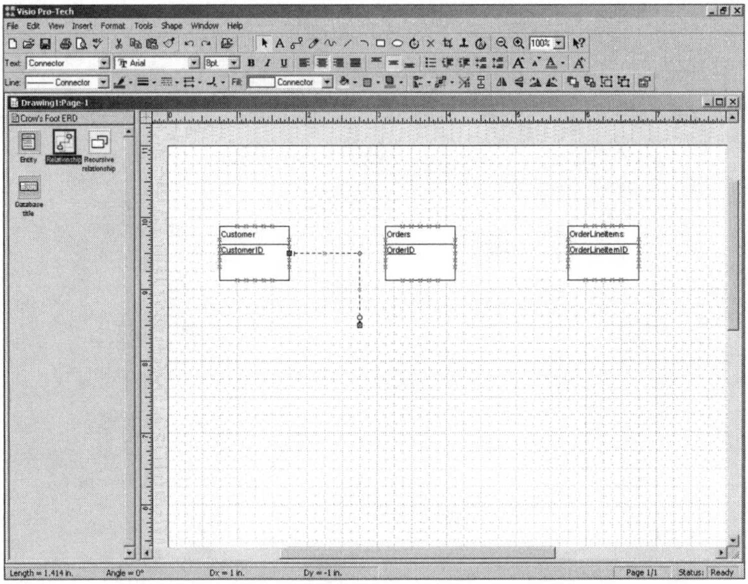

FIGURE 3.10

For the auto-
mated tasks to
work correctly, it
is important
that each side of
the relationship
line touches a
blue marker
attached to the
entities.

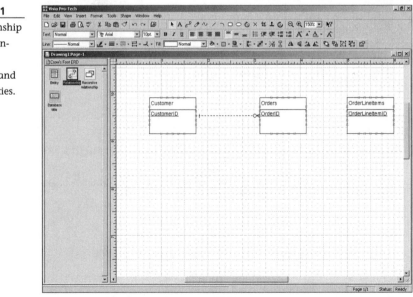

3. The next step is to attach the right end of the relationship line to the Orders
   entity. Simply click the right end of the relationship line, and drag it to one of
   the blue markers of the Orders entity. Your diagram should look similar to
   that shown in Figure 3.11. To make the illustration clearer, the diagram view
   is set to 150%.

FIGURE 3.11

The relationship
line now con-
nects the
Customers and
Orders entities.

4. Repeat step 3 for the relationship between the Orders and OrderLineItems entities.

You might be asking where the automation is. After all, you have been doing all the work. The wait is over, and here is where you will see all your hard work pay off!

From the Shape menu, select Update Foreign Keys. Voilà! Based on the relationships, the tool knew the foreign keys that had to be defined. For example, for the Order entity to support a foreign key of CustomerID, a CustomerID field had to be defined. As you will see in the next chapter, whether you elect to have some fields stored in one entity over another is optional, but the fields at this level are not optional. That is why these fields are discussed in this section. Simply put, if you don't have foreign key fields, you can't have relationships. Relationships, after all, are the heart of a relational database. If you performed the steps correctly, your diagram should look similar to Figure 3.12.

FIGURE 3.12

The database model is now complete with entities, foreign keys, and relationships.

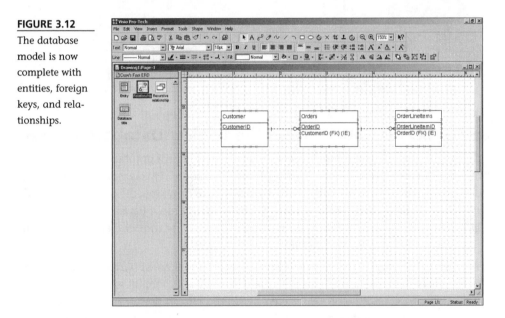

So, why do they call it a "crow's foot" model? Figure 3.13 shows why the model has this seemingly corny name.

FIGURE 3.13

A crow's foot illustrates the many-side of the relationship. A vertical line illustrates the one-side of the relationship.

Orders
OrderID
CustomerID (FK) (IE)

A crow's foot shows
many sides of relationship

A vertical line shows
one side of relationship

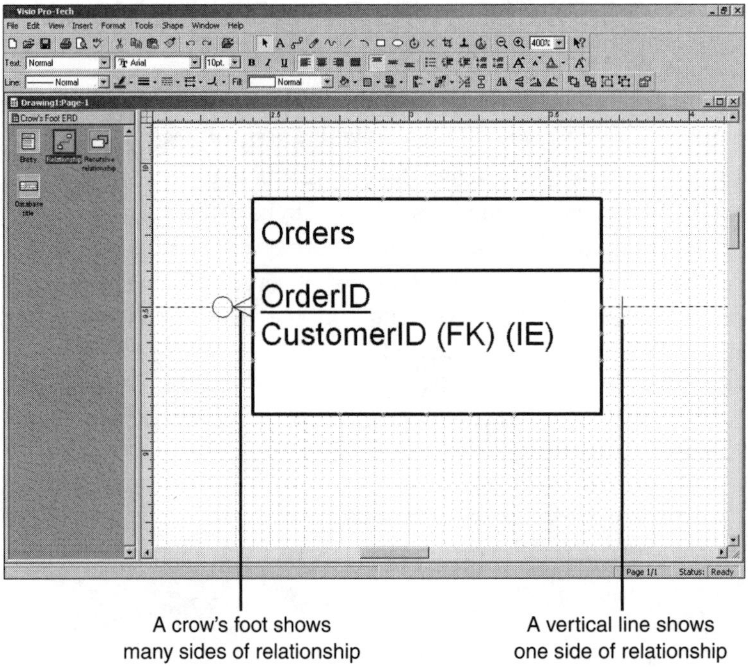

Creating a Physical Database from the Logical Database Model

An automated tool is not much use if it can't take a logical database model—the blueprint of a database—and create a physical database. This is where the worlds of designing a database and implementing a database come together. By working with models, you get a chance to visualize the concepts and ideas before implementation. This process is far more efficient than using the process of trial and error against the physical database to see whether things work correctly.

Visio and other database design tools have facilities to create physical databases from logical database models. In the case of Visio, the capability exists to create an Access database, and the process is easy because a wizard powers it. You select Tools, Macro, Database, Create Database Wizard to start the Create Database Wizard.

Be sure that no ERD errors exist. For example, an unconnected relationship results in an ERD error. If the model has errors, the resulting database will have the same errors. Before creating a database from the model, be sure to update the foreign keys before proceeding with the Create Database Wizard.

After you go through the steps of the Create Database Wizard, you will have a new Access database. The various attributes defined in the model carry through to the physical database. Figure 3.14 illustrates the results of running the Create Database Wizard.

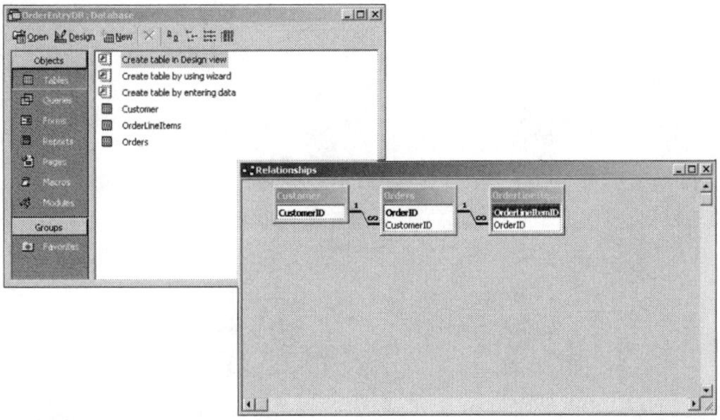

FIGURE 3.14

The Create Database Wizard used the model created in this chapter to create this Access database.

Creating a Logical Database Model from a Physical Database

How about the reverse situation in which you have a physical database and no model? Fortunately, Visio has the capability to take a physical database and reverse-engineer the database to create a logical database model.

To import a database, follow these steps:

1. From the File menu, select New, Database, Map Database Wizard.
2. Tell the wizard where the database you previously created is located.
3. Choose to map all entities.
4. Create a Crow's Foot diagram, and leave the Layout option as is.
5. Select to show all attributes and show foreign keys. Leave the other attributes as is.
6. Provide a title and description for the database diagram.
7. Click the Finish button.

Figure 3.15 shows how the resulting model should appear in Visio.

FIGURE 3.15

The Map
Database
Wizard, reading
an existing
Access database
file, created this
database model.

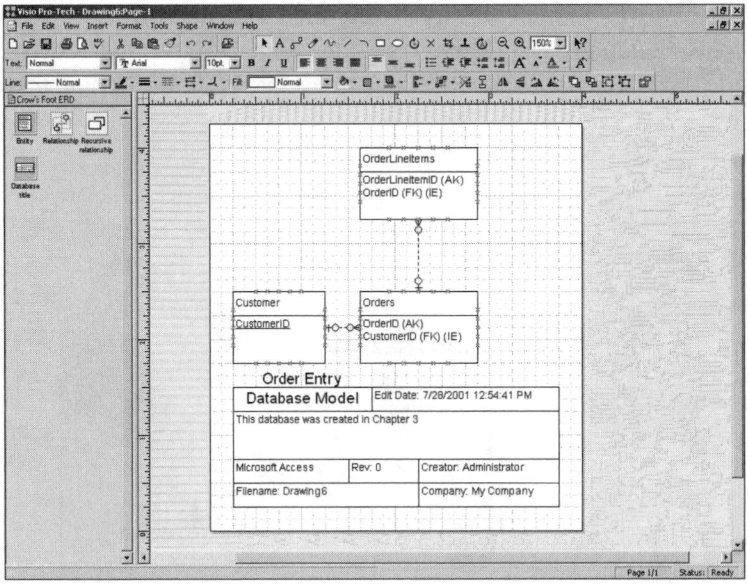

Model the Time Entry and Billing Database

Now that you have a good understanding of what database modeling is, you can
employ the techniques to your current project—the Time Entry and Billing Database.
Through the course of interviews and the analysis of business documents and forms,
you have identified the following entities:

- Clients
- Employees
- Cases
- Invoices
- TimeEntryDetail

In the course of your analysis, you have identified the following relationships:

- Clients can have one or more cases.
- Clients can have one or more invoices.
- Invoices are made up of one or more TimeEntryDetail records.
- Time is charged to a case.
- Employees charge time to a case.

Figure 3.16 shows the database model at this point in the development process. As you will soon see, there are already a few wrinkles to contend with.

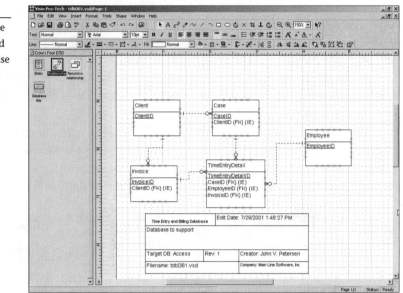

Editing the Text

Have you noticed the shape in the diagram in Figure 3.16 that contains descriptive information about the chart? The shape is called the database title and is located in the Design Symbol toolbox. After you place the database title shape onto the design surface, each text block can be edited by following these steps:

1. Click the database title shape; this selects the entire shape. A green selection marquee will surround the border of the shape.

2. At this point, you can select each rectangle contained within the database title shape. As you select each contained rectangle, a gray selection marquee surrounds its border.

3. Press the F2 key. This highlights the text, allowing you to modify the text.

Refining the Design

The design so far looks good. Is it complete? Given that this is the first iteration of the design, the answer most likely is no. This case is no different. Did you notice relationship number five is marked with an asterisk? Although this relationship might not seem ambiguous at first, it is very ambiguous. Let's look at the relationship "Employees charge time to a case" a bit more closely.

Suppose in the course of interviewing, you discover that an employee must be assigned to a case before the employee can charge time to a case. Does the current design of the database have a direct relationship between cases and employees? No, indirectly a relationship exists. From the Case entity, you can find employees who have charged time to the case by going through the TimeEntryDetail entity. As long as all employees associated with the case have charged time to the case, you can find all the employees associated with a case. What if, on the other hand, you need to get a list of all employees associated with a case and you know that some employees working on the case have not charged time? The short answer is that you are out of luck!

It is important to emphasize that relationships between entities have to be supported regardless of whether specific instances of data exist. In other words, even if an employee has not charged time to a case, that employee has to appear in a list of employees for that case. Figure 3.17 shows the refined design.

FIGURE 3.17

Version 2 of the Time Entry and Billing Database model supports a direct relationship between employees and cases.

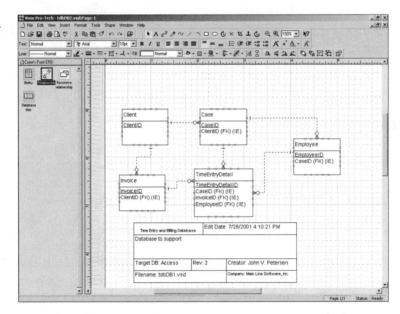

Do you see another problem? Based on this model, when it comes to associating employees with cases, you have the following situation: Each time an employee is associated with a new case, a new employee record for that employee must be created. This results in duplicate employee records. It would not take long for your database to become cluttered with a lot of redundant data. When it comes time to create queries and reports, your task will be difficult. What happens if an employee changes her name and she is associated with 10 cases? Ten different employee records would have to be modified. You have enough knowledge about relational databases to know that this scenario would be unacceptable. One of the main design goals with relational databases is to achieve data consistency by way of reducing data redundancy. So, then, how do you go about solving the problem?

Do you recall in Chapter 2 when the topic of many-to-many relationships was discussed? That is exactly the issue that exists in this case. Employees can be associated with one or more cases, and cases can have one or more employees. In Chapter 2, you were shown that breaking a many-to-many relationship down into two one-to-one relationships addresses this situation. To solve the problem, a new intermediary table, called a *junction table*, must be added to the model. Junction tables are also called *many-to-many resolver tables*—what you call it is not nearly as important as what the table accomplishes. Junction tables enable you to facilitate data consistency by way of reducing data redundancy. Figure 3.18 shows version 3 of the database model that contains the new junction table and modified relationships between the Case and Employee entities.

FIGURE 3.18

Version 3 of the Time Entry and Billing Database model supports a many-to-many relationship between cases and employees.

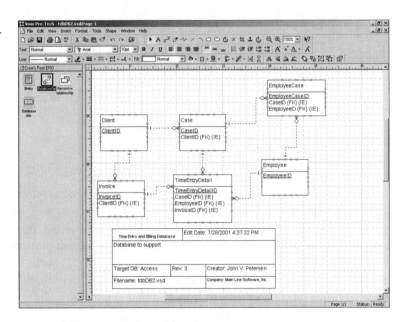

There is still a little more work to accomplish before the first draft of the database design can be considered complete. As you continue your analysis, you find that multiple clients can be associated with a case. Because of this change, the granularity of associating a TimeEntryDetail record with a case, an employee, and an invoice is not enough. Although it is true that the TimeEntryDetail record has to roll up to one case, one invoice, and one employee—because multiple clients can be associated with a case—the TimeEntryDetail entity must carry the ClientID as a foreign key. See Figure 3.19 for the complete first version of the Time Entry and Billing Database.

FIGURE 3.19

Version 4 of the Time Entry and Billing Database model represents the completed first draft of the database model.

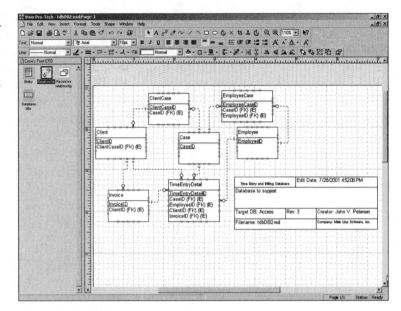

What You Have Learned

In a real scenario, you might find that many more iterations are required to get to an initial design. The time it takes to achieve a useful design is dependent on how thorough your analysis is and the frequency with which you seek input from the users of the database. Of all the sources of information you get, report requests might be the most valuable because you can often reverse-engineer reports to the base entities that are required to produce such a report. Of course, other sources of information—interviews and existing systems—are also important. In different situations, you can rely on different sources to different extents.

The result of your analysis work culminates in the form of a database model. The most common and easiest to understand modeling technique is the Entity Relationship Diagram (ERD). Tools such as Visio automate the process of creating logical database models and creating physical databases from the models. ERDs consist of entities, entity attributes, and entity relationships.

If there is one key lesson, it is this: Don't get buried in the details too quickly. As you deal with the trees, stay aware of the forest. This chapter did not delve into the details of the fields of information each entity will store. Why? Because it is not a requirement in achieving a solid initial database design. In fact, getting into the details too quickly can be a hindrance. Will the complement of entities change as the field definitions for entities are fleshed out? Most likely, the answer is yes. But that is okay; it is a basic part of the design process.

Remember the mantra of "be patient"? Remember those Paul Masson commercials: "We will sell no wine before its time"?

In the next chapter, you take the design to the next stage of development through the process of normalization. At the conclusion of Chapter 4, the design of the Time Entry and Billing Database will be complete.

4

DATABASE DESIGN CONTINUED: AN INTRODUCTION TO NORMALIZATION

CHAPTER HIGHLIGHTS:

- What Does It Mean to Normalize a Database?
- Steps to Normalize Your Data Model
- Denormalize Data—When Does It Make Sense to Break the Rules?
- Normalization Applied—Review the TEB Database and Refine the Design
- What You Have Learned

In the last chapter, you were introduced to basic database design concepts. In this chapter, you will build on those skills. If you recall one of the basic mantras of this book, it takes several iterations of work to reach an optimal database design. After your initial complement of tables has been created, the next step involves outfitting the tables with columns. At this point, the only columns that exist are the primary and foreign keys necessary to support the relations between the tables. The question at this point is, "What columns do you include in a table?" Some of the columns to include can be determined through the application of common sense. Other columns to include are not as intuitive. As you will see, whether to include a column can determine whether new tables have to be created. If you think all the tables for the Time Entry and Billing (TEB) Database have been created, you are in for a surprise! The process of determining which columns go in a table is called *normalization*. The normalization process is the focus of this chapter, and upon completing this chapter, the TEB Database design will be complete.

What Does It Mean to Normalize a Database?

Database normalization can best be characterized as the process of organizing a database. With the question of *what* out of the way, let's turn to the question of *why*. The goal of normalization is to reduce problems with data consistency by reducing redundancy. Sound confusing? The concept of normalization is probably easier understood by way of a simple example. To illustrate, let's again turn to the Northwind Traders Database that ships with Access.

Figure 4.1 shows the ERD (Entity Relationship Diagram) for the Northwind Traders Database that was introduced in Chapter 2, "The Anatomy of a Real Database." Notice the relationship between the Customers and Orders tables. As a quick review of how relationships work in a relational database, the primary key of the parent table is carried in the child table as the foreign key. In this case, the CustomerID field is carried in the Orders table. This is how order records for a specific customer can be associated with that customer.

Why then not carry other fields from the Customers table? As you will see later, sometimes you might elect to carry other fields from the parent table to the child table. As a general rule, however, you will not want to do this. For example, what if you decide you are going to carry the CompanyName field in the Orders table and the company name changes? Not only would you have to update the Customers table, you would also have to update the Orders table and any other table in which CompanyName exists. Continuing with this example, what if the various locations of CompanyName were not consistently updated? Which version would reflect the current, most accurate version of CompanyName? If you were asked to prepare a report that needed to include CompanyName, which table should you use as the source of CompanyName?

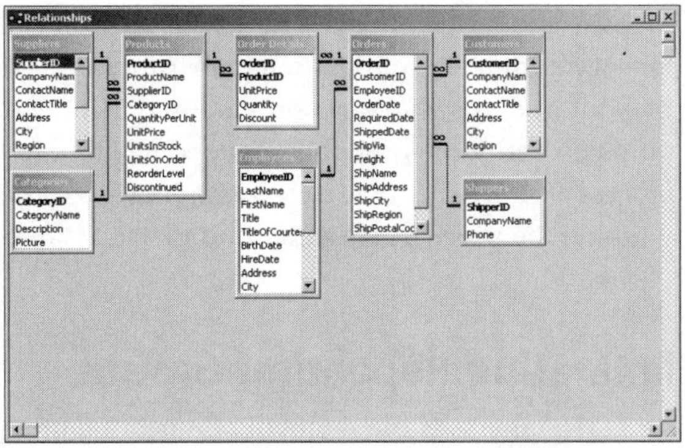

FIGURE 4.1

The Entity
Relationship
Diagram for the
Northwind
Traders
Database shows
a relationship
between cus-
tomers and
orders.

It seems clear that if you have only one instance of a given data element in a database, it leaves nothing to interpretation and guesswork. When you update CompanyName in the Customers table, you can be sure that every report that relies on CompanyName will be accurate and up to date. Why? Because CompanyName is not carried redundantly in the database, and as a result, consistency is ensured. The same concept can be seen throughout the data model in Figure 4.1. Greater consistency through the elimination of redundancy—this is the goal of normalization!

Steps to Normalize Your Data Model

Just as achieving an optimal database design is a multistep process, so, too, is the process of normalization. At a minimum, you will want to normalize to the third normal form. Quite possibly, you might need to go one step further by normalizing to the Boyce-Codd Normal Form. Fourth and fifth normal forms do exist, but their use is far less common. For informational purposes, the fourth and fifth normal forms are described briefly at the conclusion of this section.

To illustrate the normalization process, consider the following list of unnormalized data items:

- Customer ID (primary key)
- Customer Name
- Customer Type
- Contact Name (one to many)
- Category Name (one to many)

If you have ever worked with data that comes from a nonrelational data source, this scenario might be familiar to you. In this example, a customer record length is variable because each customer can have a different number of contacts and each customer can be part of multiple categories. Remember that in its raw form, information produced by your analysis efforts is nonrelational. All the attributes you have identified for a given entity are probably grouped together in a flat structure. This is where the process of normalization comes into play—to organize the attributes. Let's begin by taking the previous structure and placing it into the first normal form.

First Normal Form: Eliminating Repeating Groups

The first normal form (1NF) involves the removal of repeating groups. The question remains, "What is a repeating group?" The previous example has two repeating groups: contacts and category. Remember, for a given customer, one or more contacts and one or more categories can exist.

For each repeating group you encounter, the repeating group is moved to a separate table. In this case, you end up with two new tables that store the contact and category data. The following outlines the new structure and entities:

- Customer table:
    - Customer ID
    - Customer Name
    - Customer Type

- Contact table:
    - Contact ID
    - Customer ID
    - Contact Name

- Category table:
    - Category ID
    - Customer ID
    - Category Name

As you might guess, the Customer table is a parent to the Contact and Category tables. The two relationships are one to many. in other words, each customer can have one or more customers and can be associated with one or more categories. What about the primary keys for each new table? Think about this issue for a few minutes. The issue of primary keys is directly related to the second normal form, the topic of the next section. In the previous chapters, the primary key has always been expressed as a single field. Although this is the case for the previous Customer table, can the same be said of the Contact and Category tables? The answer is not as clear-cut as you might think. Keep thinking about this issue—it will be picked up in the next section.

Before going any further, it is important that you see the benefits derived by moving contacts and categories to separate tables. Imagine how difficult the task of managing contacts would be if contacts were kept in the Customer table. If a customer could have only one contact, the argument could be made that contact data, such as name, phone number, and so on, could be stored in the Customer table. After all, in this case, you would be dealing with a finite set of columns. But what if somebody makes a database enhancement request that involves the support of multiple contacts per customer? You have two choices:

■ Add more columns to the Customer table to support multiple contacts.

■ Add a child table that allows for any number of contacts.

Clearly, choice number two is the easier, more flexible, and more cost-effective alternative. With choice one, your database design could continually be changing whenever a specific customer has exceeded the number of contacts the Customer table can support. If there is one thing that can spell doom for a database application, it is a continually changing database structure and model. A solid and stable database model is the foundation on which everything else rests. After an application has been developed, changing the database structure can be quite expensive and time-consuming. The entire application has to be tested thoroughly to ensure bugs have not been introduced as a result of the database modifications. Attending to these issues at the beginning avoids many problems that would otherwise occur.

The various normal forms are cascading. In other words, before you can tackle the job of applying the second normal form, the first normal form must be applied. The same prerequisites apply for the succeeding normal forms. With the first normal form out of the way, let's proceed to the second normal form, which involves eliminating redundant data. How will this affect each table? The answer follows in the next section.

Second Normal Form: Eliminating Redundant Data

To get tables into the second normal form, you must analyze the fields in relation to the primary key. The question of primary keys was raised in the previous section. The Contact and Category tables' primary key is a multivalued key, so you can't look at a single field that can uniquely identify a record. Looking at the Category table, the primary key is a combination of the Category ID and Customer ID fields. Many customers can use the same category, and a customer can be part of many categories. A customer, however, can't be part of the same category more than once. This makes sense. Because of this rule, the combination of Category ID and Customer ID uniquely identifies a record in the Category table. Let's turn our attention to the Contact table. As you will see, this scenario presents an ambiguous situation.

Does Contact ID uniquely identify a contact record? It might uniquely identify a record; then again, it might not. How is that for an answer? The answer depends on the context. Is the Contact table purely about contacts? Or, is it more accurately named a Customer Contacts table? Again, the answer depends on the context. Can a contact be associated with multiple customers? Or, can a contact be linked with one and only one customer? The analysis and design efforts on your part can answer this question. Sometimes, large corporations can exist as several entries in a customer table. It is quite possible that a contact person could be linked to several customer records. It is very important that your analysis and design efforts uncover details such as this. After a system has gone into production, it can be very expensive to correct this mistake.

HOW MUCH DOES IT COST TO CORRECT THAT MISTAKE?

Using $1 as a base, correcting a mistake at the earliest possible time costs $1. The earliest possible time is when you are engaged in the process of analysis and design and modeling your database. After your database has been created, the cost to correct that same mistake is $10. After your system has begun the process of beta testing, that same mistake costs $100. If the mistake gets through beta testing and is part of the product released into production, that mistake costs $1,000 to fix.

If you think about it, this makes sense. After you get into the process of beta testing, if a mistake is found, you have to start the process over. Imagine if your application is installed in a few hundred sites. The cost of having to redistribute software and update a database can be immense. The idea to take away from this is that as you go through the various stages of development, the cost of fixing bugs increases by a factor of 10. The more effective your analysis and design efforts are, the more likely you are to stay within the budget and deliver your applications at or ahead of schedule.

For the purposes of this illustration, let's assume that a contact can be associated with a single customer. With this in mind, the Contact table is in the second normal form because attributes do not depend on part of a multivalued key, meaning the contact name depends on the contact ID alone. In this case, the Contact ID field does uniquely identify a contact record. Also in this case, no redundant data exists. What about the Category table? Is it in the second normal form? In this case, the answer is no.

Whereas a contact is specific to a customer, a category is a generic item. To illustrate, let's assume some of the valid categories are medical, marketing, and financial. A customer might be a member of both the financial and marketing categories. Each of these categories likely is associated with multiple customers. To illustrate, consider the following entries that might be found in the Category table:

Category ID	Customer ID	Category
1	1	Medical
2	1	Marketing
3	2	Financial
2	2	Marketing

There are two questions to ask:

- What is the primary key?
- Does a category depend on all or part of the primary key?

In this case, the primary key is a multivalued key that combines the Category ID and Customer ID fields. The category depends on part, not all, of the primary key. If a field exists that does not depend entirely on the primary key, a table is not in the second normal form. To get this table into the second normal form, the categories must be removed to a separate table. This increases the table count from three to four. The following illustrates the new structure of the Category table:

- Category table:
    - Category ID (primary key)
    - Category Name

The following shows the structure of the new Customer Category table:

- Customer Category table:
    - Customer Category ID (primary key)
    - Customer ID
    - Category ID

NONSURROGATE VERSUS SURROGATE PRIMARY KEYS

Do you need a Customer Category ID field in the Customer Category table? The answer is no. The combination of Customer ID and Category ID would serve as a valid multivalued primary key. This type of primary key is also known as a *compound* primary key. In a table like Customer Category, which serves the role of being a many-to-many resolver table only, a compound key is a perfectly acceptable alternative. For one thing, it is highly unlikely the Customer Category Table will ever act as a parent; that is, the Customer Category PK is unlikely to ever be carried in a child table. Whether you choose to keep a single-value PK or a multivalue compound PK is a matter of personal preference.

The reason the field is included is a matter of consistency and preference for a specific methodology. The two methodologies in question are whether you use surrogate or nonsurrogate keys.

Two schools of thought exist on how to produce primary keys. One group says that the keys should be produced in sequential order; another group says that primary keys should be a combination of existing fields. Surrogate keys are produced in sequential order by way of some incrementing device. In Access, the autonumber field type is used for this purpose. Sometimes, surrogate keys are called meaningless keys because, when viewing the value of the key, it says nothing about the record it identifies. The other type of key, often called a multivalued or meaningful key, is made up of a combination of existing fields. Sometimes, the key is a combination of customer name + address + city + state. Anything that uniquely identifies a record will work. It is easy to see why multivalue keys are meaningful. When viewing the value of the key, you immediately see data that describes the record the key identifies.

Which method is correct? Both methods have merit. Of the two methods, surrogate keys are probably the better approach. To analyze why surrogate keys are a better approach, you need to understand the purpose of a primary key. A primary key serves to uniquely identify a record. Primary keys are carried in child data records for the purpose of linking those child records to the parent. Which is easier, carrying a single integer value in a child table or carrying a character string that might be 100 or more characters in length? What happens when the company name, address, or any other component of the key changes? Not only does the key change, but the key—carried as a foreign key in child tables—must change as well. The maintenance problems multivalued keys create outweigh any advantage they might have.

The purpose of a primary key is twofold: to uniquely identify a record and to serve as the glue between related tables, period. Its value should never change. Primary keys sit in the background and keep order. In some ways, they are similar to a referee in a football game. In good football games, you don't notice the referee. End users should never see, be aware of, or control the makeup of primary keys. With all this in mind, is a primary key the only way to uniquely identify a record? The answer is no. Consider customer number fields.

No two customers would have the same customer number. Otherwise, what use would a customer number have? Often, companies have a systematic way of numbering customers. Part of the number might indicate information about the customer, such as the name. If this is the case, the customer number should not serve as the primary key because it is dependent on characteristics in the customer record. Remember, if some aspect of the customer record changes that the customer number depends on, the customer number must change as well. Of course, there is no reason the primary key could not serve a third purpose of being a customer number as well. If this is indeed the case, users should not have control over the makeup of the customer number.

The following outlines how sample data might appear in the Category table:

Category ID	CategoryName
1	Medical
2	Marketing
3	Financial

The following outlines how sample data might appear in the Customer Category table:

Customer Category ID	Customer ID	Category ID
1	1	1
2	1	2
3	2	1
4	2	2

Prior to placing the tables in the second normal form, consider the scenario of changing the description of a category. With redundant data, multiple updates would need to occur. With the second normal form, a category description exists in one location only. After that single entry has been changed, any reports would automatically be up to date. In regard to reports, consider that prior to placing the tables in the second normal form, you must create a report that displays the Category Name field. What would you use as a source for the field? With the second normal form, the answer is much clearer.

Let's take a closer look at the Customer table. Looking at the Customer Type field, it would appear that another repeating group exists. The following illustrates how the data appeaers in the Customer table:

Customer ID	Customer Name	Customer Type
1	Ace Tomato	Business
2	PMH	Hospital
3	Rutgers Law	School
4	Microsoft	Business

In order to apply the second normal form, a new Customer Type table must be created. The following outlines the structure of this new table.

Customer Type ID	Customer Type Description
1	Business
2	Hospital
3	School

Now that a new Customer Type table exists, the Customer table must be modified so that a link between the two tables can be established. The following outlines the new Customer table structure:

Customer ID	Customer Name	Customer Type
1	Ace Tomato	1
2	PMH	2
3	Rutgers Law	3
4	Microsoft	1

Figure 4.2 shows the new data model produced through normalization.

FIGURE 4.2

The tables in this data model conform to the second normal form.

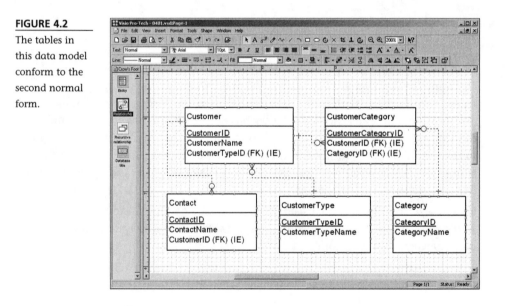

Third Normal Form: Eliminating Columns Not Dependent on Keys

You started with a single flat structure. To get to the first normal form, repeating groups were moved to separate tables. This resulted in three new tables: Contact, Category, and Customer Type. The next step is to get the tables into the third normal form. In order to illustrate this process, some new fields need to be added to the Customer table. The following outlines the new structure of the Customer table:

- Customer ID
- Customer Name
- Customer Type ID
- City
- State
- ZIP Code

The Customer table is in the first normal form because no repeating groups exist, and the Customer table is in the second normal form because a multivalue key does not exist. In this case, a single surrogate primary key exists. The question turns to whether the Customer table is in the third normal form. The third normal form requires that any field that is dependent on anything besides the primary key be moved to another table. The table the field is moved to may be an existing table or a new table. What about fields such as city, state, and ZIP Code—do they depend on the Customer ID Primary Key? The answer is no. These elements are completely independent of the Customer ID Primary Key.

Let's take a few moments to examine the relationship between city, state, and ZIP Code. A ZIP Code is specific to a city and a state. For example, 19301 is specific to Paoli, Pennsylvania. There is, however, a Paoli, Oklahoma as well. Remember the goal of normalization is to remove redundant data. You only want to have to define an element of data one time and reuse that element of data as needed. Consider a city like Philadelphia that has hundreds of ZIP Codes. As you examine the problem, it becomes clear that new tables will be required. In this case, you would create a state, city, and citystatezip table. The following outlines the various table structures:

- State table:
    - State ID
    - State Name

- City table:
  - City ID
  - City Name
- City State Zip table:
  - ZIP Code
  - City ID
  - State ID

Because you can be sure a ZIP Code is unique, you could use the ZIP Code itself as the primary key. Figure 4.3 illustrates how the data model appears after the third normal form has been applied to the Customer table. As you will see when the topic of denormalization is discussed, leaving the Customer table in the third normal form may not yield optimal results.

FIGURE 4.3

The tables in this data model conform to the third normal form.

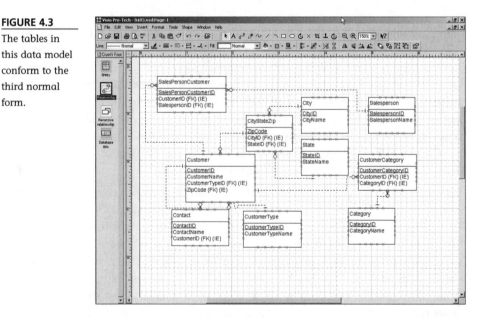

Most of the time, the third normal form is as far as you will have to go. It should be noted, though, that fourth and fifth normals do exist. Their use, however, is rare and infrequent. In the interest of completeness, the following section outlines these additional normal forms.

Fourth and Fifth Normal Forms

In most situations, the third normal form is as far as you have to go. That is not to say that is the end of the normalization story. Fourth and fifth normal forms exist. The fourth normal form isolates independent multiple relationships, and the fifth normal form isolates semantically related multiple relationships. What the heck does this all mean? It is a mouthful of words, but the concepts are not that difficult to understand. Let's start with the fourth normal form.

As you go through your analysis, you determine that categories of customers fall within certain sales volume ranges. Knowing what you know about normalization, you decide to create a sales range definition table and in turn, link that table to the Customer Category table. The following outlines the revised structure of the affected tables:

- Customer Category table:
    - Customer Category ID (primary key)
    - Customer ID
    - Category ID
    - Sales Range ID

- Sales Range table:
    - Sales Range ID (primary key)
    - Sales Range Description

The question is whether a meaningful relationship exists between the Customer Category and Sales Range tables. Most likely, the answer is no. The customer itself has sales, but sales ranges are not associated with a customer by way of the categories the customer might be associated with. To be in the fourth normal form, the Sales Range ID field needs to be moved to the Customer table. In the current hypothetical case, the Customer, Contact, Category, and Customer Category satisfy the fourth normal form already.

The fifth normal form concept is a bit harder to grasp. The fifth normal form involves breaking tables in the fourth normal form into separate tables for the purpose of reducing the amount of rows that must be inserted, modified, or deleted during various update operations. The question is whether maintaining a few extra rows of data is easier than maintaining an extra table. If you don't really need another table, it is best to avoid creating the table. To illustrate the fifth normal form, consider the following example.

Let's add a Salesperson table to the hypothetical database you have been working on. The database can record which categories are associated with a customer. In addition, the database also records which salesperson is assigned for a given customer category combination. The implication is that a customer category salesperson table would have to exist to support the association between the three entities. Because a meaningful relationship exists between categories and salespeople, the customer category salesperson is in the fourth normal form.

Now, let's assume a new rule is put into place that after a salesperson is associated with a given customer category combination, the salesperson has access to the other categories with which the customer might be associated. If a customer is associated with three salespersons, every time you associated the customer with a new category, you must add three records in the customer category salesperson table—one for each salesperson. The same situation would occur if the customer were associated with three categories and a change in salesperson were made. In this case, three records would have to be updated. The fifth normal form involves breaking up the table to reduce the number of records.

To accomplish the goal, a Customer Salesperson table and a Customer Category table would be established. This explanation assumes that a Customer Category table did not exist. Rather, the analyses lead directly to a Customer Category Salesperson table. Figure 4.4 shows the data model and new entities that are in the fifth normal form.

FIGURE 4.4

The tables in this data model conform to the fifth normal form.

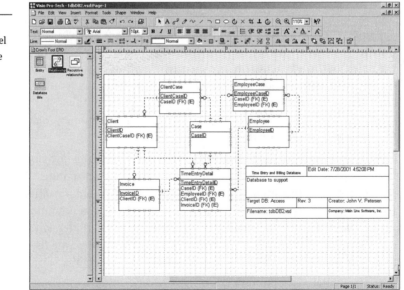

Normalization: Some Final Thoughts

As you gain experience developingdatabases, you will find that normalization becomes an implicit and less of an explicit process. In other words, as you organize and model the information acquired in the requirements-gathering activities, you will immediately create tables that conform to the third normal form so long as you use single-value surrogate keys. If you have a many-to-many relationship, as is the case between customers and categories, you might have to take the additional step of going to the fourth normal form. As long as the table that acts as the many-to-many resolver—the Customer Category table in this case—contains only the minimum data required for supporting the many-to-many relationship, you don't have to worry about getting to the fourth normal form because the table will already conform. Finally, if you don't have to be concerned about getting to the fourth normal form, you don't have to be concerned with the fifth normal form. Again, the table will already conform. It can also be argued that if you don't have to be concerned with getting to the fourth and fifth normal forms, those normal forms don't apply. As long as you get to the third normal form and as long as you have been thorough in your analysis and design efforts, your chances of success are very good.

Denormalize Data—When Does It Make Sense to Break the Rules?

Consider the case of the city, state, and citystatezip tables. On one hand, these tables conform to the third normal form. On the other hand, every time you need to write a query to extract customer data, you will need to join data from four tables. Whenever you normalize data, you always have to balance the competing goals of reducing data redundancy with the extra work that will be created when needing to extract data from the database. Most of the time, elements like city, state, and ZIP Code are carried redundantly. Consider the case of trying to assign a city to a customer but the city has not been defined in the city table. You need to maintain the city table first. Now, what would have taken only one operation now takes two. This is not to say that a valid business reason may not exist to divide the city, state, and ZIP Code information into multiple tables. In this case, it makes sense to break the rules and denormalize.

The rules of normalization are important ones to follow. At the same time, it is important to recognize that situations do arise where it makes sense to break the rules. If you do break the rules, be sure you have an important reason for doing so. Reducing the complexity of queries and improving query performance are good reasons to denormalize. Because you are breaking the rule, it should be an exception, not the norm. Therefore, if you find yourself continually denormalizing, take a moment to scrutinize what you are doing. Chances are, you are misapplying the concept of denormalization.

Normalization Applied—Review the TEB Database and Refine the Design

With a good understanding of normalization, it is time to apply the concepts to the current project, the Time Entry and Billing Database. To review, the following tables have already been identified:

- Case
- Client
- ClientCase
- Employee
- EmployeeCase
- Invoice
- TimeEntryDetail

Figure 4.5 shows the relationships between the entities.

FIGURE 4.5

Version 4 of the Time Entry and Billing Database model represents the completed first draft of the database model.

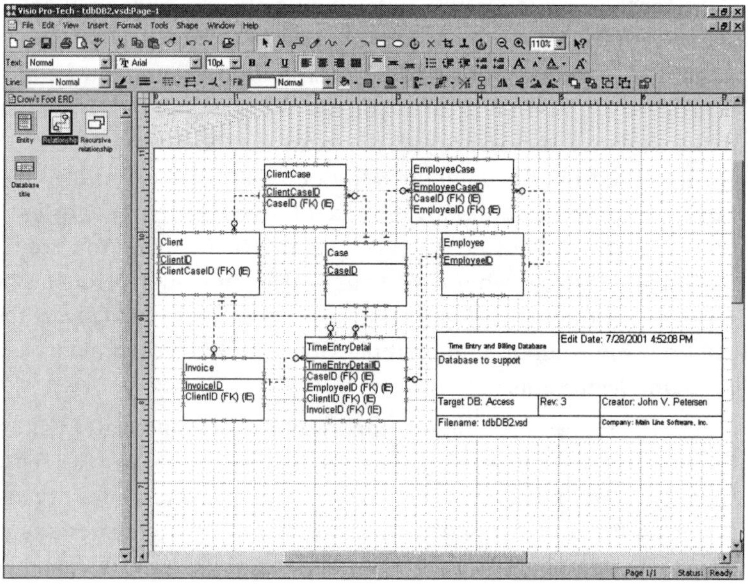

Identifying New Columns and Tables

As you might guess, the need will arise for new tables. Before getting to that step, the existing tables must be outfitted with columns. Before going any further, it is also important to note that every time-entry issue has not been contemplated. The sample you are working through contains the basic information required to illustrate and teach the database concepts covered in this book. Let's now build up the data model started in Chapter 3, "An Introduction to Database Design."

EmployeeCase and ClientCase Tables

If you recall, the EmployeeCase and ClientCase tables are many-to-many resolver tables. Clients can be assigned more than one employee. In addition, an employee can be assigned to multiple cases. The same type of relationship exists between clients and cases. Because of the nature of these tables, no additional columns are required.

Employee Table

Let's begin with the Employee table. What type of information needs be stored in the Employee table? At a minimum, the following data elements are required:

- Employee ID
- First Name
- Middle Initial
- Last Name
- Social Security Number
- Address 1
- Address 2
- City, State, ZIP Code
- Home Phone and Work Extension

In addition to those previously listed, a few more elements of information are required. One element is the Employee Classification. In the firm, you have partners, associates, paralegals, legal secretaries, and other administrative staff. Anytime you run into one of the classification items, it is a good bet that another table will be required. Do you remember the discussion on the third normal form? An employee classification is a generic item that is not dependent on the EmployeeID key. With this in mind, an EmployeeClassification table must be added, along with an EmployeeClassificationID foreign key in the Employee table.

Law firms typically have multiple departments. For example, a law firm might have some or all of the following departments: tax, antitrust, civil litigation, intellectual property, insurance, and municipal, to name a few. Sounds like another classification item, doesn't it? Yes, you will be adding another table to the database, called Department. In addition, you must add a field called DepartmentID to the Employee table.

Just to keep track of things, the Employee table has the following structure:

- Employee ID (primary key)
- Department ID (foreign key to Department table)
- Employee Class ID (foreign key to Employee Class table)
- First Name
- Middle Initial
- Last Name
- Social Security Number
- Address 1
- Address 2
- City, State, ZIP Code
- Home Phone and Work Extension
- E-Mail Address

In conjunction with the new foreign keys, the following tables have been added to the data model:

- Department
- EmployeeClass

The Department table, in addition to having a DepartmentID field, also has a Description field. The EmployeeClass table has an EmployeeClass ID and a Description field.

Client Table

The Client table is pretty straightforward. The following elements of data need to be stored:

- ClientID (primary key)
- Client Type (business or individual)
- First Name
- Middle Initial

- Last Name
- Organization Name
- Address 1
- Address 2
- City, State, ZIP Code
- Phone
- E-Mail Address

A few items need to be addressed. First, with respect to Client Type, do you need another table to hold the various types of clients the firm represents? In this case, the answer is no. While conducting your analysis, you have found that only two types of clients will ever exist: businesses and individuals. With this in mind, each client record can have a Client Type field that holds either "B" for business or "I" for individual. In a case like this, there is no practical benefit for having an additional lookup table.

How about contacts? There is no question that in the case of business clients, you will need to provide for contacts. The next question is whether you can have multiple contacts for each client. Most likely, the answer is yes. You will need contact information for the general counsel, a staff attorney, and the CEO, to name but a few. With this in mind, it would appear that clients could have multiple contacts. If you think a Contact table will need to be defined, you are on the right track!

The structure of the Contact table is straightforward:

- ContactID (primary key)
- First Name
- Middle Initial
- Last Name
- Title
- Phone
- Extension
- E-Mail Address

What about the Title field and the need for a lookup table? Job titles are a generic item. At the same time, job titles can vary from company to company. Here is where you need to make the decision between whether to store the information in a table or link the data with another table and a foreign key. The advantage of having predefined titles stored in a table is consistency. For example, you could control variances between CEO and C.E.O. At the same time, only a handful of job titles will probably exist. When attention turns to building user interfaces, you will be introduced to some techniques that can enforce standards, and at the same time, allow for variances. With this in mind, a separate job title table will not be created. Instead, the title itself will be stored in the contact record.

Case Table

The Case table holds basic information regarding a case, including the title, judge, court, docket number, department, start date, trial date, settlement date, and notes. Is a separate lookup table required for judge and court? The answer in this case is most likely yes. The firm wants to know which cases have been tried before specific judges. In addition, the firm wants to know the breakdown of which cases have been tried in which courts. Using the City of Philadelphia as an example, state, municipal, and federal courts exist. Within these classifications are many types of courts in which a case can be tried. The firm definitely wants to keep track of which cases are tried in which courts.

Note Court cases are calendar driven. In real life, a child table would be associated with the Case table that would keep track of various date-driven items, such as depositions, pretrial motions, answers, hearings, meetings with the trial judge, settlement talks, and so on. This child table would act as a tickler file to notify users when certain items are due or when appearances have to be made. Because these items are not directly related to keeping track of time and billing, this item will be ignored.

The Case table has the following structure:

- CaseID (primary key)
- DepartmentID (foreign key to Department table)
- CourtID (foreign key to Court table)
- JudgeID (foreign key to Judge table)
- DocketNumber
- Title
- Notes
- Start Date
- Trial Date
- Settlement Date

Every case has to be assigned to a department. For example, a patent case would be assigned to the Intellectual Property Department. What does this facilitate? When it comes time to assign employees to a case, you don't want to assign just any employees to the case. Rather, you want to assign only employees who are part of that department. As you know, an employee must be assigned to a department. As you will see later, organizing data in this manner enables you to filter the list of employees. This helps prevent mistakes, such as assigning a tax attorney to an intellectual property case. Later in the book, you will be introduced to the concepts of business rules and data integrity. As you will see, and as you can probably see already, a sound database design enhances the ability to enforce business rules and data integrity.

The new Court table contains a CourtID field and a Description field. The Judge table contains a JudgeID field, as well as a CourtID field to link with the Court table. In addition, the first name, middle initial, last name, and notes about the judge are stored as well. Even though you might not realize it, this brings up an interesting issue. The Case table has links to both the Court and Judge tables. The Judge table contains a link to the Court table, so the judge must be assigned to a court. If the judge already has a link to a court, why do you need a link to both court and judge in the Case table? This is because another judge could very likely get assigned to your case. Also, these multiple links aid in reporting.

TimeEntryDetail Table

Let's now turn to the TimeEntryDetail table. In the course of analysis, it has already been determined that a TimeEntryDetail record will link with an Invoice record when invoiced. Every TimeEntryDetail record must link to an employee-case-client combination. Remember that a case can involve multiple clients. Therefore, it is not enough to simply link to a case. The issue of which client the time gets billed to would be ambiguous. What else does the TimeEntryDetail need to store? If you have ever filled out a timesheet, you can probably guess what most of the required information will be. Elements such as description of work, date, hours, and rate are a good starting point. In this context, when rate is discussed, it is the billing rate, not the pay rate. What an employee gets paid is beyond the scope of this system. There are more issues with billing rate, so let's take a few moments to discuss those issues.

What does a client pay per hour for services performed? It depends on what the nature of the work is. For example, if administrative tasks, such as photocopying, are being performed, the client might pay $50 per hour for those services. If a paralegal is working on the case, the client might pay $100 per hour for those services, and if an attorney has to appear in court, the client might pay a flat rate of $1,500 for that service. Presently, information regarding default-billing rates is not stored in the database. A billing rate is stored in the TimeEntryDetail table. To ensure consistency and accuracy, a default rate must be stored somewhere. The question is where.

How about the Employee table? Can an employee perform different types of work? The answer is yes. An attorney might confer with the client on the phone, appear in court, or take a deposition. Each of these has different default billing rates. Based on this requirement, the nature of the work seems to define the default rate. Put another way, the default rate depends on the type of work. With this in mind, is the work category stored in the database presently? The answer is no. Therefore, a new table called WorkCategory is required. The details of the new WorkCategory table are discussed shortly. Before moving on, though, do you see how the analysis process of one table can lead to new tables and fields?

The TimeEntryDetail table has the following structure:

- TimeEntryDetailID (primary key)
- InvoiceID (foreign key to Invoice table)
- CaseID (foreign key to Case table)
- EmployeeID (foreign key to Employee table)
- ClientID (foreign key to Client table)
- Description
- Hours
- Rate
- Work Date
- Work Category

The question at this point is whether the TimeEntryDetail record will point to a related WorkCategory record or whether the information will be carried in the TimeEntryDetail record. In this case, the TimeEntryDetail record needs to be independent of changes to the WorkCategory table. For example, what happens if, when time is charged, the task costs $100 per hour and three weeks later the cost of that service increases to $120 per hour? If a link is all that exists, viewing the details of any TimeEntryDetail record would show the new rate. That scenario simply will not work. Further, the rate in the WorkCategory table is a default rate. The rate, after being added to a new TimeEntryDetail record, can be modified. For these reasons, the actual rate must be stored in the TimeEntryDetail record. Because the Work Category Description can change, that, too, is carried in the TimeEntryDetail record.

How do you know when a specific TimeEntryDetail record has been invoiced? You might think you need a field to indicate whether the item has been invoiced. This is where the InvoiceID field comes into play. This field serves two purposes. First, when a new TimeEntryDetail record is created, this field has a default value of 0. Then, after the TimeEntryDetail record has been included in an invoice, the new InvoiceID field is populated with a value. Therefore, any InvoiceID field equal to 0 in TimeEntryDetail has not been invoiced. This is how you know whether a specific TimeEntryDetail record has been invoiced.

The new WorkCategory table has the following structure:

- WorkCategoryID (primary key)
- Description
- DefaultRate

When you view the latest version of the database model in Figure 4.6, you will not see the WorkCategory table involved in a relationship. In this scenario, the WorkCategory table acts as a template. In other words, after the data in a specific WorkCategory record is used to populate data in TimeEntryDetail, no need exists to refer to the WorkCategory table. The need for relationships and to enforce relationships is very important. These concepts are discussed in Chapter 7, "The Basics of Referential Integrity." Suffice it to say at this point that in some cases, tables exist for the purpose of giving data-entry operations a head start. Remember, after a user picks a WorkCategory, the billing rate can be modified.

Invoice Table

Last but not least is the Invoice table. The Invoice table is very straightforward and has the following structure:

- InvoiceID (primary key)
- ClientID (foreign key to Client table)
- Invoice Number
- Invoice Date

The Invoice table in this context is nothing more than glue to tie multiple TimeEntryDetail records together. One element in the Invoice table makes it unique—the Invoice Number field. In this context, an invoice number is part static and part sequential. For example, invoice number 150 in the year 2001 would have the following invoice number: 2001-150. In this scenario, the invoice number is part static prefix and part sequential. How do you produce the invoice number? Because you are still in the modeling phase, the mechanics of how to produce invoice numbers is not an issue of concern.

Reviewing the TEB Model

It is definitely time to catch your breath! Figure 4.6 illustrates the latest version of the Time Entry and Billing Database model. It is very different and more expansive than what was completed in Chapter 3. It is said that a picture is worth a thousand words. Figure 4.6 conveys a good understanding of the functions the TEB Database is going to support. It is important to note that a physical database still does not exist. In real practice, you would present this model to the primary customers of the system to ensure the requirements have been met. From a budgetary perspective, this is the time you want to catch any shortfalls in functionality that might exist. If an application can be compared to a house, the database is the foundation. If the foundation is faulty, the house will fall. You can't begin construction until the foundation has been built and has had time to settle. Rush the process, and bad things are sure to follow. This is the time in the development process to ensure your application's foundation has settled.

FIGURE 4.6

The latest version of the Time Entry and Billing Database has been outfitted with new columns and tables and has gone through the normalization process.

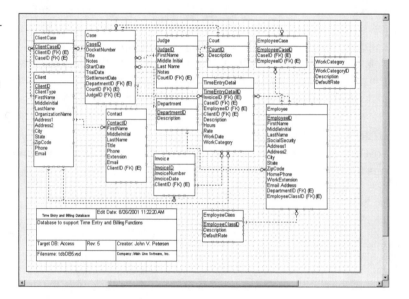

ASK QUESTIONS AND GET YOUR USERS INVOLVED!

One way you can determine whether your design is solid is to ask your database questions and determine whether the database can provide answers. For example, ask the question, "Can I determine which attorneys are working on a specific case?" Then, see whether the database can answer that question. In this case, the database can. In analyzing the design, you can see a link between cases and employees. Furthermore, employees are categorized by type in the EmployeeClass table. Obviously, if you ask a question that can't be answered, the database design is not complete.

As you might guess, catching these design gaps now, during the modeling phase, is far less expensive. Whether gaps exist can be determined by employing common sense as opposed to science. For one thing, science can't answer these questions. If you are unsure about which questions to ask, find out what the users of the system want to know. Be sure to solicit questions from all levels of the organization. Recall the earlier discussion of tactical versus strategic needs of a business? Your users will definitely appreciate being involved in the process. The more users are involved, the more likely users will take ownership and be accepting of the system.

What You Have Learned

In this chapter, you have been introduced to the concepts of normalization and the impact normalization has on database design. In most situations, a database needs to conform only to the third normal form. In some situations, however, the fourth and fifth normal forms are required. As you go through the process of normalization, you will be able to formulate which columns have to be stored in which tables. It is almost certain that your normalization efforts will lead to a few new tables that were not contemplated in your initial design efforts. This chapter and the previous chapter have outlined a roadmap and framework for conducting database analysis and design. Database analysis and design can be a complex area, so the goal in these two chapters has been to stress simplicity and common sense. To review, the following summarizes the framework:

- Gather your requirements through interviews, documents, and existing systems.

- From your requirements, identify the major things your database needs to track. These "things" are manifested as tables.

- After the major tables have been identified, identify the relationships between the tables. This process can result in additional tables.

- With the basics of your database in place, you have a framework to build on. Using normalization and information you have accumulated in your requirements-gathering efforts, data fields and additional tables can be identified.

- Finally, ask the data model questions the business needs to know. This process determines the completeness of the model. If the model can't answer a question, you will need to repeat some or all of the previous steps.

This concludes the study of database analysis and design in a formal sense. You will now embark on the more tangible aspects of building and putting your database to work. Chapter 5, "Using Access to Build the Time Entry and Billing Database," takes you through the process of building the TEB Database in Access.

USING ACCESS TO BUILD THE TIME ENTRY AND BILLING DATABASE

CHAPTER HIGHLIGHTS:

- Automatically Generate the Database from the TEB Model
- A Brief Review of the Access Database Designer
- Use the Designer to Create the Time Entry and Billing Database
- What You Have Learned

Now that you have completed your database model, it is time to create the physical database. There are two ways you can create the database. The first method generates the database automatically from the Visio diagram. The second method requires manual creation of all tables, fields, and relationships. Even with the automatic method, you will still have to manually set some field attributes. For this reason, this chapter will concentrate on the manual method. As a review, the chapter will begin with the automatic method if you choose to go down that path. Figure 5.1 illustrates your starting point, the TEB Database model created in Chapter 4, "Database Design Continued: An Introduction to Normalization."

FIGURE 5.1

The Time Entry and Billing Database model.

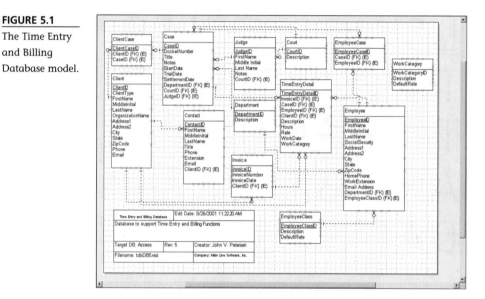

Automatically Generate the Database from the TEB Model

In Chapter 3, "An Introduction to Database Design," you were introduced to the Visio Create Database Wizard. This wizard reads a Visio database entity relationship diagram and either adds the tables to an existing database or creates a new database. For details on how this Visio feature works, take a few moments and return to Chapter 3. The following steps will be a brief review of how to use the wizard.

After you have opened the TEB Database model in Visio, from the Tools menu, choose Database Design\Create Database Wizard. Figure 5.2 illustrates the wizard dialog box.

FIGURE 5.2

The opening
screen of the
Create Database
Wizard dialog
box.

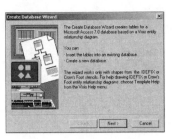

Figure 5.3 illustrates Step 2 of the wizard that requires you to specify the name of
the Visio Diagram (.vsd) file that will be used to base the new database on.

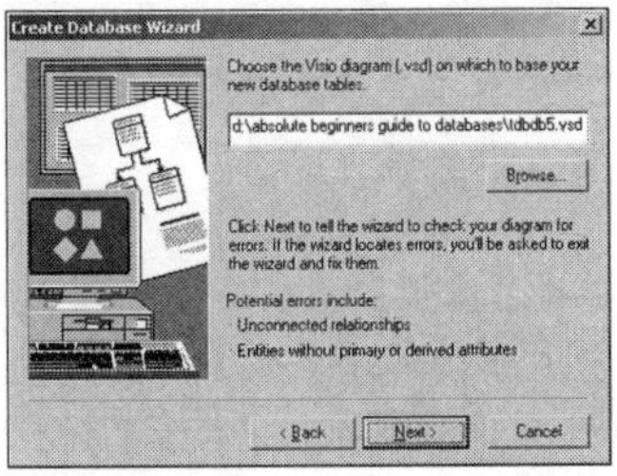

FIGURE 5.3

Step 2 of the
wizard prompts
for the Visio dia-
gram file to use.

Between Steps 2 and 3, Visio will read the file. In Step 3, you will tell Visio where
to create the new database file. In this case, name the database file TEB.MDB (see
Figure 5.4).

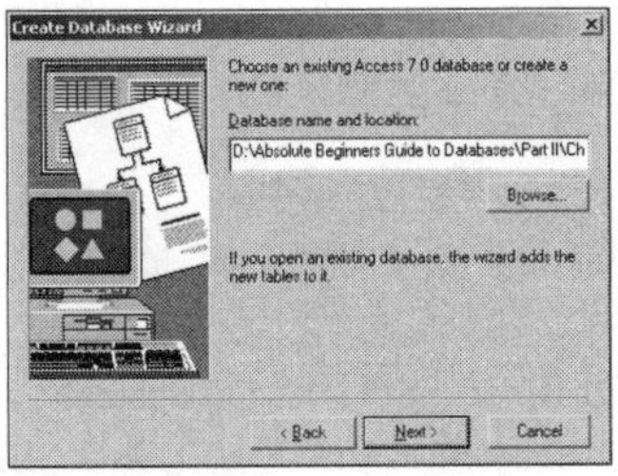

FIGURE 5.4

Step 3 of the
wizard prompts
for the database
file to create.

The last step displays the list of tables that will be created. After you click the Finish
button, the new database will be created. Figure 5.5 illustrates this step.

FIGURE 5.5
The last step displays the list of tables that will be created.

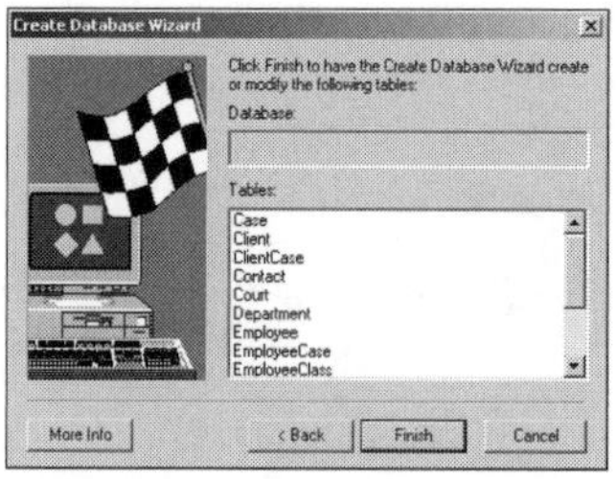

After your database has been created, double-click the icon illustrated in Figure 5.6. This will start Access and load the new Time Entry and Billing Database.

FIGURE 5.6
The new TEB Database icon displayed in Windows Explorer.

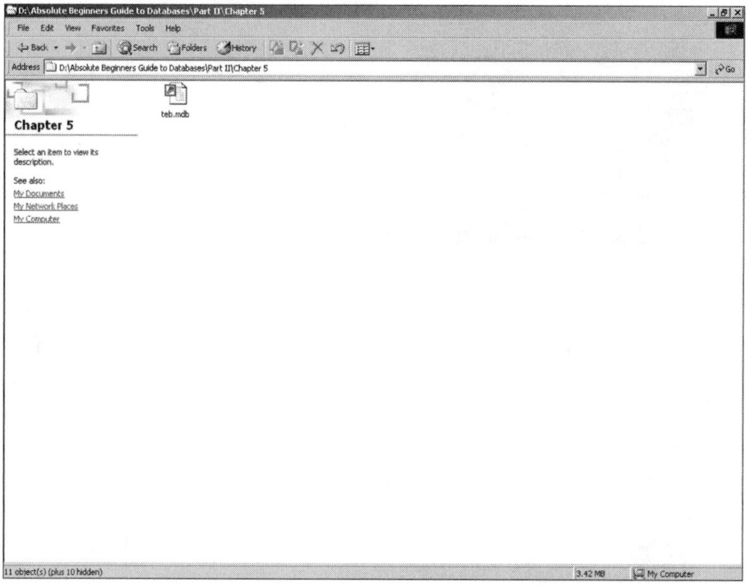

Figure 5.7 illustrates the Time Entry and Billing System Database in Access. The relationship diagram initially will look like a garbled mess. In a few minutes, by moving the entities around, you can clean things up. The mess notwithstanding, all the relationships specified in the Visio diagram are in the actual Access database.

FIGURE 5.7

The relation-
ships defined in
Visio are created
in the Access
database file.

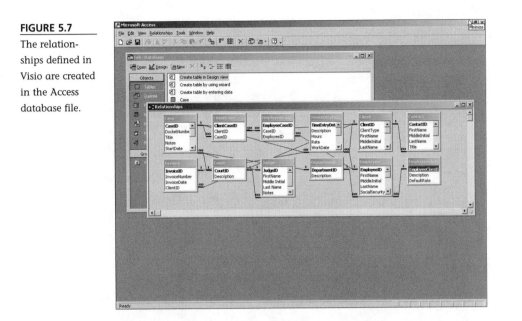

On one hand, this is a very fast and efficient method of creating Access databases.
On the other hand, you don't get an understanding of how these elements are actually created if you are new to the process. Eventually, this is how you will create the
initial versions of your databases. Because this book is about showing you the details
of how to build and work with databases, the rest of this chapter will focus on the
manual methods of creating tables, columns, and relationships.

A Brief Review of the Access Database Designer

In Chapter 2, "The Anatomy of a Real Database," you were introduced to the Access
Database Designer elements. In this chapter, you will work with these elements.
Before going further, let's take a few moments to review the lay of the land, using
the Northwind Trader's database as an example. Figure 5.8 illustrates the main components of the Access Database Designer.

The following sections briefly outline and describe the main database design components you will be working with in this chapter.

Open
object button   Delete object button

Design object button   Table designer

FIGURE 5.8

The Microsoft
Access Database
Design Interface.

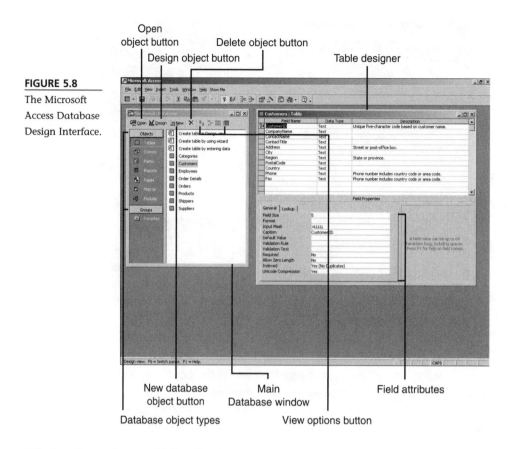

New database   Main   Field attributes
object button   Database window

Database object types   View options button

Main Database Window

There are two windows displayed in Figure 5.8. To the left is the main database window that provides access to all the objects within a database. To the right is the table
designer, which will be discussed later in this section. The main database window
itself is split into two vertical panes. The left pane outlines the different objects and
enables you to select the different object types. The list includes tables, queries,
forms, reports, pages, macros, and modules. As you select a different object in the
left pane, the contents in the right pane change to reflect the specific objects for that
type. This chapter will focus on the first object type, tables. The remaining object
types will be discussed later in the book.

Across the top of the main database window is a toolbar divided into three sections.
The toolbar operations work in the context of the currently selected object. Reading
from left to right, the first toolbar section has three options: open, design, and new.

The open button has the effect of "running" the selected object. In the case of a table, running the object means browsing the data. Figure 5.9 illustrates the data in the Northwind Customers table.

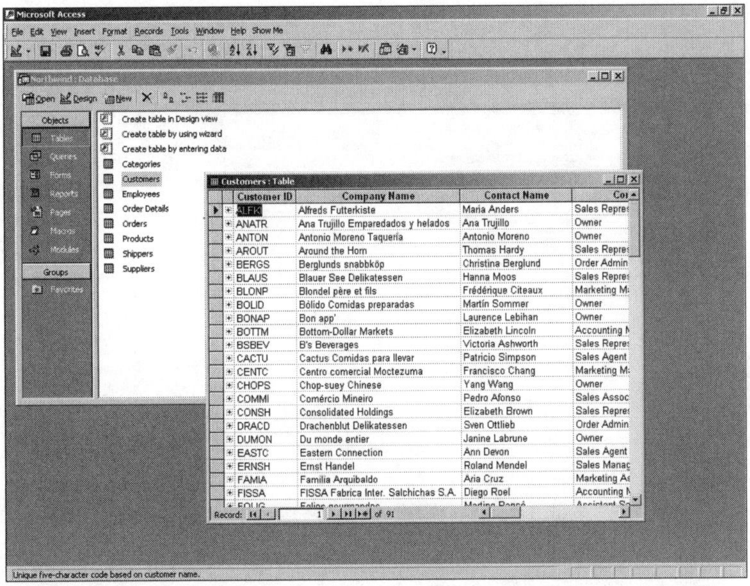

FIGURE 5.9

The Open but-
ton in the main
database win-
dow toolbar
runs the selected
database object.

The design button places the currently selected object in design mode. Double-clicking the object in the right pane will also place the selected object in design mode. Figure 5.8 illustrates the customer table in design mode. The details of the table designer components are fully discussed in Chapter 2. The new button creates a new object, based on the type selected in the left pane of the main database window.

When the New button is clicked, a New Table dialog box is displayed. Figure 5.10 illustrates the various options available when creating a new table. As you will discover, Access has many wizards that guide you step-by-step through many common tasks.

The second section of the main database window toolbar contains a single option that deletes the currently selected database object. The third section contains four options that control how the right pane in the main database window appears. The four options are large icons, small icons, list, and details. Figure 5.11 illustrates the level of object detail you can view.

FIGURE 5.10

The New Table dialog box presents a variety of ways to create a table.

FIGURE 5.11

The viewable details for each database object include the description, date modified, date created, and type.

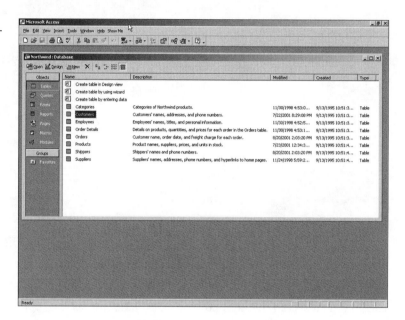

Designer Window

Let's now focus on the second major window illustrated in Figure 5.8, the designer window itself. There are several different designers in Access. The list includes the table, query, form, report, Web page, macro, and module designers. The Table Designer was introduced in Chapter 2 and will be the focus of this chapter. The other designers will be introduced when the respective object types are introduced.

Now that you have the lay of the land, let's get to work creating the Time Entry and Billing Access database.

Use the Design to Create the Time Entry and Billing Database

This section will go through, step-by-step, how to create tables, columns, and relationships. Chapter 2 gave you the 10,000-foot view on the Access design tools. Now, you are going to see and experience how these tools work through actual practice. The process will start with the creation of an empty database. After the database has been created, you will then create the tables. Within each table, you will define the columns, the attributes for each column, and the primary key. After the tables have been constructed, the relationships between the tables will be defined. After these tasks have been completed, the Time Entry and Billing Database core components will be complete. You will then be ready to undertake the next step, putting the database itself to work.

Creating the Database

Creating the database is the easiest step of all. From the File menu, select New. The New database dialog box opens and is divided into two tabs, General and Databases (see Figure 5.12). In the General tab, you can create an empty database. The General tab also provides the ability to create a database based on a predefined template (see Figure 5.13). As you develop more databases, you will find that databases will fall into distinct business classes. Databases within these classes have many common attributes.

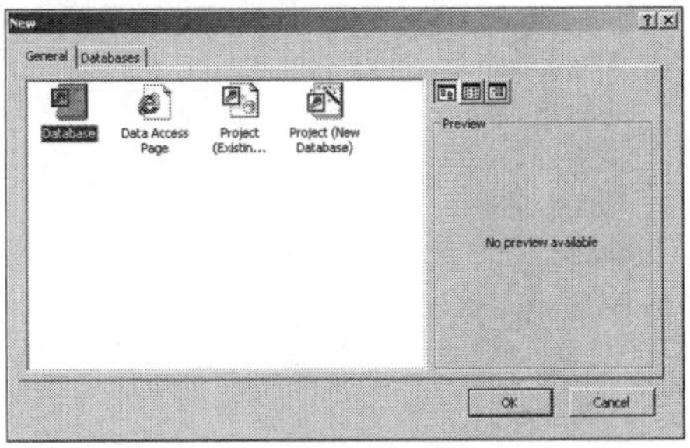

FIGURE 5.12

The General tab of the New database dialog box provides the ability to create an empty database.

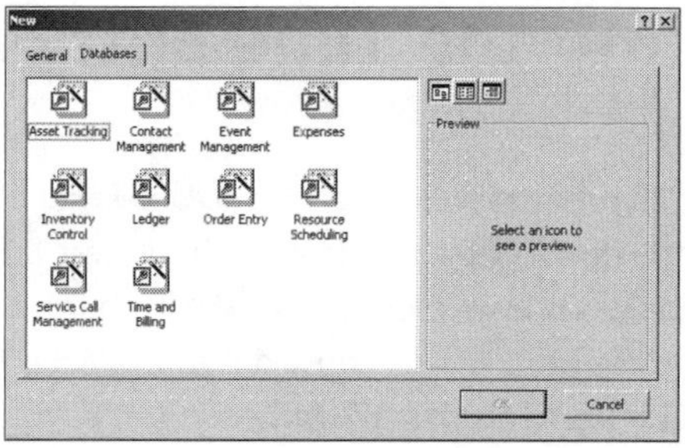

FIGURE 5.13

The Databases tab of the New dialog box provides the ability to create a database based on predefined templates.

From the General tab, select the Database icon and select the OK button. The File New Database dialog box specifying a location and name for the new database will be displayed (see Figure 5.14).

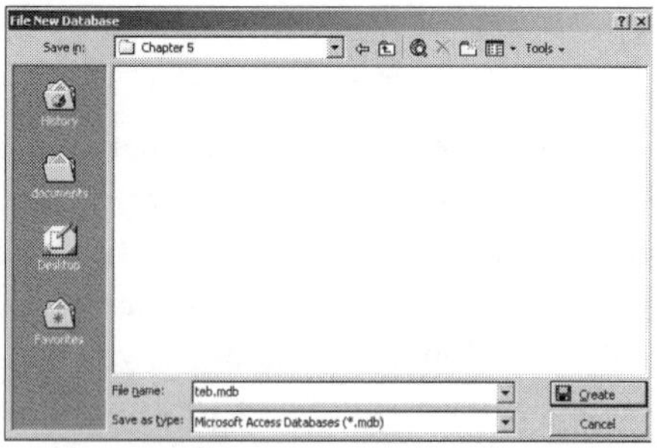

FIGURE 5.14

The File New Database dialog box provides the ability to specify the location and name of a new database file.

In the File New Database dialog box, name the new database TEB.MDB and click the Create button. Figure 5.15 illustrates the empty database that you have just created.

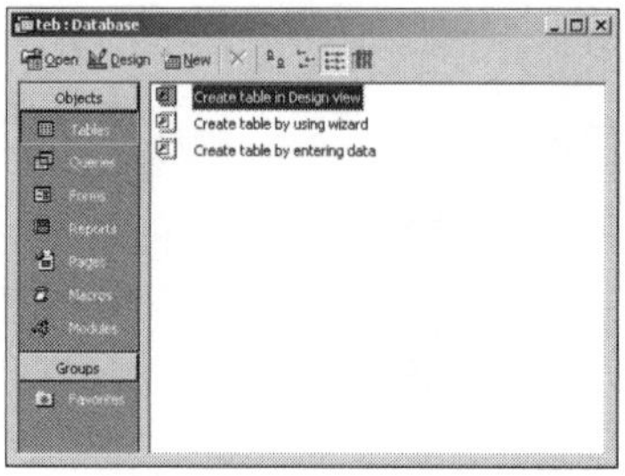

FIGURE 5.15

An empty TEB Database, ready for new table, columns, and relationships.

You may have noticed when you open the TEB Database, which is represented by the `teb.mdb` file, a `teb.ldb` file appears. Figure 5.16 illustrates this file. This file facilitates multiuser access to the database. Although you have not been introduced to multiuser concepts, it is worthwhile to take a few moments now to touch upon the subject. Consider the case when a user is working with data and another user wants to edit that data. How does the database manage that issue? This is where the `ldb` file comes into play. The `ldb` file contains information about which records are locked and which users have those locks.

For more information about `ldb` files, consult the Microsoft Developer Network Knowledge Base (MSDN KB). If you are not familiar with MSDN and the knowledge base, you definitely need to make this resource a core part of your arsenal of tools. The MSDN Web site can be found at `http://msdn.microsoft.com`. The knowledge base can be found at `http://search.support.microsoft.com/kb/`. The specific article ID for the introductory article on `ldb` files is Q208778.

Access database file
Lock file

FIGURE 5.16

Multiuser issues are facilitated with a lock file that has the same name as the underlying database.

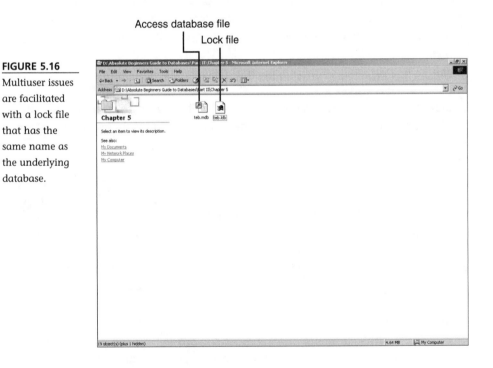

With a database created, it is time to create the tables and columns for the Time Entry and Billing Database.

Creating Tables and Columns

Creating tables and columns in Access is very simple. The first step is to create a new table. To do this, with the tables object type selected in the left pane, press the New button in the main database window toolbar. You can refer to Figure 5.8 for details on the main database window. After you click the New button, you will encounter the New Table dialog box (refer to Figure 5.10). In this case, you are going to create a table in the Design View. The Design View is the option you will more than likely use most of the time. Several new table options are available to you.

Datasheet View

Of all the options, this one is the least useful. If you do like creating your tables and at the same time, entering data, you might like this approach. You begin with what looks like a spreadsheet with 10 columns. You can rename the fields by clicking the right mouse button over the field name and typing a new name. You don't get control over other field attributes such as the data type, input mask, description, and so on. To gain control over those elements, you need to switch to the Design View.

Design View

The Design View, which is illustrated in Figure 5.8, is the preferred method of designing tables. The view is divided into two parts. The top part consists of the basic field information. The bottom part contains the extended field attributes for the currently selected field in the top part of the view.

Table Wizard

If you recall, you can create databases based on a predefined template. Even if you don't choose to go this route in creating the database, you still have access to the table templates via the Table Wizard. Wizards have their place, but they are no substitute for learning and understanding how the base tools work. As you gain more proficiency, you will find that wizards lengthen the time it takes to complete a task. As you will quickly see, like all rules, this one regarding wizards is not absolute.

Import Table

The Import Table Wizard guides you through the process of taking a table definition from an external source such as another Access database or any other ODBC data source and using that design as the basis of a new table in your Access database. In this scenario, the Wizard makes what would otherwise be a complex task very simple. It is in cases such as these where wizards have great utility.

Link Table

The Link Table Wizard is like the Import Table Wizard with one notable exception. The table definition you create in Access links to an external data source. The external data source is what actually stores the data.

Continuing on with the new table, in the New Table dialog box, select Design View and click the OK Button. An empty table designer will appear, ready to accept new fields (see Figure 5.17).

FIGURE 5.17

This is how the table designer appears when a new table is created.

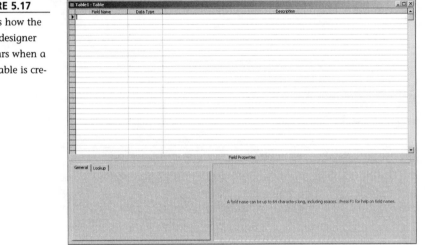

You cannot save a table until at least one field has been added. Every table must have a primary key. The first field you should add is the primary key field. Reviewing the database model, the primary key field for the Clients table is called ClientID. Figure 5.18 illustrates how the newly added field appears.

Field creation is easy. Simply follow these steps:

1. Type the field name in the Field Name column (ClientID).
2. Assign a data type in the Data Type column (AutoNumber).
3. Type a description in the Description column (Primary Key field for Client table).

The AutoNumber data type is used for primary keys. Access keeps track of the next sequential ID that will be used for new records. There is still one more task that has to be done. This involves designating the ClientID field as the Primary Key field. To do this, simply press the Primary Key button illustrated in Figure 5.18. Notice the Primary Key indicator that appears to the left of the field name.

Primary Key indicator

Primary Key button

AutoNumber
Data Type

FIGURE 5.18

Before saving a
table, you must
have at least
one field and a
primary key
defined.

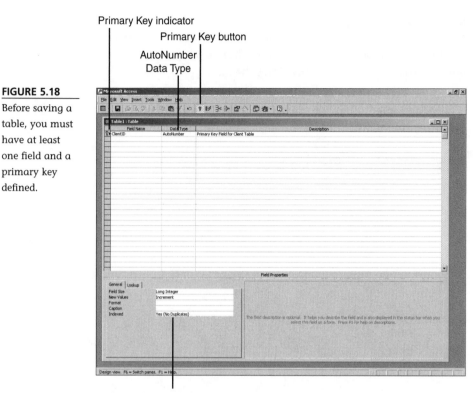

No duplicate values allowed

After you have added the primary key column, it is a good idea to immediately save
the table. You do this by clicking the Save button on the main Access toolbar or,
alternatively, from the File menu, you can select Save. In either method, you will see
the Save As dialog box (see Figure 5.19). In this case, name the table "clients" and
press the OK button.

Figure 5.20 illustrates the new Client table, which is now part of the TEB Database.

What if you want to change the name of the new object? Changing object names is
easy. The first rule is that the object cannot be open when you change the name. When
you are ready, simply select the object in the Main Database window and click the right
mouse button. Figure 5.21 illustrates the context-sensitive menu that pops up. Simply
select Rename. The cursor will be positioned at the beginning of the name, providing
the ability to type a new name. Alternatively, you can select the object in the Main
Database window and then click the object name once.

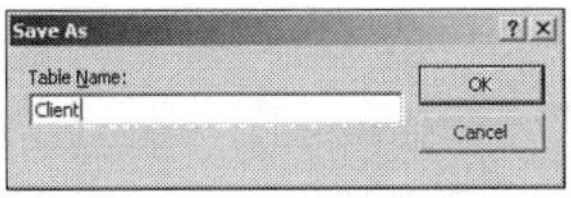

FIGURE 5.19

The Save As dialog box allows you to specify a name for the new database object.

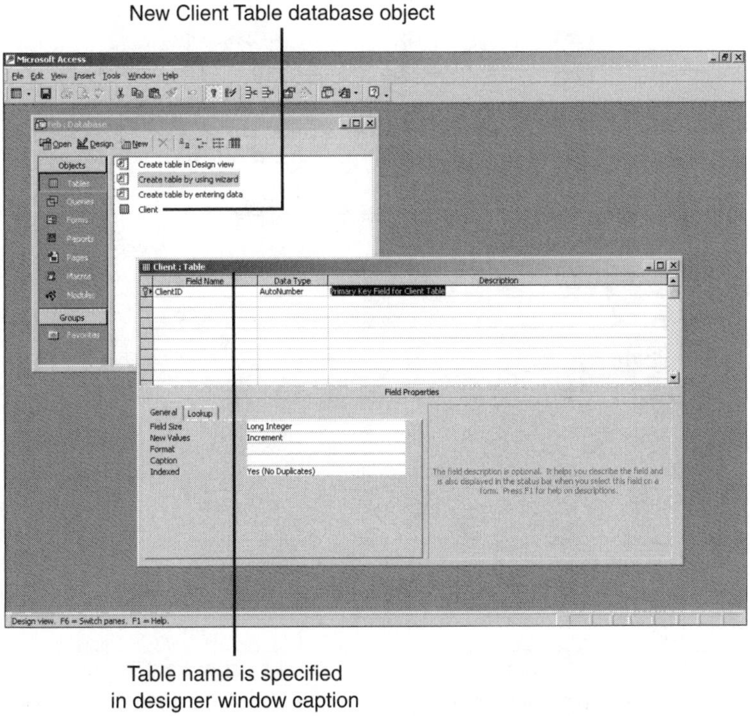

New Client Table database object

FIGURE 5.20

After a database object is saved, the object immediately appears in the Main Database window.

Table name is specified
in designer window caption

Now that you know how to add a field, it is a matter of repeating the process. Table 5.1 outlines the details for each field.

Table 5.1 Client Table Field Information

Name	Type	Size	Description
ClientID	Autonumber	LI*	PK Field for Client Table
ClientType	Number	LI	Foreign Key to Client Type Tab
FirstName	Text	30	First Name
MiddleInitial	Text	1	Middle Initial

Table 5.1   (continued)

Name	Type	Size	Description
LastName	Text	30	Last Name
OrganizationName	Text	50	Organization Name
Address1	Text	50	Address 1
Address2	Text	50	Address 2
City	Text	30	City
State	Text	2	State
ZipCode	Text	9	ZIP Code
Phone	Text	10	Phone Number
Email	Text	50	E-mail Address

LI stands for Long Integer.

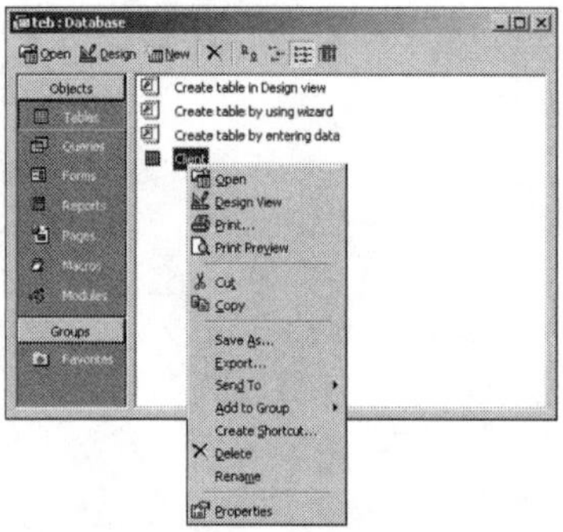

FIGURE 5.21

Clicking the right mouse button on any database object provides a context-sensitive menu with options that will operate on the selected object.

Note

As you enter field information, you will see a set of field attributes (whether a field is required or whether zero-length entries are allowed, for example). Don't worry about the settings for these additional properties. In later chapters, you will be introduced to these properties and at that time, you will learn what they are for. At this point, the following properties are the only ones of concern:

- Name
- Type
- Description
- Size

After you have added the previously enumerated fields, compare your Clients table to Figure 5.22.

In order to demonstrate how to build relationships, at least two tables have to exist. Using the information in Table 5.2, go ahead and build the Contact table. Check out Figure 5.23 to check your work. As a reminder, follow these basic steps:

1. Click the New button to add a table.

2. Create the field that will be the primary key.

3. Designate the field created in step 2 as the primary key.

4. Save the table to the database.

Table 5.2 Contact Table Field Information

Name	Type	Size	Description
ContactID	Autonumber	LI	PK Field for Contact Table
ClientID	Number	LI	FK Field to Client Table
FirstName	Text	30	First Name
MiddleInitial	Text	1	Middle Initial
LastName	Text	30	Last Name
Title	Text	30	Title
Phone	Text	10	Phone Number
Extension	Text	5	Extension
Email	Text	50	E-mail Address

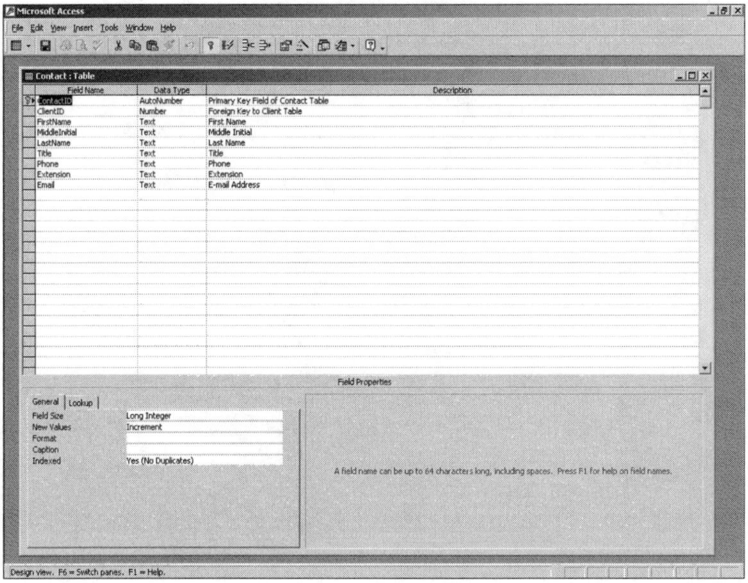

FIGURE 5.23

The Time Entry
and Billing
Database
Contact table.

At this point, you may want to create the rest of the Time Entry and Billing
Database tables. The detailed structure for each table is in Appendix A, "The
Structure of the TEB Database." Alternatively, you can wait until you have completed this chapter because the next section on relationships uses only the Client
and Contact tables.

Creating Relationships

With two tables created, you can now establish a relationship between the Client
and Contact tables. Reviewing the model, there is a one-to-many relationship (1:M)
between the tables. That is to say a client can have many contacts. Now that you
know what the relationship characteristics are, the next step is to create the relationship in the Access database.

From the Tools menu, select Relationships. Figure 5.24 illustrates the relationship
builder and the Show Table dialog box that appear. In case the Show Table dialog
box does not appear automatically, simply select Show Table from the Relationships
menu.

FIGURE 5.24

The Access
Database
Relationship
Builder.

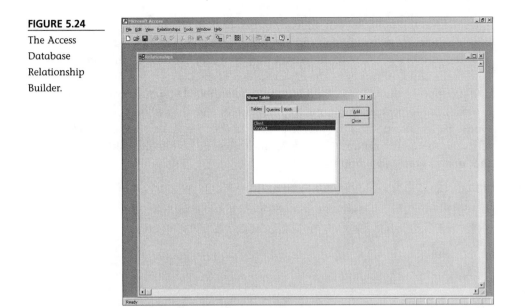

In the Show Table dialog box in Figure 5.24, be sure the Client and Contact tables
are highlighted. You highlight a choice in a list by holding the shift key down while
clicking the option with your mouse. After the tables have been selected, click the
Add button. Your relationship builder should resemble Figure 5.25.

FIGURE 5.25

The Access
Database
Relationship
Builder with the
Client and
Contact tables
added.

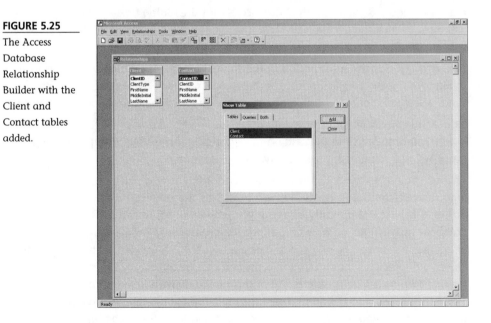

After the two tables have been added, you can click the Show Table dialog box Close button. There are two ways you can create relationships. The first way involves dragging the primary key field of the parent and dropping the field on the foreign key field of the child. In this case, the ClientID field of the Client table would be dragged and dropped on the ClientID field of the Contact table. Drag-and-drop operations are not hard to perform. Simply select the parent field, and while holding the left mouse button down, drag the mouse pointer to the foreign key field of the child, releasing the mouse button. Figure 5.26 illustrates the Edit Relationships dialog box that appears after you drop the field.

FIGURE 5.26

The Edit Relationships dialog box allows you to specify the characteristics of a relationship between two tables.

The second way you can create a relationship is to select Edit Relationship from the Relationship menu. This will display the same Edit Relationships dialog box displayed in Figure 5.26. The only difference is that the dialog box will be empty. You will need to click the Create New button to display the Create New Relationships dialog box (see Figure 5.27).

After you provide the information in the New Relationships dialog box as illustrated in Figure 5.26, the Edit Relationships dialog box will look like Figure 5.27. The Create New Relationships dialog box takes the place of the drag-and-drop operation.

Notice in Figure 5.27, the Edit Relationships dialog box knows that the relationship is one to many. Anytime the field on the right side of the relationship is not a primary key, the relationship will always be one to many.

The next step is to check the Enforce Referential Integrity check box. The details regarding Referential Integrity (RI) will constitute the subject of Chapter 7, "The Basics of Referential Integrity." To give you a quick preview, think of RI as giving the database instructions on how to manage the relationship between the tables. For example, should you be allowed to delete a client without deleting the contacts first? Or, if you do delete a contact, should the contacts be automatically deleted? The latter is known as *cascading deletes.* All of this has to do with Referential Integrity. There is a lot more to the topic. This brief overview should give you a good preliminary understanding of why databases support relationships in the first place.

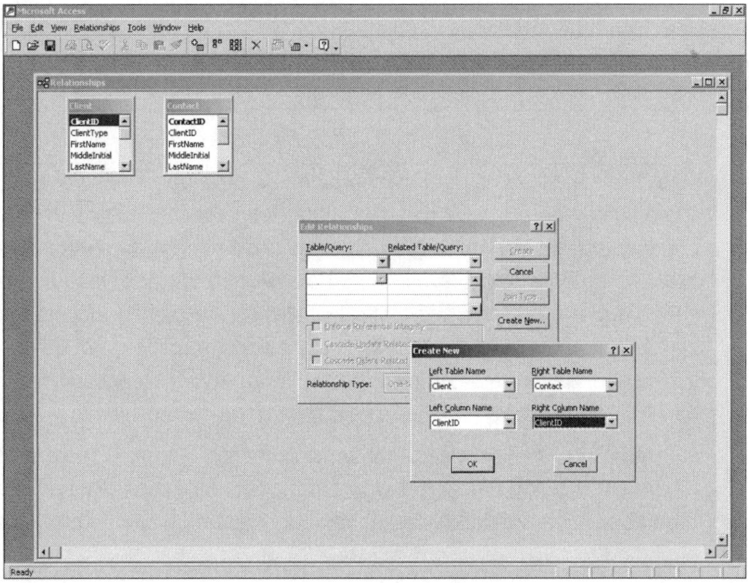

FIGURE 5.27

The Create New
Relationships
dialog box
allows you to
manually spec-
ify the charac-
teristics of a
relationship.

FIGURE 5.27

The Create New
Relationships
dialog box
allows you to
manually spec-
ify the charac-
teristics of a
relationship.

After you check the Referential Integrity check box, click the OK button. Figure 5.28
illustrates the newly created relationship. Notice the number 1 on the one side of the
relationship and the infinity sign, which looks like the number 8 resting on its side,
on the many side of the relationship.

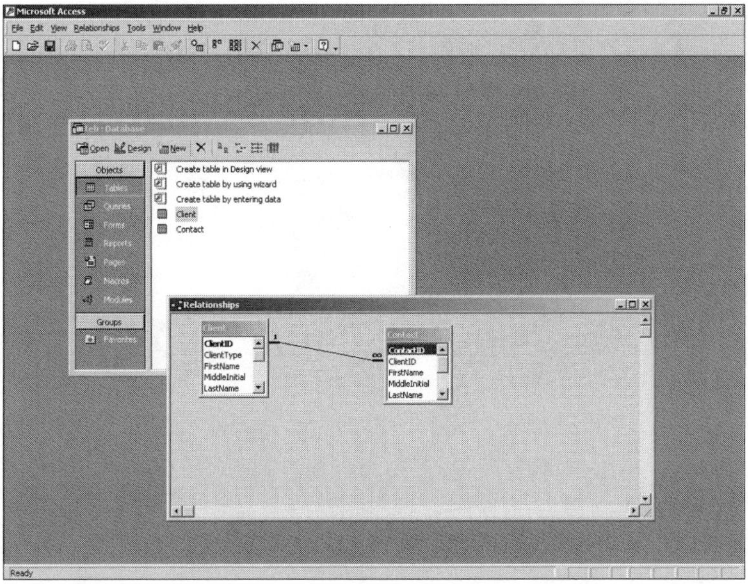

FIGURE 5.28

The new one-to-
many relation-
ship between the
Client and
Contact tables
in the
Relationship
Builder.

Any two fields involved in a relationship must be of the same type and length. If you attempt to create a relationship between two fields of different types and/or different field sizes, Access will generate an error.

One of the most important tasks in database development is documenting the work. At some point, you will have to make changes and/or train new team members. Your memory may be good, but no memory is good enough to remember every detail of a project. The only way to avoid the pitfalls of memory lapse is to accurately document your database. Truth be told, nobody really likes to prepare documentation. And although most managers and clients want documentation, nobody really likes to pay for it. The goal is to create complete documentation quickly and efficiently. As you might have guessed, Access provides a nice solution to the problem.

From the Tools menu, select Analyze, Documenter. Figure 5.29 illustrates the Documenter dialog box and the output produced by the documenting utility. All database objects can be documented. The documentation can be printed from Access or published to Microsoft Word or Excel.

FIGURE 5.29

The Documenter Utility makes quick work of documenting your database.

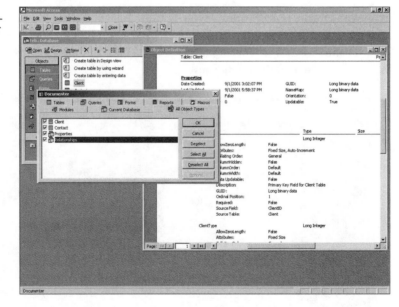

What You Have Learned

In this chapter, you were introduced to how you can take your model and turn it into a database. Two methods were introduced. The first method was an automated method of reading the model. The second method involved the manual generation of tables, columns, and relationships. You were also introduced to how relationships are built in Access. In the future, after you have a solid understanding of the details, the automated method of constructing these items will be much faster and more efficient.

This chapter concludes Part II, which focused on the design and building phases of your database. Right now, only the basic database components exist. Part III will take your database to the next level, which includes adding the intelligence to enforce business rules and database integrity.

PART III

MAINTAINING YOUR DATABASE—AN INTRODUCTION TO DATABASE INTEGRITY

6

MAINTAINING INTEGRITY THROUGH DATA VALIDATION RULES

CHAPTER HIGHLIGHTS:

- An Overview of How Validation Rules Work in Databases
- Implement Field-Level Rules
- Implement Row-Level Rules
- What You Have Learned

In Chapter 5, "Using Access to Build the Time Entry and Billing Database," you completed the process of building the core parts of the Time Entry and Billing database. The core parts included the tables, fields, and relationships. At a minimum, this is all you need to store data. The big issue now is how do you control what gets into the database? Should the user be able to enter whatever he wants? Should a user be able to save a client record without a complete address? Should there be some element of control? If there should be some control, how should that control be implemented? These issues fall under the broad category of database integrity.

Most relational database management systems (RDBMSs) have some capacity of maintaining database integrity. Database integrity falls into two broad categories: data validation rule enforcement and referential integrity. Validation rules deal with issues such as whether a value is valid for a specific field or whether the data is in a state that can be saved. For example, if the user has not specified a city for a client, the data should not be saved. This chapter is concerned with how field-level and record-level rules are defined. Referential integrity is concerned with maintaining the logical relationship between tables. For example, should you be able to delete a client record if a related contact record exists? Referential integrity is discussed in detail in the next chapter, Chapter 7, "The Basics of Referential Integrity."

This chapter will illustrate field- and row-level rules using the TEB Client table.

An Overview of How Validation Rules Work in Databases

Databases support two levels of rules. The first level is at the field-level. Field-level rules are sometimes called field-level validations. For example, if the user should be prevented immediately from entering invalid data into a field, a field-level rule would be used. Have you ever entered data into a field only not to be able to get out of the field until you enter a valid value? This is an example of a field-level rule.

Field-level rules are often criticized because they tend to interrupt the flow of work. It can be quite aggravating to continually get interrupted with validation error messages prior to saving a record. This gets to a fundamental issue of whether field-level rules are of much use if an attempt to save the record is not made. Why not check the value of all the fields at once when the record is saved? This leads to the concept of row-level rules.

Sometimes, the state of one field depends on the state of one or more other fields. In this context, field-level rules do not apply. You can only check the state of all fields just prior to saving the record. Often, database developers will rely on row-level rules exclusively. For example, rules that would otherwise be field-level rules are implemented as part of the overall row-level rule scheme. In order to provide more clarity, the next section will implement these field- and row-level validation rule concepts.

Note	One question you may have is whose job is it to ensure valid data is stored in the database? Traditionally, this has been the job of the application programs. For example, ensuring a complete address has been entered, including the address, city, state, and ZIP Code, was the responsibility of the order-entry system software. At one time, databases were merely storage devices. Perhaps in the past, this was not a big deal because it was often the case that a database was accessed by only one application. Today, databases are made available to multiple applications. What would happen if one application omitted an important validation rule? The last line of defense for data integrity is the database itself. If you recall from Chapter 1, "An Introduction to Databases," and Codd's 12 rules, Rule 5 deals with the idea that a relational database needs to support a language that facilitates data integrity.

Just because a database supports a language and complies with Codd's Rule 5, it does not necessarily follow that you have to use those database features. If, however, you are concerned with employing "best-practices," it is highly recommended that you determine which rules are essential for database integrity, and, in turn, implement those rules in the database. Then, no matter which application is used to interact with your database, your database will take care of itself and you can be assured of continued data integrity.

Implement Field-Level Rules

Before delving into how field-level validation is implemented, a study of the relevant field-level properties that support validation must be undertaken. In Chapter 2, "The Anatomy of a Real Database," you were briefly introduced to these properties. In this chapter, you will be introduced to how these properties actually work to help enforce data integrity.

Field-Level Properties

Figure 6.1 illustrates the various properties of the ClientType field of the Client Table. Depending on how you want to configure your rules, you may use some or all the properties. Depending on the field data type, some properties may not apply. For example, the Allow Zero Length property would apply only to a text field and the Decimal Places property would apply only to a numeric field. In the case of Autonumber fields, the Required property does not apply because the user does not have control over how this data is stored in the database.

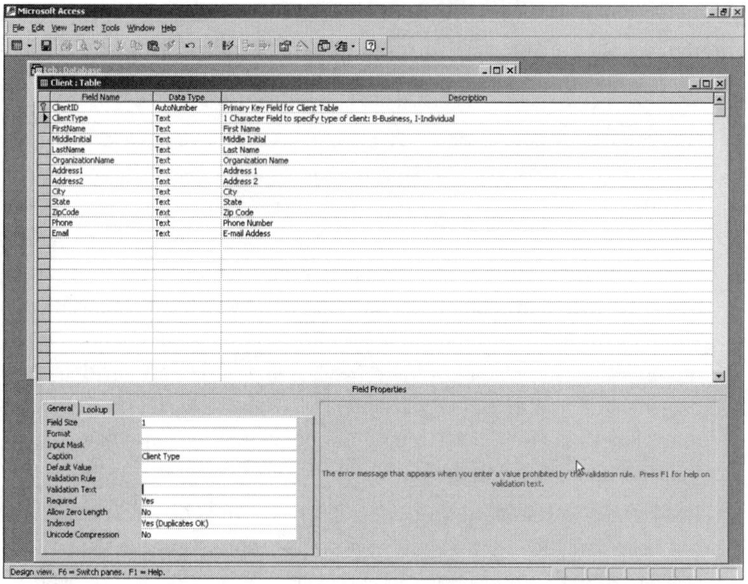

FIGURE 6.1

Access supports a variety of field-level properties to support data validation and integrity.

This section will illustrate how to establish field-level rules for the Client table of the TEB Database.

Required

If a field requires a value, the Required property is set to yes. Figure 6.2 illustrates how to set this value. This is a Boolean-type property. A Boolean can accept only two values: Yes or No. Sometimes, the values are either True or False, 1 or 0. A Boolean is like a switch—it is either in the on or off position.

> To toggle the Required property value, simply select the value with your mouse and double-click the left mousekey. Alternatively, you can single-click the down arrow and select an item from the drop-down list.

Common sense and the fruits of your analysis and design efforts will often dictate whether a field requires a value. In the case of the Client table, ClientType, Address1, City, State, Zip, and Phone are required. What about the Address2 field? Not every client is going to have the need for a second address line. The same is true for the Email address; not every client will have one. What about FirstName, MiddleInitial, LastName, and OrganizationName? These fields represent a tricky problem. Some clients will be individuals and some will be businesses. If the client is an individual, where the ClientType field = "I", the FirstName and LastName will be required. The

MiddleInitial field will not be required because not every person has a middle name. If the client is a business, ClientType field = "B," then the OrganizationName field will be required. As you can see, in these last cases, whether some fields are required or not depends on the values of other fields. This is where row-level rules come into play. This scenario will be discussed in the next section on row-level rules.

To recap, Table 6.1 illustrates the Required property settings for the Client table.

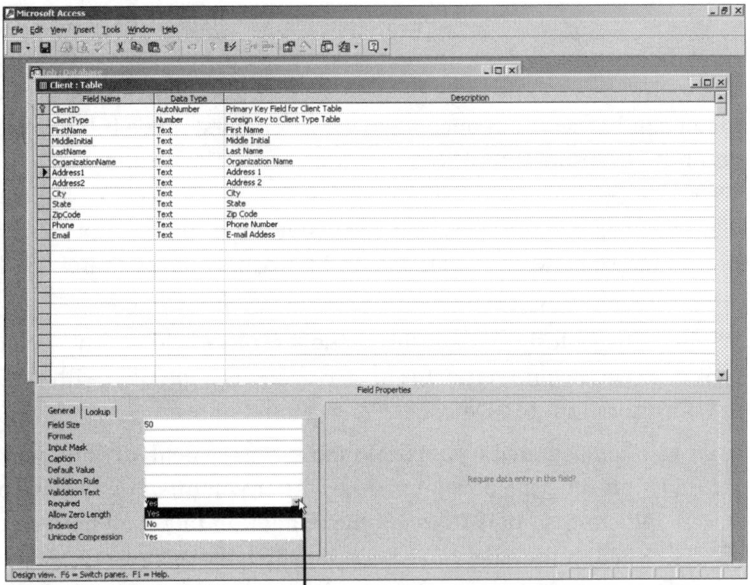

FIGURE 6.2

The Required property specifies whether data entry is required for the field.

A drop-down list stores the valid property settings for the Required property

Table 6.1 Client Table Field Required Property Settings

Field	Value
ClientID	-
ClientType	Yes
FirstName	No
MiddleInitial	No
LastName	No
OrganizationName	No
Address1	Yes
Address2	No
City	Yes

Table 6.1 (continued)

Field	Value
State	Yes
ZipCode	Yes
Phone	Yes
Email	No

Now that you have made the necessary Required property settings, it is time to see what effect this will have on data entry. If you recall from the previous chapters, tables can be viewed in one of two views. The first mode is the Design View, which you have been working with quite extensively. The second view is the Datasheet View. The Datasheet View, introduced in Chapter 2, acts like a spreadsheet. In this view, you can view, modify, and delete data in a specific table. Figure 6.3 illustrates how to toggle between the Design and Datasheet Views. Simply click the View button on the Main Access toolbar and select the desired view.

While in the Datasheet View, tab to the FirstName field and type your name. Notice that after you begin typing, the ClientID field is populated with a new value. Figure 6.4 illustrates how the Datasheet View should appear.

After you have entered a value into the FirstName field, attempt to move off the record by pressing the down-arrow key. After you attempt to move off a record, Access will check to make sure all the validation rules you have put in place have been satisfied. If the rules have been satisfied, the record will be saved. If the rules have not been satisfied, an error message, will be generated indicating that an exception has occurred (see Figure 6.5). As you can see, this is not what you would call a user-friendly message. Later in this section, you will learn additional techniques to provide your users with more intuitive and friendly messages.

At this point, if you click the OK button to get rid of the dialog box and press the Escape Key, the new record you may have thought was created is removed. No matter how hard you try, Access is not going to let you bypass the validation rules you put in place! Let's turn our attention to the Allow Zero Length property, which is closely related to the Required property.

FIGURE 6.3

The View button allows you to toggle between the Design and Datasheet Views.

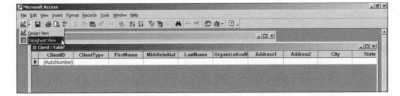

FIGURE 6.4

As soon as you enter data into a new record, the AutoNumber field will be populated with a new value.

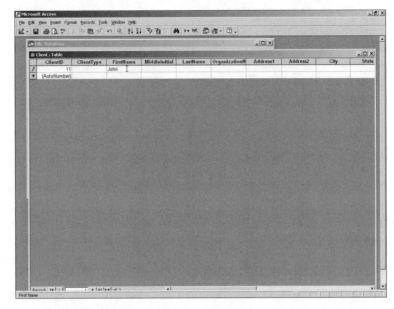

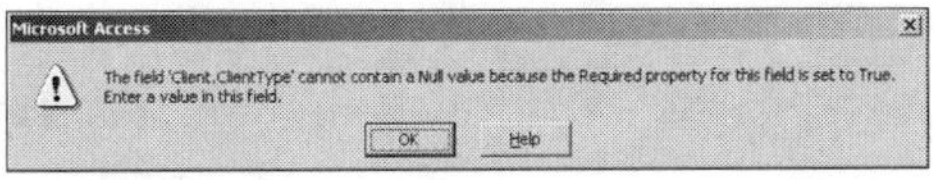

FIGURE 6.5

You will not be allowed to save the record until all validation rules have been satisfied.

Allow Zero Length

The Allow Zero Length property at first will seem confusing. The property will require you to differentiate between a null and a zero-length string.

Nulls initially can be a difficult concept to understand. Consider an empty field for a customer record. Is the field really blank or is the real value of the field unknown? Nulls indicate a situation where the value is not known as opposed to being empty.

The combination of values between the Required and Allow Zero Length properties will affect how the validation will work. The best place to start is when the Required property is set to yes. In that case, a null is never allowed. Remember that a null represents an unknown value. The fact that you are required to enter a value into a field precludes it from being unknown. Therefore, if nulls are not allowed, what about an empty string? An empty string, unlike a null, is a known value and in the case of a field where a value is required, an empty string may be valid. If that is the case, you will then want to set the Allow Zero Length property to yes.

Let's turn our attention to when the Required property is set to no. A field that is not required can always accept a Null Value. The question is whether you are allowed to enter a zero-length string. The issue turns on whether you need to know the difference between a zero-length string and a null. Take, for example, an e-mail address. If there is nothing in the field, does this mean the client does not have an e-mail address? Or, does this scenario mean that the client's e-mail address is not known? Later in this section, the Format property will be discussed. The Format property provides a way to control how a null is displayed. If you want to have the null appear as an empty string, you can. What the user sees is not nearly as important as being able to tell the difference between a null and an empty string. To the user, they are the same thing. To you, the database developer, they represent very different things. Let's take a few moments to go down the list of fields to see what the settings should be.

The ClientType field must be either "B" or "I." By definition, it is required and because there are only two possible values, a zero-length string should not be allowed. How about FirstName, MiddleInitial, LastName, and OrganizationName? Would it make sense to have an empty-string valid LastName value? The answer is most likely no. You are either going to have a value in these fields or you are not. When you think about it for a moment, a zero-length string will almost never be valid. Therefore, in the case of the Client table, the Allow Zero Length field property will be set to no for all fields. In cases where you try to enter a zero-length string, Access will automatically replace the string with a null.

Try as you might, you will not find a null key on your keyboard! If a field has an Allow Zero Length property set to null—that is, the field accepts nulls—simply remove all the characters from the field. This will tell Access to replace the field value with a null. As soon as you enter a field, all the characters will be highlighted. Simply press the spacebar and all the characters will be removed.

Format

As you might have guessed, all of these properties tie together to one degree or another. Just as the Allow Zero Length property related to the Required property, the Format property ties to the Allow Zero Length property. The Format property performs two tasks. First, the Format property controls how fields are displayed. Second, the Format property controls how nulls are displayed.

Regardless of how data is stored, the Format property can alter how the data appears. For example, even if all the characters in the FirstName field are stored in lowercase, the Format property can force the characters to be displayed in uppercase characters without disturbing how the data is actually stored. The Format property is quite complex with many different settings depending on the data type you are working with.

The primary goal of this book is twofold: first, to teach you how to design databases and second, to get you up and running as quickly as possible in Access. The help documents that ship with Access are quite good. Regurgitating the information found in the help docs will provide little value to you. Demonstrating how the features work, on the other hand, has incredible value. After that is done, you can go on to experiment with the different settings. With this in mind, if you want extended information on a specific property or feature, simply select the property and press the F1 key. Figure 6.6 illustrates the Format property help topic for an example.

The irony is that the help system is often the most valuable yet most underutilized feature of application software.

FIGURE 6.6

Pressing the F1 Key when the cursor is positioned in a specific property will display help for that property.

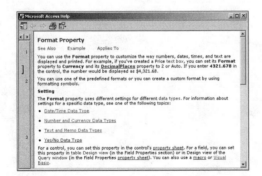

The Format Property comes in handy when you have specially formatted fields that have to be displayed. Two specially formatted fields that come to mind are phone numbers and ZIP codes. Figure 6.7 illustrates the Format property setting for the ZipCode field.

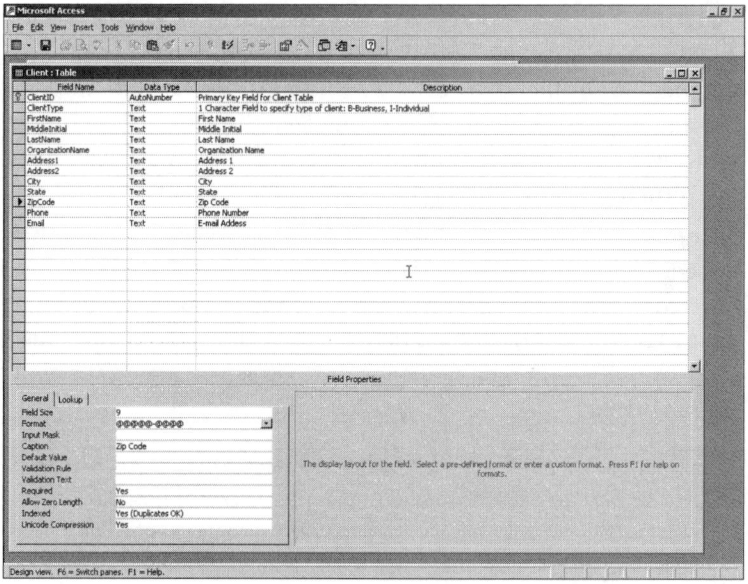

FIGURE 6.7

The @@@@@-@@@@ Format property setting ensures that a ZIP Code will be displayed with five characters, a dash, and then four characters.

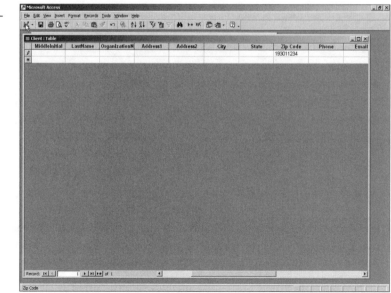

Let's see how the Format property works. Go back to the Datasheet View and tab over to the ZipCode field and enter 193011234. Be sure to not tab to the next field. Figure 6.8 illustrates how your Datasheet View should appear.

FIGURE 6.8

While you are still positioned in the field, the Format property will not take effect.

Now, tab to the Phone Number field. Figure 6.9 illustrates what the Format property setting has done. After you leave a field, Access will conform the display to the Format property. Be sure to hit the Escape key to get rid of the data so that you can get back to the Design View mode. Remember, there are validation rules in effect that will prevent you from saving data.

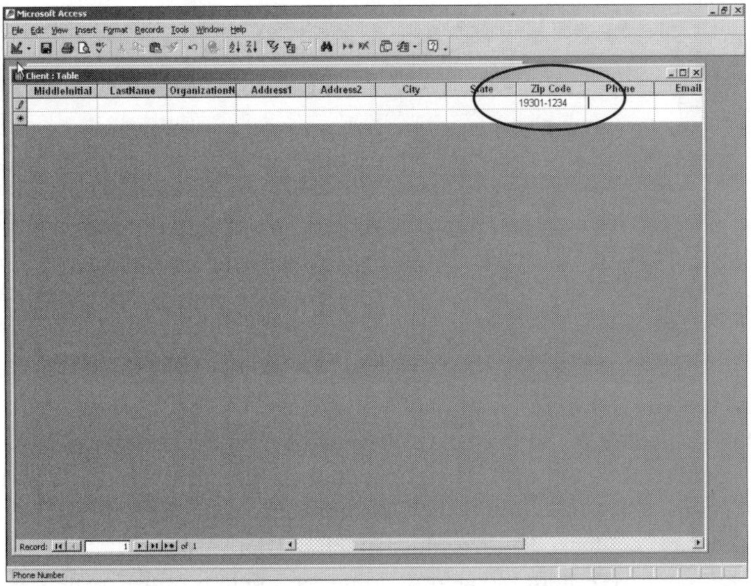

FIGURE 6.9

After you tab out of a field, the Format property will take effect.

Access will not allow you to leave your data in a state of limbo. For example, if you are entering data and then decide that you either want to switch to the Design View mode or move to a new record, you will need to deal with the data in the current record first. You have two options. You can either save the data, which may require you to go through the fields one by one to get those values to satisfy the rules, or two, discard the data. There is no middle ground here. This concept will be important when you create data entry forms to maintain your data. If your user is in the middle of a data entry session and decides to close the form, the user will need to make the decision of either committing or discarding the data. This is what data integrity is all about, not being able to store "half-baked" data.

Let's now turn the focus to the second task of the Format property, controlling how nulls are displayed. In the case of text fields, the Format property consists of two sections. The first section deals with how the data is to be displayed. The second section indicates how nulls will be displayed. For the TEB Database, "N/A" will be used to display null values. A semicolon separates the sections of the Format property (see Figure 6.10).

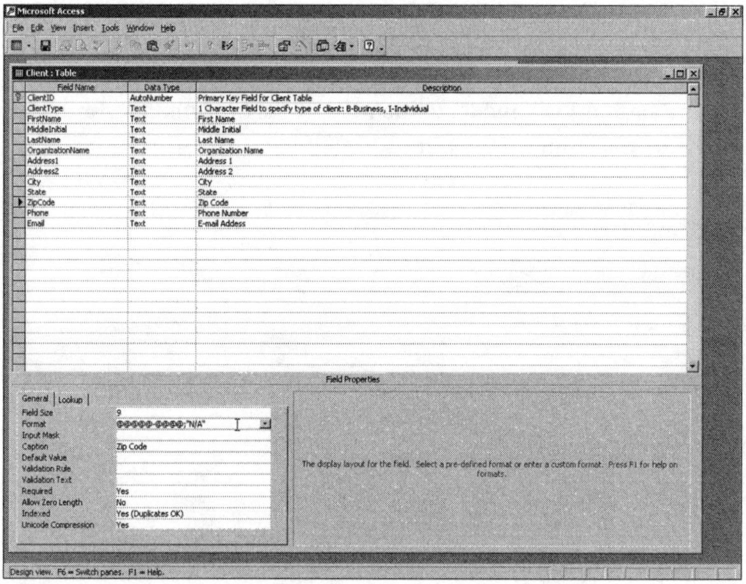

FIGURE 6.10

The second sec-
tion of the text
field's Format
property controls
how a null
value is dis-
played.

Now go back to the Datasheet View and tab to the ZipCode field. Notice that the field contains N/A. But wait! The ZipCode field is a required field and therefore cannot accept nulls. How can this be? The answer is quite simple. When a new record is created, except for a default value, which is another property that will be discussed later in this section, the default value for a field is null. The field is literally waiting for you to provide an initial value. Because the ZipCode is a required field, you would not be able to save the record with a null ZIP code. Figure 6.11 illustrates how the ZipCode field will initially appear.

Is the Format property alone sufficient to ensure data integrity? The answer is most definitely not. Figure 6.12 illustrates the problem. Remember, the Format property is concerned with controlling how data is displayed, not with how the data is entered. In order to control input, you need to look to the Input Mask property.

In actual practice, you won't need to control how nulls are displayed in the ZipCode field because it is a required field. Remember, nulls cannot be stored in required fields. The previous illustration using the ZipCode field was for demonstration purposes only. Table 6.2 outlines the settings for each Client table field that requires a Format property setting.

FIGURE 6.11

In the absence of a default value, fields in a new record are initialized as nulls.

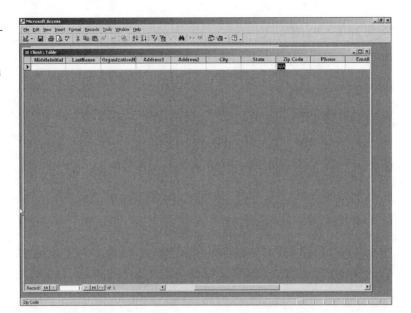

FIGURE 6.12

The Format property does not prevent invalid characters from being entered into a field.

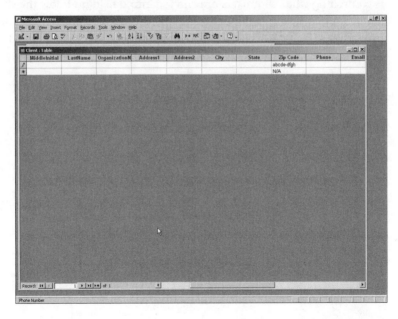

Table 6.2 Client Table Field Format Property Settings

Field	Value
FirstName	@;"N/A"
MiddleInitial	@;"N/A"
LastName	@;"N/A"
OrganizationName	@;"N/A"
Address1	-
Address2	@;"N/A"
ZipCode	@@@@@-@@@@
Phone	@@@-@@@-@@@@
Email	@;"N/A"

Input Mask

What the Format property does not address, the Input Mask property does. The issue is controlling what characters are entered into a field and how the characters are entered into a field. The Input Mask property can be entered manually or generated by a wizard. Figure 6.13 illustrates the Input Mask Wizard. Table 6.3 outlines the settings for each Client Table field that requires an Input Mask property setting.

FIGURE 6.13

The Input Mask Wizard makes quick work of generating a value for the Input Mask property.

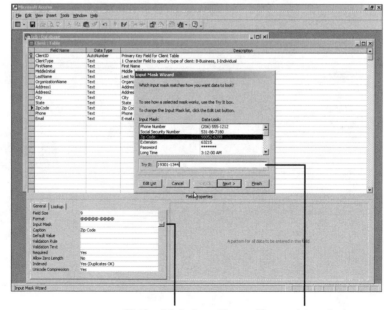

Clicking this button will start the Input Mask wizard

You can interactively test the Input Mask

Table 6.3   Client Table Input Mask Property Settings

Field	Value
ZipCode	00000-9999;;_
Phone	(999) 000-0000;;_

The Input Mask for the ZipCode field is 00000-9999. The Input Mask is a template to which data entry must conform. In this case, the first five characters must be digits between 0 and 9. The last four characters must be digits between 0 and 9 or a space. Why allow spaces in the plus 4 part of the ZIP Code? You may not know what the plus 4 part of the ZIP Code is.

Like the Format property, the Input Mask property is divided into sections. In this example, the Input Mask for the ZipCode field is 00000-9999;;_. The first section is the input mask itself. The second section specifies whether the actual display, including the template characters, is displayed or whether the core data is stored. In this case, if the second section were set to 0, 19301-1344, Access would attempt to store 10 characters to the ZipCode field. The tenth character, in this case, would be the dash that separates the two parts of the ZIP code. If you leave the second section empty, no template characters would be stored. In this case, "193011344" is what will be stored in the ZipCode field. The setting of this section is very important because in this example, the ZipCode field is only nine characters in length. In this case, if the template characters were stored, the ZIP code would be truncated. This means that if you entered 19301-1344, what would actually be stored would be 19301-134. The last section specifies the placeholder for the space where data should be entered. In this case, an underscore character is used. You can specify any placeholder character you want. The Input Mask Wizard has three steps. Each step corresponds to each section. Most of the time, you will simply leave the default settings the wizard provides. Figure 6.14 illustrates how the Zip code Input Mask property will appear after the wizard is closed. As you gain a better understanding of how the Input Mask property works, you can enter the input mask directly instead of using the wizard.

Now that you have one input mask setting under your belt, go ahead and create the setting for the Phone Number field. Figure 6.15 illustrates how your results should appear. Notice the exclamation point that precedes the input mask for the Phone Number field? This forces characters to be displayed from right to left.

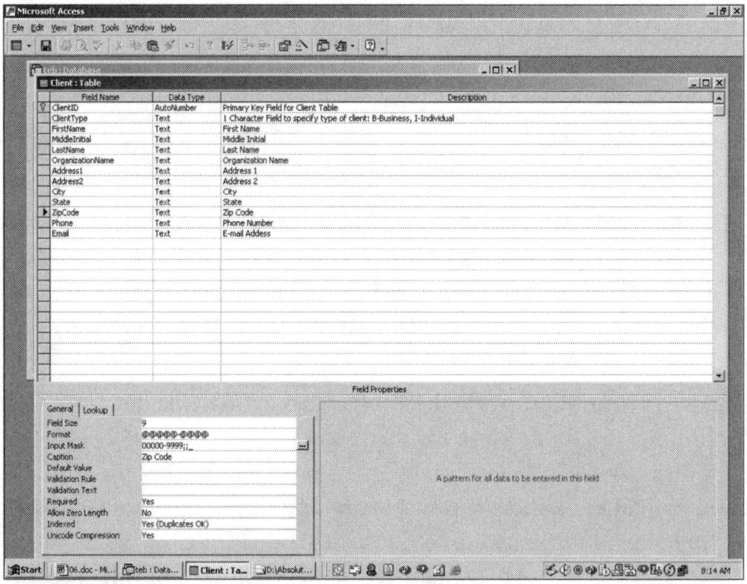

FIGURE 6.14

You have the choice of using a wizard to generate a property setting or of entering the property manually.

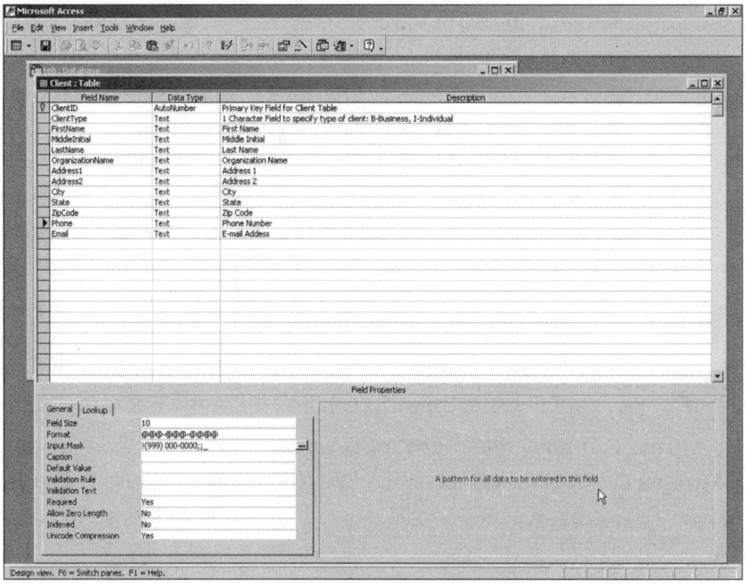

FIGURE 6.15

The ! character forces characters to be displayed from right to left.

When you save the table, you may have noticed the Input Mask property for the ZipCode and Phone fields have changed. The input mask for the ZipCode field changed to 00000\-9999;;_ and for the Phone field, it changed to !\(999") "000\-0000;;_. The \ character causes the character that follows to be displayed as a literal character. For the most part, you do not need to be concerned with how Access stores this information.

Let's take a few moments to test things by going back to the Datasheet View. Tab over to the zipCode field and enter 19301 and then tab over to the Phone field. Figure 6.16 illustrates the problem that results.

The solution to this problem is very simple. The ! character works in a slightly different manner for the Format property. When you precede the Format property with an ! character, the data is left aligned. Therefore, if you change the Format property to !@@@@@-@@@@, the data will be properly displayed when the plus 4 part of the ZIP Code is not entered (see Figure 6.17).

FIGURE 6.16

It is important to make sure the Format and Input Mask properties are coordinated.

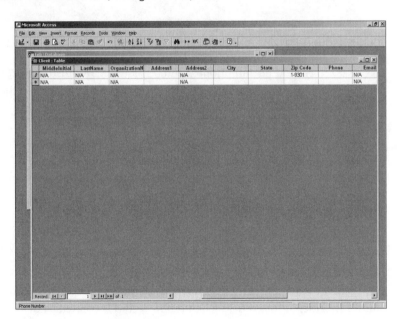

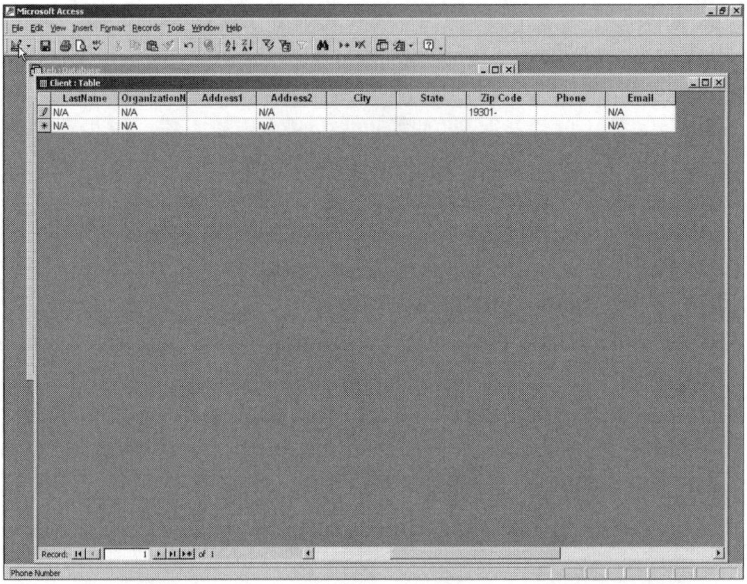

FIGURE 6.17

The ! character in the Format property forces the character display to be left aligned.

Next, try to enter a partial phone number. Figure 6.18 illustrates the exception Access generates. Access will require that entered data conform to the input mask specification.

FIGURE 6.18

Access will require data input to conform to the input mask specification.

Default Value

The Default Value property does as its name infers—it specifies a value that is automatically entered into a field when a new record is created. A default value of I will be specified for the Client Type field because it has been concluded that most of the clients will be individuals. Figure 6.19 illustrates the Default Value property setting for the Client Type property. The Client Type field is the only field with a Default Value property setting.

Validation Rule

The discussion now turns to one of the most important features of Access and any database product, for that matter—the ability to specify validation rules. Rules can be specified at the field and row levels. The first type you will be introduced to is the field-level rule. If you recall, the Client Type field can be only one of two values: I or B. Right now, there is no way to enforce that rule. Although a default value of I is specified, there is nothing to stop you from entering any value for Client Type. If you navigate to the Validation Rule property, you will see a small button. This button launches an expression builder you can use to build your rule. Alternatively, you can enter the rule manually, bypassing the Expression Builder.

> **Note**
>
> Expressions and the use of the Expression Builder can be a complex topic. This chapter focuses on very simple rules. If you are not familiar with Boolean logic, it is highly recommended you take a few moments to review the Validation Rule help documentation.

Figure 6.20 illustrates the Client Type Validation Rule property setting. The logic is clear—the Client Type field has to equal B or I.

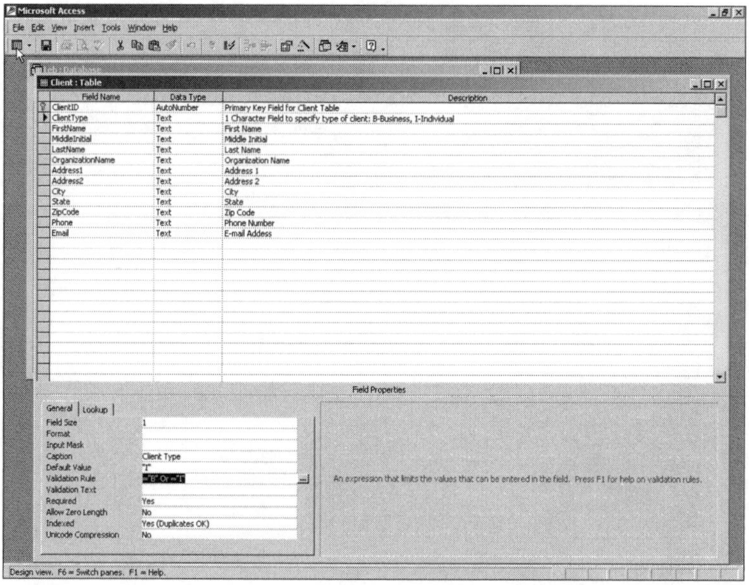

FIGURE 6.20

The Client Type
Validation Rule
property requires
the value to be B
or I.

Let's take a few moments to test the rule by going back into the Datasheet View. Try
to enter a value other than B or I and tab out of the field. Figure 6.21 illustrates the
exception generated by Access.

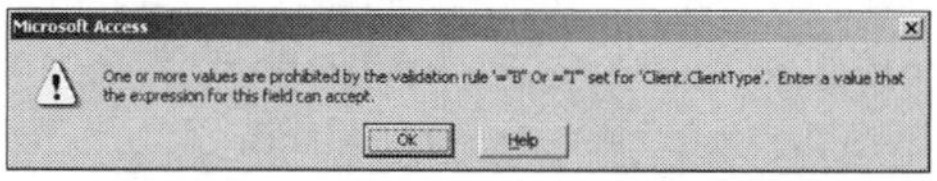

FIGURE 6.21

Whenever a val-
idation rule
fails, Access
generates an
exception and
corresponding
dialog box to
inform the user
of the problem.

It would be an understatement to say the message is not user-friendly. To address
that problem, let's turn to the Validation Text property. Table 6.4 outlines the field-
level rules for each field that requires the setting.

Table 6.4   Client Table Validation Rule Property Settings

Field	Value
ClientType	="B" or ="I"
Address1	Is Not Null
City	Is Not Null
State	Is Not Null
ZipCode	Is Not Null
Phone	Is Not Null

Validation Text

The Validation Text property is very straightforward. You simply specify text that should be displayed to the user when a validation rule fails (see Figure 6.22).

Now, go back to the Datasheet View and enter an invalid value for the Client Type field. Figure 6.23 illustrates the blunt error message that appears.

FIGURE 6.22

The Validation Text property specifies the text that should be displayed to the user when a validation rule fails.

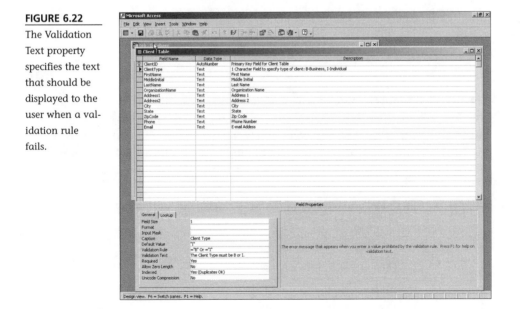

FIGURE 6.23

When the
Validation Text
property is speci-
fied, Access will
use that text in
the dialog box
informing the
user of a failed
validation rule.

Before continuing, let's try another Validation Rule/Text example. Figure 6.24 illustrates the error a user will receive if the Address1 field is left empty. Again, this is not
a very user-friendly message.

FIGURE 6.24

This is the
default error
message gener-
ated by Access
when leaving a
required field
blank.

Figure 6.25 illustrates the Address1 Field Validation Rule and Validation Text properties. The rule specifies that the field cannot be null and the text provides a user-
friendly message. Figure 6.26 illustrates how the dialog box will appear to the user if
the Address1 field is left empty when attempting to move off the current record. Table
6.5 outlines the Validation Text settings for each field that requires a setting.

Table 6.5   Client Table Validation Text Property Settings

Field	Value
ClientType	The Client Type must be B or I.
Address1	You must specify an address.
City	You must specify a city.
State	You must specify a state.
ZipCode	You must specify a ZIP Code.
Phone	You must specify a phone number.

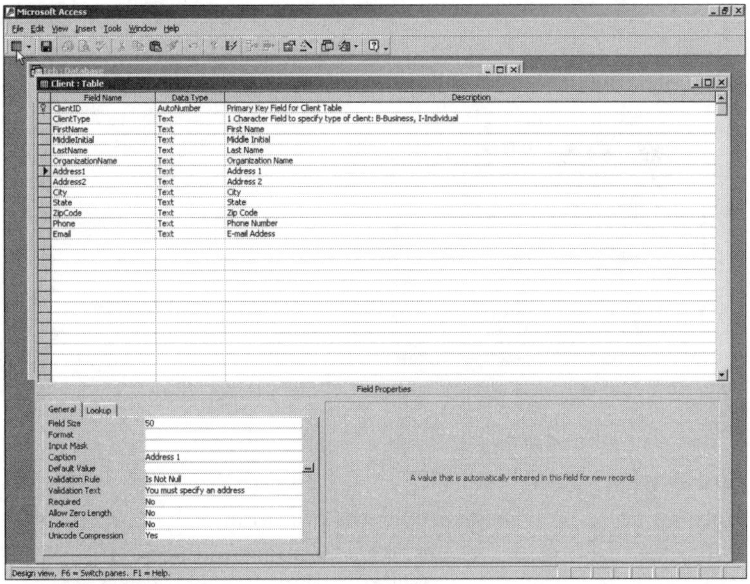

FIGURE 6.25

The Address1
Field Validation
Rule specifies
that the
Address1 field
cannot be left
empty.

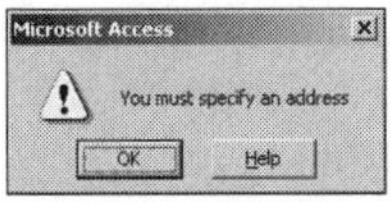

FIGURE 6.26

The Validation
Text property
provides a user-
friendly error
message.

Implement Row-Level Rules

When you attempt to save a record, Access will first check to see that all the field-level validation rules are satisfied. You have seen this behavior in the previous examples. If all the field-level rules are satisfied, Access will then check the row-level, sometimes also referred to as table-level rules, to ensure that rule is satisfied as well. Table-level rules come in handy when you have to compare multiple fields to determine whether the condition passes or fails. The validation rule logic at the table level is often more complex because multiple fields have to be checked. This concept is best illustrated through an example.

Row-Level Properties

If you recall, either the first and last name or the organization name must be specified. Figure 6.27 illustrates the Table properties dialog box that is accessed by pressing the Properties button of the Main Access toolbar. The Table Properties dialog box allows you to specify several table-level properties, including validation-related properties. As you can see, a table, like a field, has a Validation Rule and Validation Text properties.

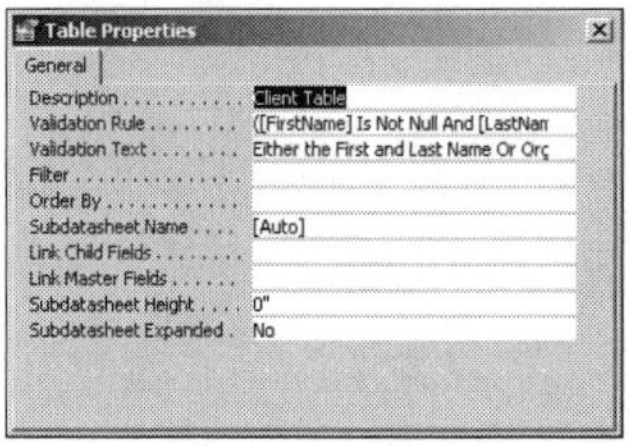

FIGURE 6.27

The Table

Properties dialog

box allows you

to specify the

Validation Rule

and Validation

Text properties

for a table.

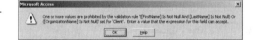

Validation Rule

Continuing on with the example, the following validation rule will ensure that either the first and last names or the organization name is specified for a client:

```
([FirstName] Is Not Null And [LastName] Is Not Null) Or
([OrganizationName] Is Not Null)
```

Go ahead and specify values for Address1, City, State, ZipCode, and Phone, leaving the FirstName, LastName, and Organization Name fields blank. Figure 6.28 illustrates the error dialog box displayed to the user. You will use the table's Validation Text property to deal with this issue.

FIGURE 6.28

After all the

field-level rules

are satisfied,

Access will test

the row-level

rule.

Validation Text

As you have already seen, the Validation Text property allows you to create user-friendly messages. In this case, set the Validation Text property to the following setting: Either the First and Last Name or Organization Name must be specified. Go ahead and repeat the previous test. Figure 6.29 illustrates the user-friendly message that will now appear.

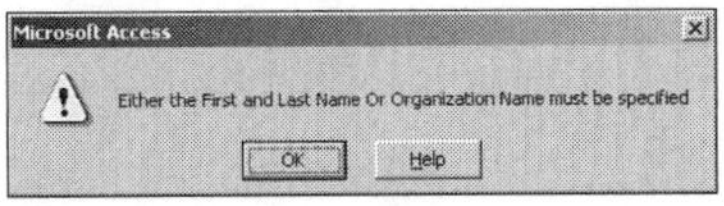

FIGURE 6.29

The Table
Validation Text
property pro-
vides a user-
friendly
message.

After you specify a first and last name, or an organization name, and have satisfied
all other rules, you will then be able to move to a new record, saving the existing
record.

What You Have Learned

A database by default will not prevent a user from entering invalid data. To guard
data integrity, either the application programs that sit on top of a database or the
database itself must have the necessary logic to validate data. If you host the validation logic in the database, you will always be assured of data integrity because ulti-
mately, all applications will have to rely on the database itself to save the data. As
you have seen, there are two levels of validation: field-level and row-level. Row-level
rules are also known as table-level rules. The terms row and table are synonymous.
When saving data, the database will first check to ensure the field-level rules are satisfied. If all the field-level rules pass, the database will then check the table-level
rules. If table rules pass, you are one step closer to being able to save your data. As
you will see in the next chapter, you are not totally out of the woods yet. The concept of data integrity extends to the relationships that exist between entities. This is
known as *referential integrity* and is the focus of the next chapter.

THE BASICS OF REFERENTIAL INTEGRITY

CHAPTER HIGHLIGHTS:

The last chapter introduced you to the concept of data validation. In review, data validation whether at the field or row level, is concerned with ensuring only valid data is saved in the database. Data validation is concerned with the table in which the rules are defined. In other words, Client Table validation rules are concerned only with the impact new data may have on the Client table. The impact that new client data may have on the Contacts table is beyond the scope of validation rules. Where validation rules are concerned with intratable issues, referential integrity (RI) rules are concerned with intertable issues. For example, should you be allowed to delete a specific record? If you are allowed to delete a record, what should happen to data in related tables? Should you be allowed to create data in a child table? All of these questions cannot be answered in the context of only one table. The answers to and the subject matter of these questions are the topic of this chapter. Appendix B, "TEB Referential Integrity Rules," contains a detailed listing of the referential integrity rules for the Time Entry and Billing Database.

What Is Referential Integrity?

Referential integrity, also known as RI for short, is a system that ensures that relationships between tables remain valid. Consider the classic example of orders and order line items. For every order, you can have one or more line items. Based on what you have learned thus far, you know this is a one-to-many relationship. You also know that carrying the primary key of the order in the order line item records facilitates the relationship. The inference of the last sentence is that if you don't have an order, you cannot have an order line item. The question then is "How do you enforce the rules that exist between tables?" The answer is to create what are known as *RI constraints*. Although databases such as Access have the capability to support referential integrity, you must equip a database with the knowledge to use that capability.

Why Maintaining Referential Integrity Is Important

Maintaining referential integrity is important for the same reasons that were enumerated in the last chapter on data validation. A database's capability to provide accurate information is directly tied to the quality of data. The capability to provide accurate information is directly tied to the quality of the relationships between tables as well. The importance of maintaining referential integrity will be abundantly clear when the Structured Query Language (SQL) is introduced in the next chapter. In the meantime, the following will serve as a brief preview of what is to come.

Consider the simple hypothetical example of customers and customer types. A specific customer type can be assigned to one or more customers. This means the primary key of the customer type is carried in the customer table. This is a simple one-to-many relationship and by now it should be a concept you are familiar with. Continuing on with the hypothetical example, let's assume you want to create a data extract that is grouped by customer type. In other words, the extract would include the customer type description along with selected customer data. To facilitate this extract, you would need data from the customers and customer type tables. As you will see in the next chapter on SQL, to accomplish the task, you will have to employ a technique known as a "join" between the customers and customer type tables. A question you may have is "How do you join the tables?" The key rests with the relationship between the tables. Remember that each table contains a common piece of information; the customer type id. This common piece of information is the linkage required to facilitate the join between the tables. The join between the tables is what allows you to combine data from different tables. What happens if this linkage is allowed to be broken? Consider the following questions:

- What if you could assign a customer to a nonexistent customer type?
- What if you could delete a customer type that has been assigned to at least one customer?

Each question has one thing in common: a broken link. The consequence of the broken link will be missing data. Specifically, any customer that references a nonexistent customer type will be omitted from the data extract. Consider the case of being allowed to delete a customer type when the type is in use by at least one customer. If the deletions are not restricted, you run the risk of compromising the integrity of the relationship. It is these very scenarios that referential integrity constraints guard against. The best measure of database integrity is the quality and accuracy of the information it produces. The concepts introduced in this section will become clearer when you study the Structured Query Language (SQL), which will be introduced in the next chapter.

How Referential Integrity Works

There are four types of referential integrity constraints that can be employed. The four types are restricted deletes, restricted inserts, cascading deletes, and cascading updates. The name of each constraint accurately describes the respective function. The following section describes the different types of referential integrity constraints as well as how to employ the constraints. Each constraint will be illustrated in the context of Client and Contact tables of the Time Entry and Billing Database.

Establishing Referential Integrity Rules for the TEB Database

Before you can see how the various constraints work, the database needs to be equipped with the capability to support referential integrity. In Chapter 5, "Using Access to Build the Time Entry and Billing Database," you created relationships between the Time Entry and Billing Database tables. Defining how tables are related is the first step in giving a database the capability to enforce referential integrity. The Edit Relationships dialog box appears, allowing you to specify how referential integrity constraints will be enforced (see Figure 7.1).

FIGURE 7.1

The Edit Relationships dialog box enables you to specify how referential integrity constraints will be enforced.

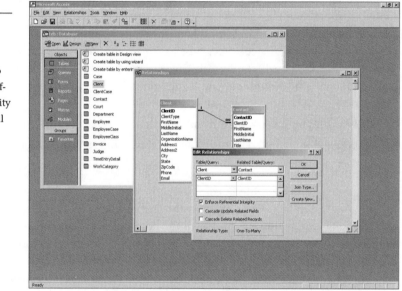

If you want referential integrity to be enforced, you must turn that option on. Figure 7.1 illustrates the check box that activates referential integrity support. After referential integrity support has been activated, there are two optional constraints that can be activated. The optional constraints are cascading updates and cascading deletes. What implication does this have for the other two types of constraints? The one constraint that is not optional is restricted inserts. It would never make sense to allow a child record to reference a nonexistent parent.

Restricted deletes can be considered the converse of cascading deletes. One of two scenarios must exist with respect to parent records. First, if you try to delete a parent, the child records must be deleted. Otherwise, you would run into the situation of child records referencing a nonexistent parent. Second, if you try to delete a parent record with related child records, you will be denied permission to delete the parent record. If you want to delete the parent, you would first have to delete the child records. As you can see, the cascading and restricted delete constraints are mutually exclusive.

Restricted Deletes

Restricted deletes mean that a parent record cannot be deleted if one or more related child records exist. In order to support restricted deletes, the Cascade Delete Related Records check box in the Edit Relationships dialog box must be unchecked. Figure 7.2 illustrates the Client and Contact Records that will be used to demonstrate how referential integrity works. Figure 7.3 illustrates Access's capability to view parent and related child records in a single view.

FIGURE 7.2

The Datasheet Views of the Client and Contact tables.

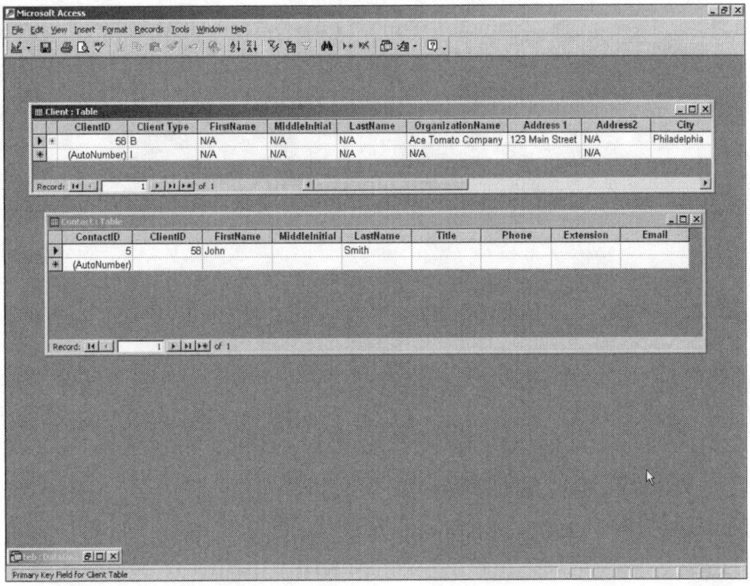

If you recall, you can perform all data operations from within the Datasheet View. To delete a record, you simply highlight the entire row by selecting the record marker on the far-left side of the Datasheet View. With restricted deletes in effect, Figure 7.4 illustrates the error dialog box Access generates when you attempt to delete a Client Record with a related Contact Record.

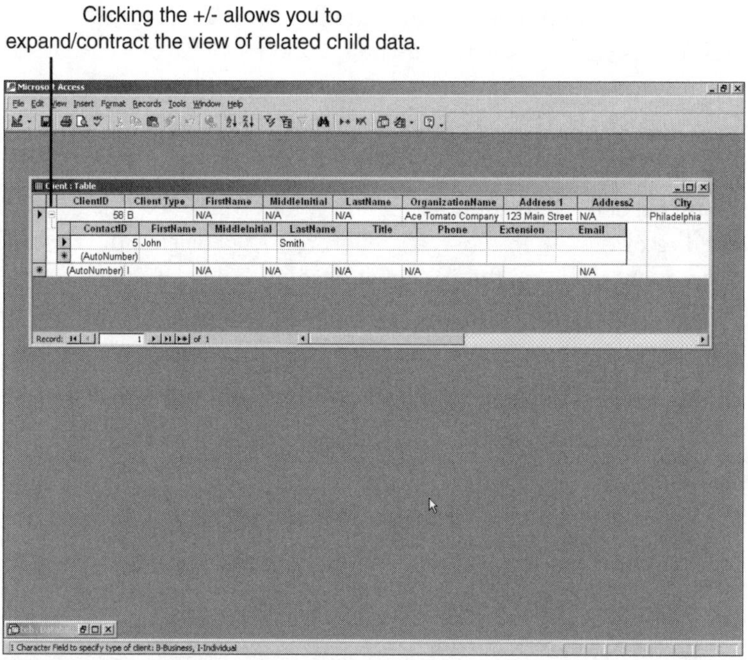

Clicking the +/- allows you to
expand/contract the view of related child data.

FIGURE 7.3

Access has the
capability to
view parent and
related child
records in a sin-
gle view.

FIGURE 7.4

Access will gen-
erate an error
dialog box if the
restricted delete
constraint fails.

Restricted Inserts

Restricted inserts means that a child record cannot reference a nonexistent parent.
Child records that reference nonexistent parent records are known as orphaned
records. Restricted inserts are a mandatory referential integrity constraint.

Figure 7.5 illustrates the error dialog box Access generates when the restrict insert
constraint fails.

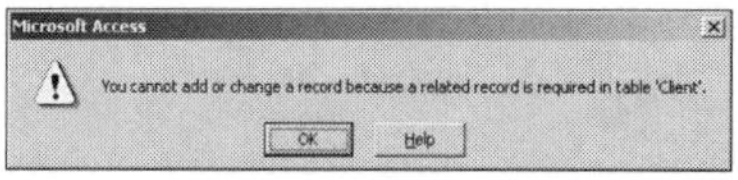

FIGURE 7.5

Access will gen-
erate an error
dialog box if the
restricted insert
constraint fails.

Cascading Deletes

Cascading deletes means that if a parent record is deleted, all related child records are deleted automatically. Figure 7.6 illustrates the required options that must be set in order to activate this referential integrity constraint. After you attempt to delete a parent record, Access will generate a dialog box informing the user that related records will be deleted if the operation is allowed to continue (see Figure 7.7).

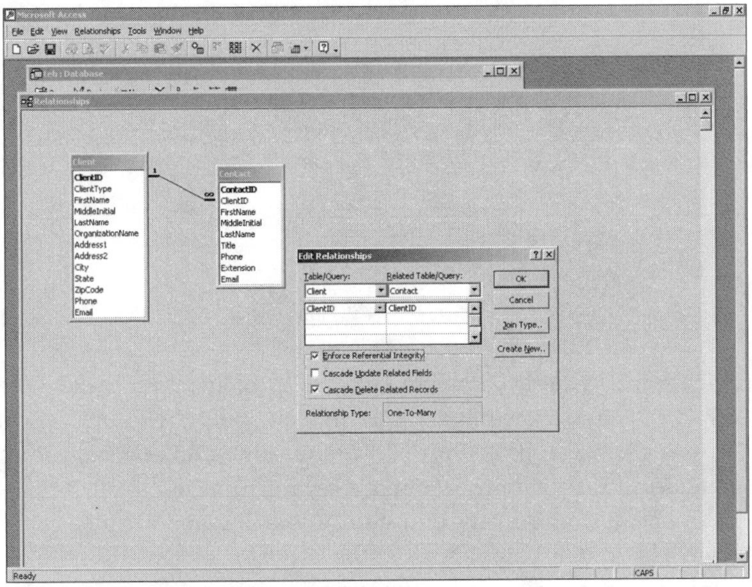

FIGURE 7.6

Checking the Cascade Delete Related Records activates that referential integrity constraint.

FIGURE 7.7

Before related records are deleted, Access provides a dialog box for the user to confirm for the operation to continue.

Cascading Updates

Cascading updates means that if the primary key of a parent has changed, the foreign key in all related child records is updated automatically. To activate this referential integrity constraint, you must check the Cascade Update Related Records check box. Figure 7.8 illustrates the required setting to activate this option.

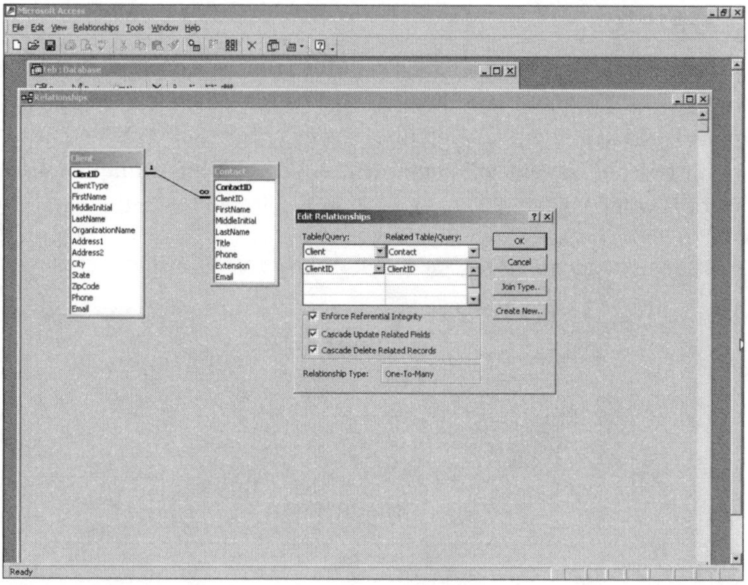

FIGURE 7.8

Checking the
Cascade Update
Related Records
check box acti-
vates that refer-
ential integrity
constraint.

If you recall in the TEB database project, surrogate primary keys are used. Surrogate
keys don't contain meaningful information about the record they uniquely identify.
Surrogate keys can be contrasted with a meaningful key that is composed of two or
more fields. For example, a primary key might be made up of the combination of
last name, first name, city, and state. Cascading updates take care of the situation
when one or more components of the key change. Remember, to support referential
integrity and the relationship among tables, the primary key of the parent has to be
carried in all related child records. Otherwise, the system will not work. The benefit
of surrogate keys is clear in that you don't have to worry about the primary key
changing. As a result, you don't have to worry about the need for cascading updates
and the need for additional complexity. If you want a review of the two types of keys
that exist, take a few moments now and refer to Chapter 4, "Database Design
Continued: An Introduction to Normalization."

What You Have Learned

In this chapter, you have been introduced to one of the most important database
concepts you will encounter—referential integrity. The four referential integrity constraints discussed in this chapter are restricted deletes, restricted inserts, cascading
deletes, and cascading updates. Referential integrity, in addition to field- and row-
level rules, is a tool that you should employ to ensure the quality of the data within

a database. The point that an application is only as good as the database it rests upon has been emphasized multiple times in this book. Taking this point one step further, a database is only as good as the quality of data it stores and the information it can provide. This chapter concludes Part III. To recap, Part I introduced basic database concepts. Part II took you through the process of designing and building a database. Part III concentrated on database maintenance through validation rules and referential integrity. The next part, Part IV, will concentrate on how to extract information from a database through the Structured Query Language (SQL).

USING YOUR DATABASE TO PROVIDE INFORMATION— AN INTRODUCTION TO SQL

SQL BASICS

HAPTER HIGHLIGHTS:

- SQL Overview
- Select Statement
- Filter Results I: Use the Where Clause
- Organize Output I: Use the Order By Clause
- Combine Multiple Tables: Use the Join Statement
- Combine Multiple Resultsets: Use the Union Clause
- What You Have Learned

The first half of this book has focused on the design and construction of the database. The second half, which begins with this chapter, focuses on putting the database to work. Remember, the value of a database is measured by the usefulness of the information that can be extracted. This chapter and the next introduce a new language called the *Structured Query Language*, or *SQL* (pronounced *sequel*) for short. SQL is a database-independent language that allows you to query data and to perform what are known as CRUD operations. *CRUD* stands for *Create, Update, and Delete*. Because the language is database independent, the language constructs you learn will be applicable to SQL Server, Oracle, Informix, Sybase, and DB2, to name a few.

SQL Overview

Just as computer programming languages such as Basic, C, C++, Java, and Pascal go through different versions, so, too, does SQL. The latest version of SQL is known as ANSI-SQL 92. *ANSI* stands for the *American National Standards Institute*. The latest standard of the SQL language was codified in 1992. A standard is nothing more than a specification of how something is supposed to work. If the database product you are working with supports the ANSI standard, you can be assured the core parts of the language are supported. This does not mean that a specific database has to support all parts of the standard. Rather, this means the Select statement in Oracle will work the same way as the Select statement works in SQL Server.

Specific database products will often extend their respective versions beyond the standard. For example, SQL Server's language is called *T-SQL*. Oracle's language is called *PL/SQL*. Each of these languages is known as a superset of the ANSI standard. In other words, the T-SQL and PL/SQL flavors of the ANSI standard not only support the ANSI-92 standard; language constructs that are specific to the database are supported as well. Access's version of SQL conforms very closely to the ANSI standard.

SQL actually consists of three sublanguages:

- **DDL**—Data Definition Language
- **DML**—Data Manipulation Language
- **DCL**—Data Control Language

This chapter and the next will concentrate on the DML sublanguage, the sublanguage you are likely to use most often. The DML consists of the Select, Insert, Update, and Delete commands. This chapter will focus on the Select command and its associated clauses. The next chapter will focus on advanced uses of the Select command as well as the Insert, Update, and Delete commands. As far as the DDL is concerned, most of the time, you will use the graphical tools for creating tables and columns. As far as the DCL is concerned, Access does not support this sublanguage. Nonetheless, the DDL and DCL sublanguages will be introduced briefly in the following section.

Interactively Working with SQL in Access

Some database products have a window that allows the user to interactively type SQL instructions. Access has a SQL Window feature. However, to use the feature, you have to jump through a few hoops.

Most of the time, when you use the SQL Window in Access, it is for the purpose of creating SQL Select queries. As you will see, there are SQL Language constructs that allow you to define database objects as well. Although the Access SQL Window was not intended for this purpose, it nonetheless supports the Data Definition Language features of SQL.

To gain access to the SQL Window in Access, follow these steps:

1. Start Access and choose to create an empty database.

2. Choose Queries from the Objects list of the main database window. The Objects list is in the left pane of the main database window.

3. In the right pane, choose the option that creates a query in Design View.

4. Close the Show Table dialog box that facilitates adding tables to the Select query. Because this is an empty database, no tables exist!

5. After you close the Show Table dialog box, choose the SQL View from the toolbar. The SQL View is the first option on the left and is labeled SQL.

6. After you complete this step, the query design window will disappear. In its place, a Select Query window will appear. To run a specific query, you need to click the Run Query button on the Query toolbar. The Run Query button is represented as an exclamation point. Figure 8.1 illustrates how your results should appear.

Throughout this chapter, you will see steps that begin with opening a SQL window. Follow the steps outlined in this note. In most cases, you will merely close the query session without saving the query. This will be especially true for Data Definition Language (DDL) commands. As far as Data Manipulation Language (DML) commands are concerned, some of those will be saved. In any case, if you want to save any SQL command, you can do so by clicking the Save button on the main Access toolbar.

Run Query button   SQL window

FIGURE 8.1

The SQL
Window allows
you to interac-
tively send SQL
commands to
Access.

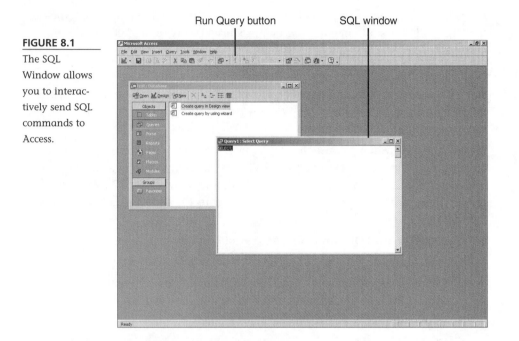

The DDL and DCL SQL Sublanguages

Access has limited support of the Data Definition Language (DDL) and no support
for the Data Control Language (DCL). Databases such as SQL Server, Oracle, and
DB2, to name a few, fully support both of these sublanguages.

The DCL allows you to grant various permissions such as Select, Insert, Update, and
Delete to specific users. The following is an example of a SQL statement that grants
select permissions on the Customer table to a user named Bob:

```
Grant Select
    On Customers
    To Bob
```

In this scenario, when Bob logs onto the database, he will be allowed to execute the
following SQL statement:

```
Select *
    From Customers
```

Although Access supports and provides specialized user interfaces to support a
security scheme like this, the means to control and define security permissions has
not been implemented through the SQL DCL sublanguage. The specifics of how
to implement the security features of Access are beyond the scope of this book.

For more information on how security is implemented in Access, please consult the help file.

The Data Definition Language (DDL) acts upon tables and columns. You can add, alter, and drop a table definition. Like tables, you can add, alter, and drop column definitions as well. Like the DCL, databases such as SQL Server, Oracle, and DB2 provide full support for the DDL. Unlike the DCL, Access does have limited support for the DDL sublanguage. Running the following code in the SQL window will create a Customers table:

```
Create Table Customers
```

Normally, when you create tables, you will create columns at the same time. The following code creates a Customers table along with two fields: custid and name:

```
Create Table Customers
    (custid counter Primary Key,name text(40))
```

As the code implies, the custid field is an AutoNumber field and serves as the primary key. The name field is a text data type with a length of 40 characters. Figure 8.2 illustrates the results of running the Create Table statement. In addition to these operations, you can modify the structure of a table as well. The following code changes the length of the name field from 40 to 50 characters:

```
Alter Table Customers
    Alter name text(50)
```

FIGURE 8.2

Access provides limited support for the SQL Data Definition Language sublanguage.

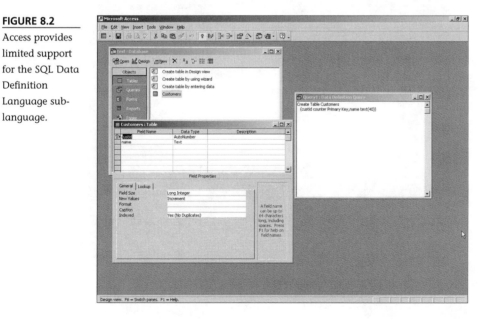

The DDL in Access also provides limited support for defining relationships between tables as well as table- and field-level validation rules. Because of this limited support and the way the Access product was designed, you are more likely to use the graphical tools for table and column maintenance. At this stage, all that is important is that you know what the DDL is and that these capabilities do exist in Access to a limited degree and are more robust in other products.

With a brief introduction to the Structured Query Language and the sublanguages that make up SQL, it is time to move on to the Data Manipulation Language (DML), the sublanguage that you will use most of the time when working with SQL. The DML is composed of the Select, Insert, Update, and Delete commands. Some of these commands have additional clauses that affect how they work. Let's put the TEB Database to work!

Select Statement

Of all the SQL statements that exist, the Select statement is the one you will use most of the time. Queries are entirely about extracting data out of a database. To accomplish this feat, you use the Select statement. Figure 8.3 illustrates a very simple Select statement.

FIGURE 8.3

The * symbol in a Select statement is a shorthand way of telling the database to return all fields in a table.

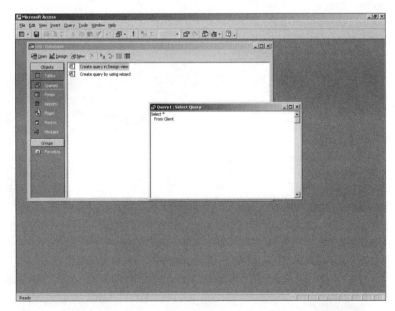

When you run a SQL statement in the SQL window, the SQL window is replaced with the Datasheet view. If you recall from previous discussions, when you open a table to look at data, you are presented with a Datasheet view of the data contained in the table. When you open the Client table to look at the data, it is just like issuing the SQL statement `Select * From Client`. Figure 8.4 illustrates how your results may appear.

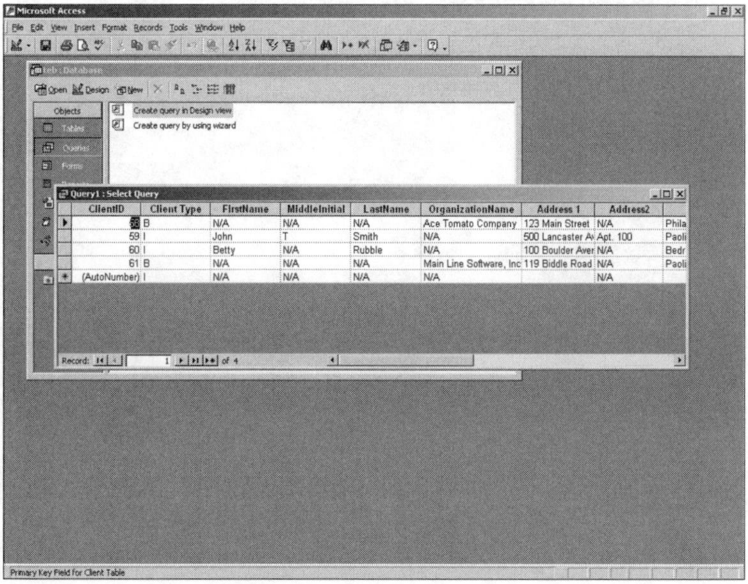

FIGURE 8.4

The Datasheet view that holds the results of a query is just like the Datasheet view you see when opening a table.

Be careful when disrupting data in the Datasheet view of a query. Depending on the circumstances, changing data will result in changing the data that is actually stored in the base tables. If you use the graphical query design tools, results can be marked to have read-only status. The query designer is discussed in detail in Chapter 10, "Making SQL Queries a Part of Your Database."

Selecting Specific Fields

Most of the time, you will not want to select all the fields in a table. Rather, you will be interested in a few. For example, the ClientID has no meaning outside the database. In a simple client listing report, elements such as phone number or e-mail address may not be required. Instead of the * symbol, you can list the specific fields in the order in which you want the fields to appear in the resultset.

To illustrate, let's assume you want to fetch the first name, last name, and organization name. The following SQL Select statement would do the trick:

```
SELECT firstname, lastname, organizationname
   FROM Client;
```

Figure 8.5 illustrates the results of this query.

FIGURE 8.5

SQL Select queries allow you to fetch specific columns of data.

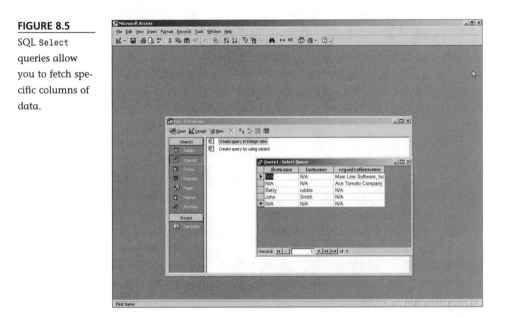

Renaming Fields with the As Clause

Not only can you control which fields you pick and the order of the fields, you can assign a different name to the selected fields. You accomplish this feat with the As clause. Take note of the following SQL Select statement:

```
SELECT firstname As fname,
          lastname As lname,
          organizationname As org
   From Client
```

Figure 8.6 illustrates the results of this query.

FIGURE 8.6

The As clause
allows you to
rename a field
in the resultset.

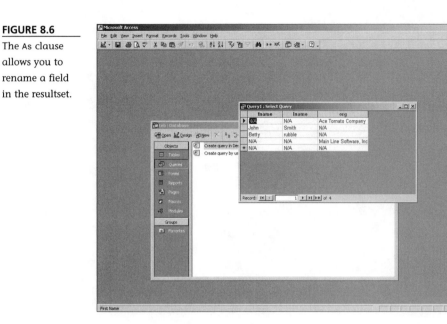

Combining Field Data

Sometimes you will want to combine data from multiple fields and return that data
as a single field in the resultset. For example, instead of returning the first and last
names as single fields, you may want to combine that data into a single field called
name. The following SQL Select statement accomplishes this task:

```
SELECT firstname + " " + lastname As name,
          organizationname As org
    From Client
```

Figure 8.7 illustrates the results of this query.

There is one caveat to combining, or as it is often called, *concatenating,* data. The
data you combine must be the same data type. Usually, you combine text data.
Numeric and datetime data is added when the + operator is used. If you want to
concatenate these items instead of adding them together in an arithmetic operation,
you would need to convert those fields to text data types and then combine the con-
verted items. To illustrate the difference, consider the following SQL code:

```
SELECT 1+2+3 as combinedfield
    FROM Client;
```

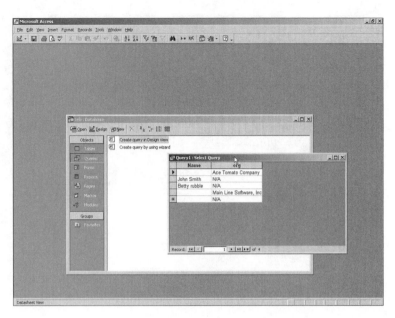

Figure 8.8 illustrates the results of this query. As you can see, not only can you reference actual fields in a Select statement, you can also reference static numeric, date, or text expressions (these static values are called *literals*). Depending on the database engine you use, you can reference any function the database engine understands.

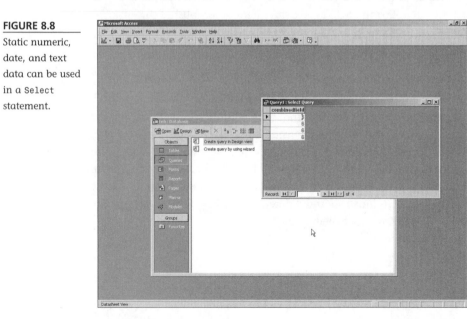

In this case, the numbers 1, 2, and 3 are added together. The reason you see 4 records, each with the value of 6, is because you get a record in the resultset for each record you would have returned in the resultset.

If, on the other hand, you wanted the field to contain the value 123, you would need to convert each item to text and then combine the text values. Yes, you could easily select the string "123"; however, you would then not get the chance to see how to convert numeric values to text! The following code achieves the desired results:

```
SELECT Str(1)+Str(2)+Str(3) as combinedfield
    FROM Client;
```

Figure 8.9 illustrates how the results of the query will appear.

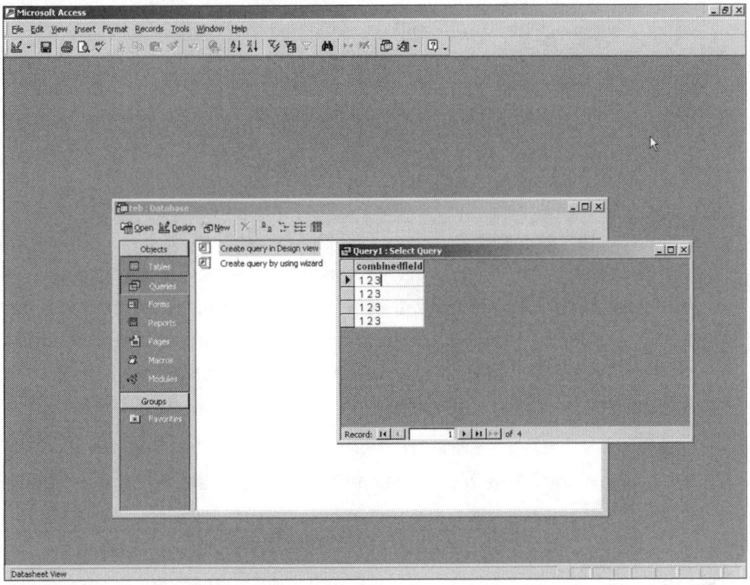

FIGURE 8.9

Database functions, such as the string conversion function Str(), can be used to combine data.

Top *n* Select Statements

The last topic as far as the Select statement is concerned deals with Top *n* Select statements. These are also known as Top *n* queries. Many times, you may want only the top 1, 10, or 100 items in a resultset. Using the preceding example where the number of rows in the resultset depends on the number of rows in the base table, a Top *n* query can control the number of rows in the resultset. The following code forces the resultset to have only 1 row:

```
SELECT Top 1 Str(1)+Str(2)+Str(3) as combinedfield
    FROM Client;
```

Figure 8.10 illustrates the results of this query.

FIGURE 8.10

A Top *n* query
controls the
number of rows
that appear in a
resultset.

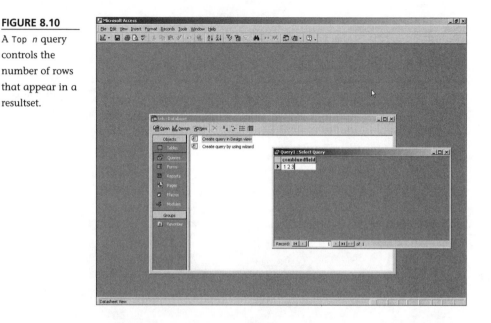

Just because you want to return the top 10 records, it is very likely that more than 10 records can be returned. Consider this example: You want to return the top 10 products based on price. Furthermore, the tenth highest-priced product is $10, and five different products cost $10. How many records will be returned? At a minimum, you are going to get 10 records. The tenth record will be the first product that costs $10. However, because there are four additional products that cost $10, those records will be returned as well. In this hypothetical situation, 14 records would be returned.

The bottom line? Top *n* queries can return more than *n* rows when there are multiple rows with the same value for the order by expression.

Now that you know how to extract and manipulate data, the next step involves filtering data and organizing. Top *n* queries are a filtering mechanism of sorts. However, the Top *n* constraint is applied *after* the filter specified in the Where clause has been applied. Filtering and organizing data is the topic of the next two sections.

Filter Results I: Use the Where Clause

In practice, you will always apply a filter to your queries. For example, let's extend some of the previous examples by qualifying for a specific client type. If you recall, clients can either be business or individuals. The Client Type field indicates which type applies. To illustrate how the Where clause works, consider the following example that extracts the first- and lastname data for clients that are individuals:

```
SELECT  lastname  + ",  " + firstname As client
   From Client
   Where ClientType = "I"
```

A few additional modifications were made. Did you notice the first- and lastname positions were reversed and separated by a comma? With regard to how the Where clause works, that is fairly straightforward. You can use a single criterion or multiple criteria. Figure 8.11 illustrates how the results will appear.

FIGURE 8.11

The Where clause allows you to filter out irrelevant data.

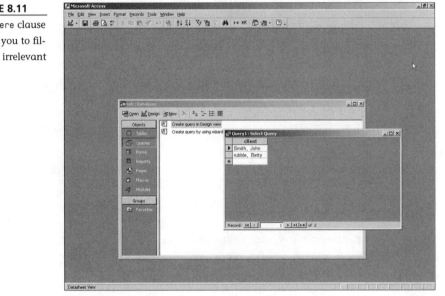

Extending this example, let's say you want to extract all the individual clients that have a lastname that begins with s. The following code will accomplish this task:

```
SELECT  lastname  + ",  " + firstname As client
   From Client
   Where ClientType = "I" And lastname Like "S*"
```

This example requires close examination of a few points. First, as previously stated, you can combine multiple criteria in the Where clause. Second, notice in this case the use of the word Like. In this example, you want to pull any individual client that has a lastname that begins with the letter s. One could say the criteria in this case are looser. Typically, when the Like comparison is used, a wildcard character is used. In Access, the wildcard character is an asterisk (*). In SQL Server, the wildcard character is a percent sign (%). Had you used the equal sign instead, Access would have looked for records that had a lastname that exactly matched s*. Figure 8.12 illustrates how the results of the query that uses multiple criteria and wildcard matches will appear.

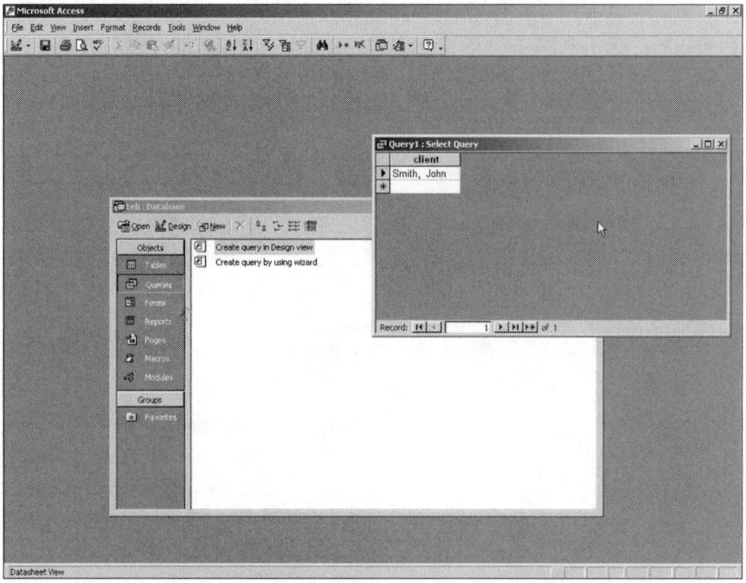

FIGURE 8.12

The use of wild-card criteria allows for looser matches.

This will not be the only coverage of the Where clause in this chapter. The Where clause has important uses when it comes to joining tables. That discussion of the Where clause will be deferred to that section later in this chapter.

Organize Output I: Use the Order By Clause

Just as you will always use the Where clause to filter irrelevant data, you will always use the Order By clause to sort the data in your resultset. Furthermore, based on the fields you choose to sort the data, you will want to sort the data ascending, descending, or some combination thereof. All of these operations are accomplished with the Order By clause. To illustrate how the Order By clause works, consider the following code:

```
SELECT  lastname  + ",  " + firstname As client
   From Client
   Where ClientType = "I"
   Order By lastname
```

Figure 8.13 illustrates the results of this query.

FIGURE 8.13

The Order By clause allows you to sort the data in your resultset.

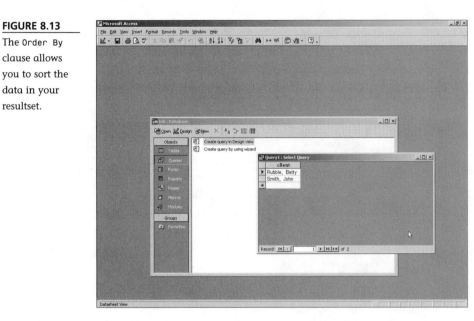

By default, any field you select to order by will be in ascending order. If you want to sort in descending order, you will need to make that choice explicitly. Except for the descending order qualifier, the following code is identical to the previous code block:

```
SELECT  lastname  + ",  " + firstname As client
    From Client
    Where ClientType = "I"
    Order By lastname Desc
```

Figure 8.14 illustrates the results of this query.

Compound Sort Orders

Let's say you want to list all individual clients that output their name, city, and state. In addition, you want to sort by state, city, and lastname. Typically, when you sort by multiple fields, the order in which the fields appear in the select list will conform to the sort order. This is not a requirement. However, it makes the output more readable. The following code outputs the state, lastname, and the combination of first and last name. In addition, the output is sorted by state, city, and lastname:

```
SELECT  state,city,lastname  + ",  " + firstname As client
    From Client
    Where ClientType = "I"
    Order By state, city,lastname
```

Figure 8.15 illustrates the results of this query.

FIGURE 8.14

With the Desc qualifier, you can specify whether the sort should be in descending order.

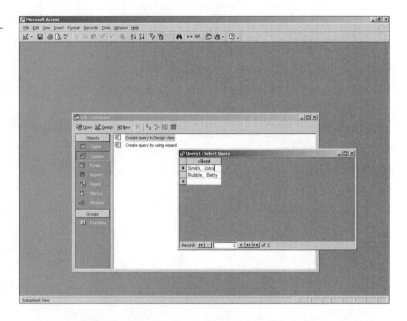

FIGURE 8.15

You can sort the resultset based on the characteristics of multiple fields.

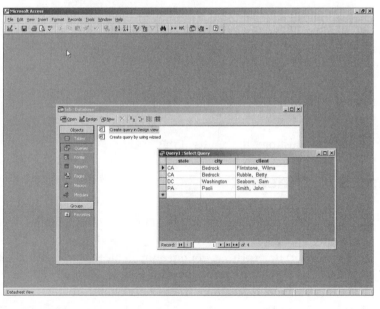

As you can see, you don't necessarily have to choose a specific field in order to use it in a sort. In this scenario, the lastname field itself was not returned in the resultset. Rather, the lastname was combined with the firstname field. Nonetheless, you can sort by the field so long as the field is available in the base table. Most of the time, however, the data you use to sort by will be available in the resultset either in its own field or within a field of combined data.

Let's extend the previous example by electing to sort by state, by city descending, and then by lastname descending. The following code accomplishes this task:

```
SELECT  state,city,lastname + ",  " + firstname As client
    From Client
    Where ClientType = "I"
    Order By state, city Desc,lastname Desc
```

Figure 8.16 illustrates the results of this query.

FIGURE 8.16

Within each of the sort elements, you can elect to sort specific items in descending order.

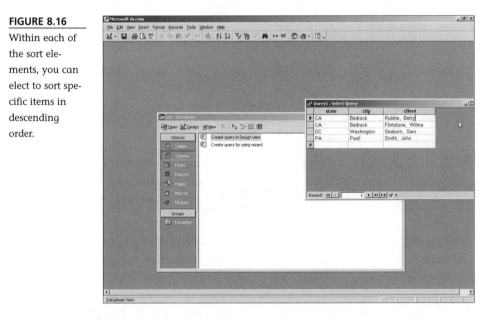

As you can see, the first sort is still by state. However, if you compare Figures 8.15 and 8.16, you will see that Betty Rubble and Wilma Flintstone have switched positions in the resultset. Remember the sorts on city and lastname were descending. What would happen if Wilma Flintstone lived in Copper Falls, instead? Because sorting is controlled first by state, then by city, and then by lastname, in this case, Wilma Flintstone would again appear in the resultset before Betty Rubble. A good exercise is to play around with a small set of data, change the data, and then rerun various queries to see the effects.

Combine Multiple Tables: Use the Join Statement

Much of the time, you will want to extract data from multiple tables. For example, you might get a request to create a list of business clients and their associated contacts. This is the basic framework that will be used to introduce the concepts of joining tables. There are four types of joins: inner, left outer, right outer, and full outer. Figure 8.17 provides a graphical illustration of how the various types of joins work together in relation to the tables that are joined. Throughout this discussion, you will continually be referred to Figure 8.17. To illustrate how the different join techniques work, the Client and Contact tables will be used.

FIGURE 8.17

There are four ways two tables can be joined: inner, left, right, and full.

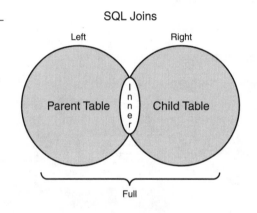

Before going any further, let's first establish the basic query that will be used. In this context, only business clients will be considered. To see what you are starting with, the following query can be used to fetch all business clients:

```
SELECT  organizationname
    From Client
    Where ClientType = "B"
    Order By organizationname
```

Figure 8.18 illustrates the list of business clients that you will start with.

A QUICK NOTE ABOUT JOIN TERMINOLOGY

With respect to left, right, and full outer joins, the use of the word *outer* is often omitted. If somebody says he is going to employ a "left join," it is inferred to be a "left outer join." Whether the word *outer* is used is a matter of preference. Just know and understand that regardless of whatever source of information you read, left, right, and full mean the same thing as left outer, right outer, and full outer.

FIGURE 8.18

The complete list
of business
clients in the
client table.

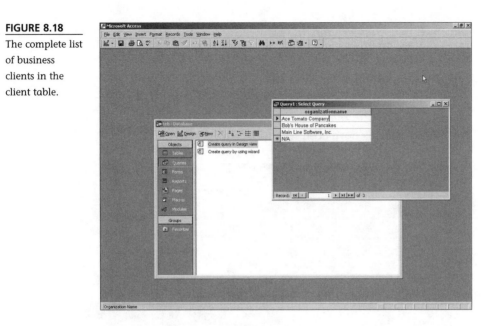

Now that you have a complete list of clients and a baseline query to work from, the
topic of SQL joins can be discussed.

Inner Joins

Referring to Figure 8.17, you can see that an inner join represents the intersection
between a parent and child table. What is the intersection in this case? If you recall
the relationship between the Client and Contact tables, the clientid primary key field
of the Client table is carried as a foreign key in the Contact table. As far as the syntax is concerned, the Join clause appears after the From clause. The following code
illustrates how to employ the Join clause:

```
Select  organizationname
   From Client
    Inner Join Contact On (contact.clientid = client.clientid)
   Where ClientType = "B"
   Order By organizationname
```

There is an alternative way you can join tables. Instead of using the syntax in the
previous code block, you can use the following syntax instead:

```
SELECT  organizationname
   From Client,Contact
   Where ClientType = "B" And
         contact.clientid = client.clientid
   Order By organizationname
```

It is important to note that when you incorporate the join as part of the From and Where clauses, an inner join is assumed. If you want to employ a different type of join, it will not be possible unless you employ the Join clause itself. This alternative is shown for illustrative purposes only. All code samples in this book will employ the Join clause.

Figure 8.19 illustrates the effect of adding the Join clause. Take note of the fact that no additional fields have been returned to the resultset.

FIGURE 8.19

The results of joining the Client and Contact tables.

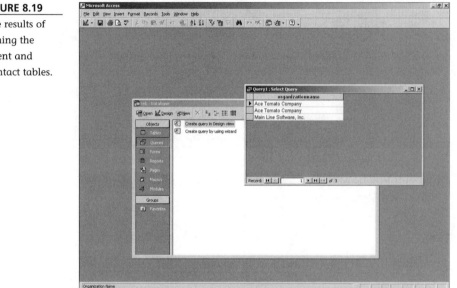

Two items should be apparent. First, there are two instances of the Ace Tomato Company. Second, Bob's House of Pancakes disappeared from the list. The reason Ace Tomato Company appears twice is because Ace has two contacts. The reason Bob's House of Pancakes disappeared is because Bob's does not have a contact defined. Remember, an inner join is the intersection between two tables. Put another way, an inner join will return data if and only if the table on the left has a corresponding record in the table on the right. In this example, if the clientid in the Client table can be found in the Contact record, a matching record is deemed to exist. In the case of the Ace Tomato Company, two matches were found because two contact records exist.

Use the Distinct Clause to Eliminate Redundant Data

What if you were tasked with providing a list of only those business clients that had a contact? You would definitely want to make use of an inner join so that clients that did not have a contact would fall off the list. At the same time, you want only one instance of the client on the list. In the previous section, you were introduced to Top *n* Queries. However, in this case, a Top *n* Query will not work. What you want is a distinct list of clients (see Figure 8.20). Fortunately, SQL provides the perfect solution and is illustrated in the following code block:

```
Select  Distinct organizationname
    From Client
      Inner Join Contact On (contact.clientid = client.clientid)
    Where ClientType = "B"
    Order By organizationname
```

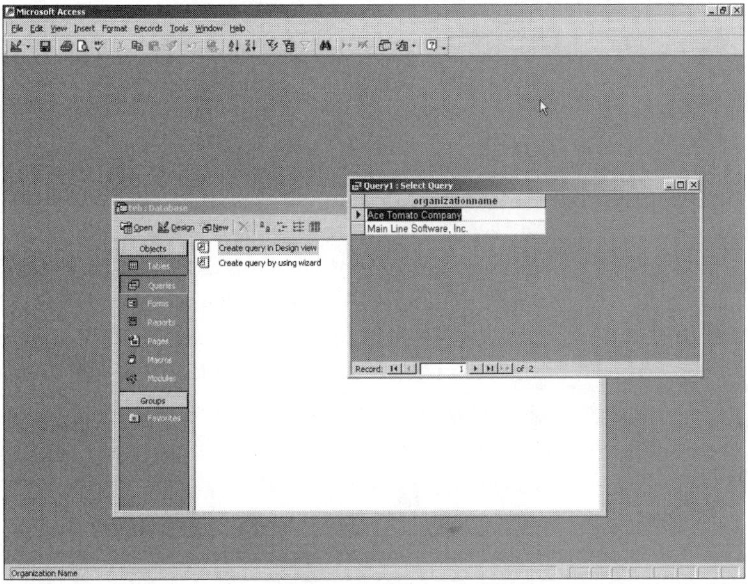

FIGURE 8.20

The Distinct clause allows you to ensure every row in the resultset is completely unique.

Return Data from Multiple Tables

Extending the previous example, let's now grab the firstname and lastname from the contact table. The following code appears to do the trick:

```
Select  organizationname, firstname, lastname
    From Client
      Inner Join Contact On (contact.clientid = client.clientid)
    Where ClientType = "B"
    Order By organizationname
```

Figure 8.21 illustrates what happens when you attempt to run this code.

FIGURE 8.21

Column names
that appear in
more than one
table listed in
the From and
Join clauses
must be quali-
fied in order to
resolve the ambi-
guity.

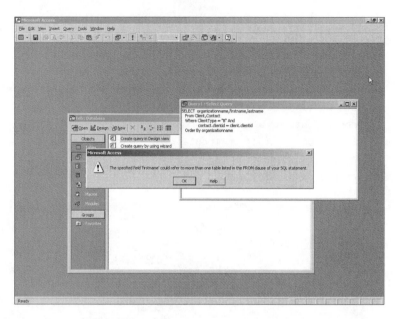

If you recall, the firstname and lastname fields exist in both the Client and Contact
records. Unless you tell the database which table to use as the source, the database is
left to resolve the ambiguity. Because databases cannot resolve these ambiguities,
you end up with an error message such as the one illustrated in Figure 8.21.

To resolve the ambiguity, you need to qualify which field you want. The following
code addresses this problem, and Figure 8.22 illustrates how the results will appear:

```
Select  organizationname, contact.firstname, contact.lastname
   From Client
    Inner Join Contact On (contact.clientid = client.clientid)
   Where ClientType = "B"
   Order By organizationname
```

Left Outer Joins

An inner join requires that matching records be on each side of the join. What if you
want records from the left table regardless of whether a matching record in the right
table exists? Getting the required data is easy if you use a left outer join. Often, *left
outer joins* are called simply *left joins* for short. The following code illustrates how to
use the left join:

```
Select  organizationname, contact.firstname, contact.lastname
   From Client
    Left Outer Join Contact On (contact.clientid = client.clientid)
   Where ClientType = "B"
   Order By organizationname
```

Figure 8.23 illustrates the results of this query.

FIGURE 8.22

When you join
tables, you can
return data from
multiple tables
into a single
resultset.

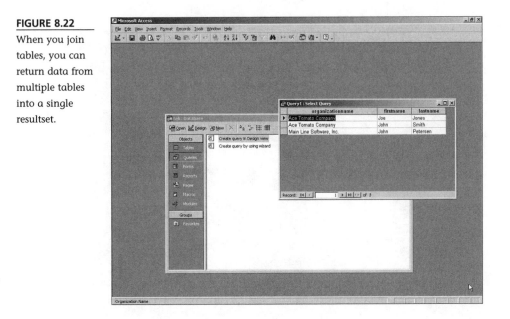

In the case of Bob's House of Pancakes, any field that would correspond to the
Contact table has a null value. Why are they null? Because a contact record does
not exist for Bob's House of Pancakes. You could say the null values are placeholders
for data that would be there had a contact record existed.

Limit Results to Only Those Records That Do Not Have a Matching Record in the Right Table

What if you needed to perform the reverse of a Left Join—only pulling client records
that did not have a corresponding record? You would still make use of the Left Join
so that you could see all records in the Client table. To achieve the desired effect, you
would add criteria to the Where clause to bring back only those records that had
ContactID fields that evaluated to null. Only those client records that did not have
corresponding contact records would satisfy these requirements. The following code
block accomplishes this task:

```
Select  organizationname
    From Client
     Left Outer Join Contact On (contact.clientid = client.clientid)
    Where ClientType = "B" And Contact.ContactId Is Null
    Order By organizationname
```

Figure 8.24 illustrates the results of this query.

FIGURE 8.23

A left outer join
pulls all records
from the left side
of the query
regardless of
whether a
matching record
in the right table
exists.

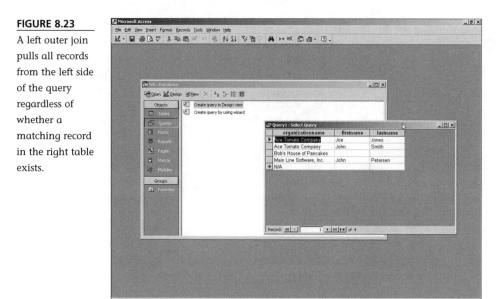

Right and Full Outer Joins

The topics of right and full outer joins are combined in this book because they are joins you are not likely to use that often. In the case of full joins, Access does not support that type. For completeness, both the right and full joins are discussed here.

A left join is useful because it is permissible to have a parent with zero children. A right join is the reverse scenario—a child without a parent. If you recall in Chapter 7 when the topic of referential integrity was discussed, the prospect of having a child record without a corresponding parent record was a violation of referential integrity.

FIGURE 8.24

In addition to
the left outer
join, you can
also extract only
those records
that do not have
a corresponding
record in the
right table.

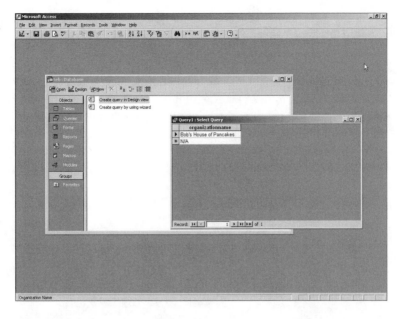

Note

The first thing you learn about rules is that given time, you will encounter a case where
the rule should be broken. Very few rules in life are immutable. There might be times
when you have a child without a parent. Consider the case of a cash invoice. All you
care about is selling something to somebody. You don't care who the person is and you
don't want to take the time to record the information about the customer. There are
other times when that exact same system needs to capture customer information. In this
example, you have a hybrid situation. A simple solution would entail creating a cash customer and having all cash invoices associated with that cash customer. Although it
would work, it might be seen as an unacceptable extra step. Perhaps the better
approach is to allow some invoices to exist regardless of whether a parent record exists.
Design issues such as these are beyond the scope of this book. Just know that there are
times when it makes sense to break the rules and that the SQL language has the capability to account for these contingencies.

These types of records are known as orphaned records. When a database enforces
referential integrity, it is impossible to add children without a parent. Still, there are
cases when the parent-child relationships are purely semantic. In other words, the
relationships exist in name only and the database does not enforce the rule. The
following code illustrates how to employ the right outer join:

```
Select  organizationname, contact.firstname, contact.lastname
    From Client
```

```
Right Outer Join Contact On (contact.clientid = client.clientid)
Where ClientType = "B"
Order By organizationname
```

Figure 8.25 illustrates the results of this query. As you can see, Bob's House of Pancakes has again disappeared from the list. Remember, the purpose of a Right Join is to pull records from the right table regardless of whether a matching record is in the left table. Every record in the right table, which is the Contact table, has a matching record in the left table, which is the Client table. None of these contact records link to Bob's House of Pancakes.

FIGURE 8.25

A right outer join selects records from the child table regardless of whether a matching record in the parent table exists.

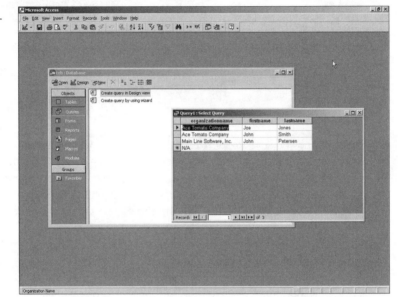

A Full Outer Join combines the Left and Right Outer Joins. All data in both tables is selected regardless of whether matching data exists. Although many databases such as SQL Server, Oracle, and DB2 support the Full Join, Access does not. Even if Access did support this type, it would be a relatively rare situation where you would need a full outer join.

Combine Multiple Resultsets: Use the Union Clause

Combining multiple resultsets is a bit of an advanced topic. However, the basics of what the Union clause does are easy to understand. The Union clause enables you to take two `Select` statements and combine them into one resultset. There are many times when you will need to use the `Union` clause. Consider the task of providing a consolidated list of clients. At first, the task may sound trivial, but in reality, it is not.

Earlier in this chapter, you were introduced to the `Select` statement. In the sample code, you were introduced to techniques that enabled you to extract client data from the Client table. In the case of individual clients, the client name is found in the first- and lastname fields. In the case of business clients, the name is found in the organization name field. Creating an extract that has all three fields is not difficult. What if the task required you to return two fields? The first is the client type field that signifies whether the client is a business or individual. The second is a field called *clientname* that holds the name of the client. As you know, there is no such field called *clientname*. You also know that with the As clause, it is easy to rename the field in the resultset. Still, you are left with the task of getting both the data in the firstname and lastname fields as well as data in the organizationname field marshaled into a single clientname field. Now that you have some scope of the problem, let's go about solving the problem. The following code block achieves the desired results:

```
SELECT  clienttype,lastname  + ",  " + firstname As client
    From Client
    Where ClientType = "I"
Union
SELECT  clienttype,OrganizationName As client
    From Client
    Where ClientType = "B"
Order By Clienttype
```

Figure 8.26 illustrates the results of this query.

The requirements for a UNION are that each unioned select fetch the same number of fields and that those fields be of the same data type. Remember, there is only one resultset. The first query will define the structure of the resultset. From that point on, any subsequent selects must output the same number of fields. In addition, the data type of each field must be the same. In this case, although the second field is different in that the first query selected firstname + lastname and the second query selected organization, both are text fields. Finally, because the first query dictates the structure of the resultset, the As clause that follows the Organizationname field in the second query is not required. In fact, the second As clause is ignored. For consistency purposes, however, it is a good idea to label the fields appropriately.

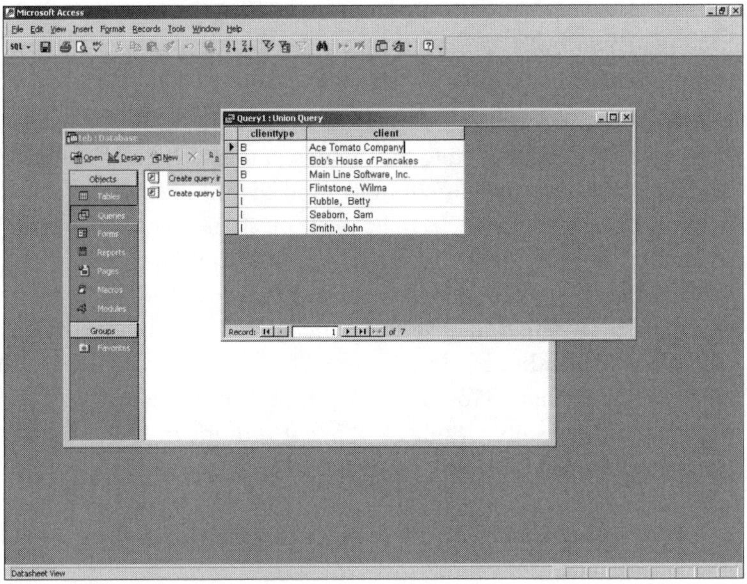

FIGURE 8.26

The Union clause
allows you to
combine data
from multiple
Select state-
ments into a sin-
gle resultset.

FIGURE 8.26

The Union clause allows you to combine data from multiple Select statements into a single resultset.

What You Have Learned

This chapter has provided you with a quick overview of what SQL is and how one of the most used parts of the language, the Select command, is used. You have learned how to use the SQL Select command to extract data from tables in a database. The From clause specifies the primary table used to support the query. The Where clause provides a mechanism for filtering data in the resultset. Top *n* Queries and the Distinct clause are other tools for limiting the data returned to the resultset. The Join clause allows you to extract data from multiple tables. In addition to these features, you also learned how to use the Union clause to combine data from multiple queries into a single resultset. In addition, you learned the As clause specifies the name of the field in the resultset. This feature is particularly useful when combining data from multiple fields to form a single field in the resultset. Now that you have a basic understanding of SQL, you are ready to learn some advanced SQL features.

SQL—GOING BEYOND THE BASICS

CHAPTER HIGHLIGHTS:

- Organize Output II: Use the Group By Clause
- Use Aggregate Functions
- Filter Results II: Use the Having Clause
- Filter Results III: Create Parameterized SQL Statements
- Modify Data with the Insert, Update, and Delete Statements
- What You Have Learned

In the last chapter, you were introduced to one of the most powerful programming languages in existence—SQL. SQL is the language of databases. If you are going to be a database application developer, it is a language you will need to learn and understand. In the previous chapter, you learned how to select and organize data from multiple tables. In this chapter, you will take those skills a few steps further by learning how to aggregate and summarize your data. In the last chapter, you learned how to get a listing of clients organized by client type. What if you needed to produce a query that produced a list of client types and the number of clients for each type? This type of query requires you to calculate the total number of clients for each type. SQL is equally suited to this task. These types of data aggregation operations, as well as data manipulation operations that involve inserting, updating, and deleting data, are the focus of this chapter.

Organize Output II: Use the Group By Clause

The first step in aggregating data involves the use of the Group By clause. The Group By clause is a mechanism for summarizing data. To illustrate, consider this query:

```
Select clienttype
    From client
    Order By clienttype
```

Figure 9.1 illustrates the output produced by this query.

FIGURE 9.1

A simple listing of client type instances in the Client table.

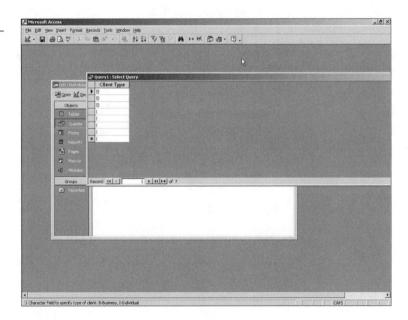

Not terribly useful output, is it? Still, there is some useful information that can be gleaned with a little work. From the output, you can see that only two client types— B and I—exist. And, if you take the time to manually count the different instances, you will find that three business clients and four individual clients exist. Although this is good information to have, you should not have to exert a lot of effort to get the information. One of the advantages of having a database is to organize data so that information like this can be obtained quickly. The value of data is time-sensitive. The older data is, the less valuable it becomes. If somebody has to aggregate and summarize data manually, by the time the task is complete, the data may be obsolete. And, there is always the risk that computation errors exist. Enter the Group By clause.

The Group By clause enables you to summarize data. Summarizing data is the first step to aggregating and subtotaling data. The following query illustrates the Group By clause and Figure 9.2 illustrates how the output will appear:

```
Select clienttype
    From client
    Group By clienttype
    Order By clienttype
```

FIGURE 9.2

The Group By clause provides the capability to summarize data.

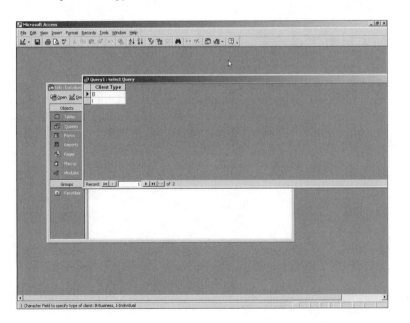

The previous query is the functional equivalent of the following query:

```
Select Distinct clienttype
   From client
   Order By clienttype
```

Therefore, to accurately state the record, the Group By clause is the second method you have learned that summarizes data in SQL. The key difference between Distinct and Group By is that the latter method allows you to aggregate and subtotal your data. Aggregation is the topic of the next section.

Use Aggregate Functions

You will rarely use the Group By clause without also employing one of the SQL aggregate functions. The five SQL aggregate functions are Count(), Sum(), Avg(), Min(), and Max(). Their names give a good indication of what they do. For example, Count() tallies the number of records, Sum() calculates the total of a mathematical expression of fields, and Avg() calculates the average of a mathematical expression of fields. Details on how each of these aggregate functions works are presented in the following three sections.

The Count() Function

The Count() function counts the number of records for each group. In this case, there are two groups, one each for business and individual clients. The question you are attempting to answer is "How many clients of each type does the firm have?" The following code illustrates how the Count() function works and Figure 9.3 illustrates the output:

```
Select clienttype,count(*) As count
   From client
   Group By clienttype
   Order By Count(*)  Desc
```

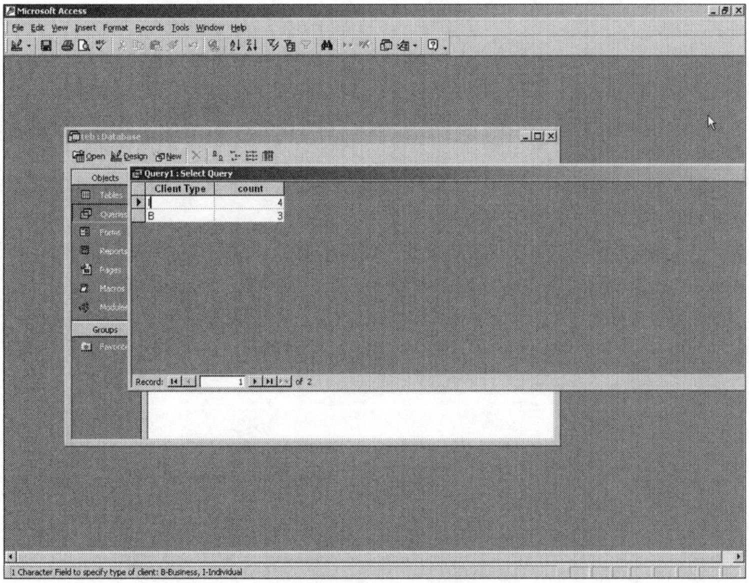

FIGURE 9.3

The Count()
aggregate func-
tion allows you
to determine the
number of
occurrences for
each group.

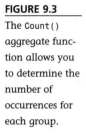

Anytime you use one of the SQL aggregate functions, you will want to use the As
clause to specify a column name in the resultset. Otherwise, the database engine is
likely to supply a name of its own that will not be as descriptive as one of your
choosing. In addition, you can choose to order the resultset based on the contents of
the aggregate field. In this case, the output is composed of the number of occurrences in descending order.

Combining what you learned in the last chapter, you may want to filter the resultset
with the Where clause. The following code is identical to the previous example with
one exception. In this case, only those clients in the state of California are totaled:

```
Select clienttype,count(*) As count
    From client
    Where state = 'CA'
    Group By clienttype
    Order By Count(*)  Desc
```

Figure 9.4 illustrates how the output will appear. As you can see, there are 2 clients
from California and both are individual clients.

FIGURE 9.4

By combining the Where clause, you can aggregate and filter data at the same time.

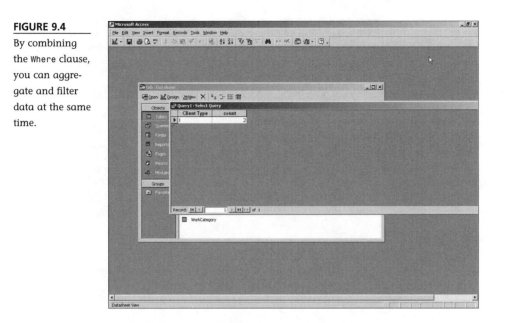

Advanced Operations: A Methodology for Putting It All Together

Let's take a few moments to examine the power of SQL through a more complicated example. You have been asked to extract the following information from the database:

- Listing of cases and associated employees
- Listing of cases and number of assigned employees
- Listing of cases and number of assigned employee types

Whenever you are presented with a request to extract data, the first step should involve identifying the required tables. In looking at the three requests, at a minimum, you know you will need the following tables:

- Case
- Employee
- EmployeeClass

If you recall, a direct relationship does not exist between the Case and Employee tables. A case can have multiple employees and an employee can work on multiple cases. A many-to-many resolver table called EmployeeCase was required. Therefore, a fourth table will be required. Figure 9.5 illustrates a portion of the database diagram of the TEB database that illustrates the required tables and the relationships.

FIGURE 9.5

Identifying required tables and the relationships between those tables is the first step in building a SQL statement.

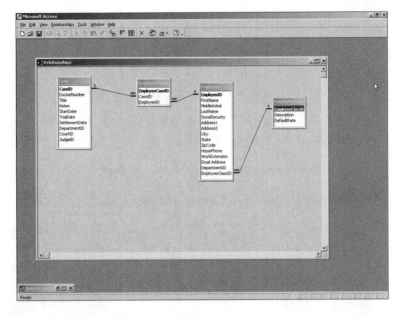

With Figure 9.5 in mind, the `From` and `Join` clauses can be determined:

```
FROM (EmployeeClass INNER JOIN Employee ON EmployeeClass.EmployeeClassID =
      Employee.EmployeeClassID)
   INNER JOIN (Case INNER JOIN EmployeeCase ON Case.CaseID =
EmployeeCase.CaseID)
      ON Employee.EmployeeID =  EmployeeCase.EmployeeID
```

The next step involves determining the fields of data that need to be returned in the resultset. Based on the requirements, the following fields will be needed:

- `case.title`
- `employee.firstname` and `employee.lastname`
- `employeeclass.description`

In addition to specific fields, you will need to capture some counts as well:

- Number of employees
- Number of employee types

Let's tackle the first query: the listing of cases and associated employees. This query will serve as the foundation for the subsequent queries that will aggregate and summarize the data. The following code will provide the required listing:

```
Select Case.Title, EmployeeClass.Description, Employee.FirstName,
Employee.LastName
        From (EmployeeClass
            Inner Join Employee ON EmployeeClass.EmployeeClassID =
Employee.EmployeeClassID)
            Inner Join (Case Inner Join EmployeeCase On Case.CaseID =
EmployeeCase.CaseID)
On Employee.EmployeeID =  EmployeeCase.EmployeeID
        Order By Case.Title, EmployeeClass.Description, Employee.LastName;
```

Figure 9.6 illustrates how the output for this query will appear.

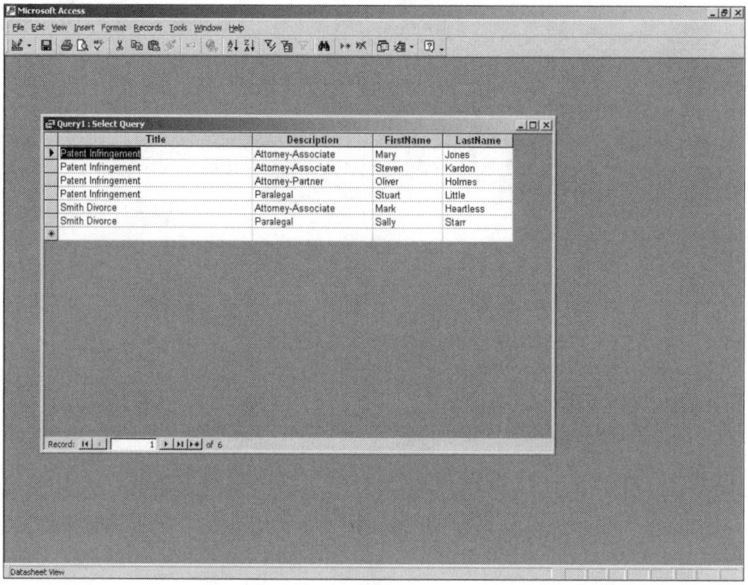

FIGURE 9.6

This resultset contains data from the Case, EmployeeClass, and Employee tables.

It is important to note that the only purpose the EmployeeCase table serves is to facilitate the join between the Employee and Case tables. If this intermediate table did not exist, it would not be possible to associate multiple cases with multiple employees.

With the foundation query out of the way, let's move to the next query—a listing of cases and number of assigned employees. Because you are not concerned with returning the employee names, the Employee table can be dropped from the query. If the only item of interest is the number of employees, the EmployeeCase table will provide this information. In addition, you can also drop the EmployeeClass table for this query as well.

When you aggregate data, it automatically means that the Group By clause is required. For this query, a listing of cases and the number of employees assigned to each case is required. This means the resultset must be grouped by case. The following code will accomplish this task:

```
Select Case.Title,Count(employeecase.employeecaseid) As employees
    From Case
    InnerJoin EmployeeCase On Case.CaseID = EmployeeCase.CaseID
    Group By case.title
    Order By Case.Title
```

Figure 9.7 illustrates how this output will appear.

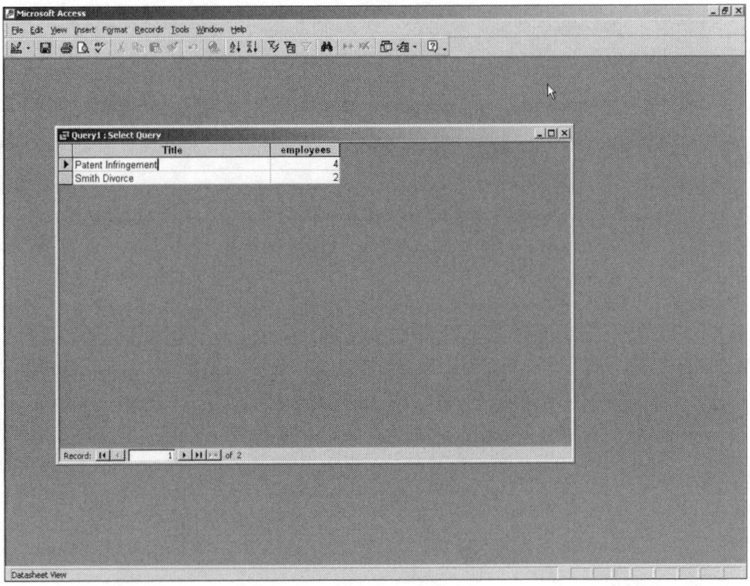

FIGURE 9.7

This resultset
contains the
number of
employees
grouped by case.

The next query takes the previous query and drills down a level. In the previous query, you were concerned with the number of employees. In this query, you are concerned with the count of employee types within the total number of employees for each case. To illustrate, within the patent infringement case, there are four assigned employees. What is the distribution of employees within that total? That is the question you are attempting to answer here. The following code accomplishes this task:

```
Select Case.Title, EmployeeClass.Description,
Count(EmployeeCase.Employeeid) As Employees
```

```
From (EmployeeClass
        Inner Join Employee ON EmployeeClass.EmployeeClassID =
Employee.EmployeeClassID)
        Inner Join (Case Inner Join EmployeeCase On Case.CaseID =
EmployeeCase.CaseID) On Employee.EmployeeID =  EmployeeCase.EmployeeID
      Group By Case.Title,EmployeeClass.Description
      Order By Case.Title, EmployeeClass.Description
```

Figure 9.8 illustrates how this output will appear.

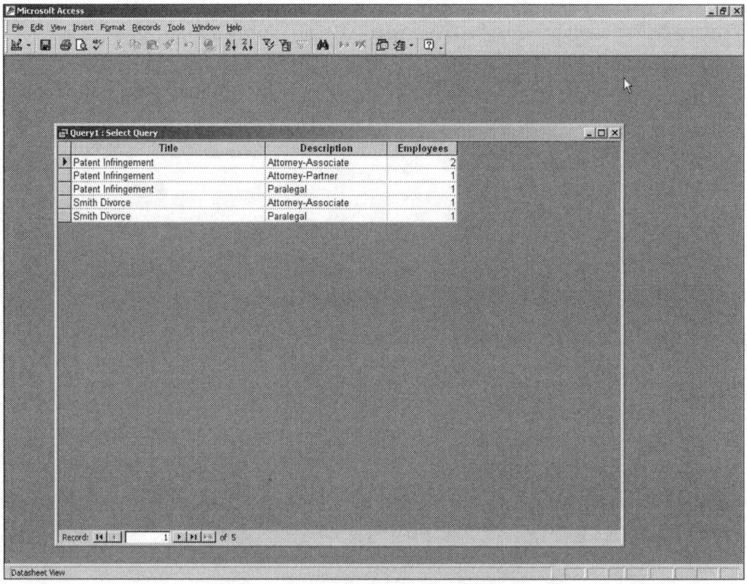

FIGURE 9.8

This resultset contains the number of employee types grouped by case.title and employeeclass. description.

As you drill down through data, you will find more fields listed in the Group By clause. In this query, although the employee name was not returned, the table was required in order to return the employee type. In other words, to get from the Case table to the EmployeeClass table, the EmployeeCase and Employee tables have to be present in the query to facilitate the join.

The Sum() Function

Often, you will need to sum data from different records instead of counting the number of records. This is where the Sum() aggregate function comes into play. Fortunately, you have already done a good part of the heavy lifting in the previous section. The same concepts of Count() apply to Sum().

To illustrate Sum(), consider the following requests:

■ Listing of cases, employees, hours, and rate billed

■ Listing of cases, sum of hours, and rate billed grouped by employee

■ Listing of cases, sum of hours, and rate billed grouped by employee class

■ Listing of cases, sum of hours, and rate billed grouped by case

■ Listing of cases, sum of hours, and rate billed grouped by work category

Employing the methodology you learned in the previous section, the first step involves identifying the required tables to support the requests. Right off the bat, you know you will have the Employee and Case tables. You might think the EmployeeCase table is also required. As you will see, the EmployeeCase table is not required for these queries. In addition, you will also need to have the EmployeeClass and WorkCategory tables. Finally, to get the actual hours and rate worked, you will need the TimeEntryDetail table. The TimeEntryDetail table takes care of joining the Employee and Case tables. Figure 9.9 illustrates the portion of the TEB Database diagram that is relevant to these sets of queries.

FIGURE 9.9

These tables are required to fetch time and rate data grouped by employee, case, work category, and employee class.

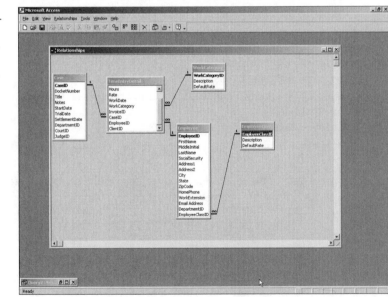

The joins depicted in Figure 9.9 are facilitated with the following SQL code:

```
FROM WorkCategory INNER JOIN ((EmployeeClass INNER JOIN Employee ON
EmployeeClass.EmployeeClassID = Employee.EmployeeClassID)
    INNER JOIN ([Case] INNER JOIN TimeEntryDetail ON Case.CaseID =
```

```
TimeEntryDetail.CaseID) ON Employee.EmployeeID =
TimeEntryDetail.EmployeeID) ON
        WorkCategory.WorkCategoryID = TimeEntryDetail.WorkCategory
```

Note By now, you have taken stock of the fact that as you increase the number of tables in a query, the more complex the Join statements get. Don't worry! In the next chapter, you will see how queries can be graphically created. The Access Query Designer provides a user-friendly interface. Behind the scenes, the SQL code is constructed for you. The goal of this and the previous chapter has been to introduce you to SQL, independent of a specific query designer. Remember, you may find yourself in an environment that requires you to manually craft SQL statements!

The first query to produce is the raw listing of data that will be aggregated and summarized by the subsequent queries. The following SQL code produces this data:

```
SELECT employee.firstname+' '+employee.lastname AS employee,
        EmployeeClass.Description AS employeeclass,
        Case.Title, WorkCategory.Description AS workcategory,
        TimeEntryDetail.Description AS workdescription,
        TimeEntryDetail.Hours, TimeEntryDetail.Rate,
        (timeentrydetail.hours*timeentrydetail.rate) AS total
    FROM WorkCategory INNER JOIN ((EmployeeClass INNER JOIN Employee ON
EmployeeClass.EmployeeClassID =
        Employee.EmployeeClassID)
        INNER JOIN ([Case] INNER JOIN TimeEntryDetail ON Case.CaseID =
TimeEntryDetail.CaseID) ON
        Employee.EmployeeID = TimeEntryDetail.EmployeeID) ON
        WorkCategory.WorkCategoryID = TimeEntryDetail.WorkCategory
```

Clue Take special note of the total field. The query returns the hours and rate fields from the TimeEntryDetail table. In addition, a calculated field that multiplies hours and rate is returned.

Clue The As clause helps with avoiding ambiguity. The Description field of the EmployeeClass, WorkCategory, and TimeEntryDetail tables is part of the resultset. To resolve ambiguities, the As clause is used to provide a more descriptive field name in the resultset.

Figure 9.10 illustrates the raw data resultset.

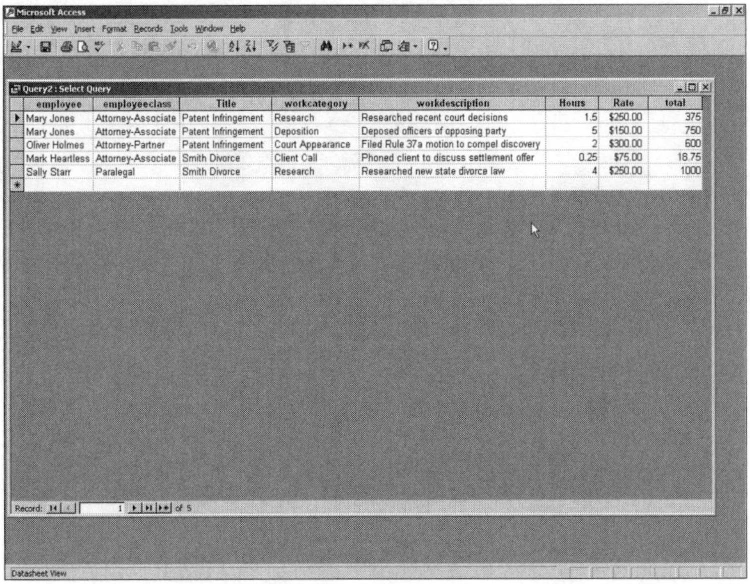

FIGURE 9.10

The raw data
listing to support
hour and rate
summaries
groups
employee, case,
work category
and employee
class.

It is important to note that not all the tables are required for every query. As you drill down into more detail, that is when you need more tables to support a more granular level of detail. Figure 9.10 illustrates the greatest amount of detail. Now, you will start with the 10,000-foot view and work your way down.

The first query involves summarizing data by employee. The following code supports this query:

```
SELECT employee.firstname+' '+employee.lastname AS employee,
        Sum(timeentrydetail.hours*timeentrydetail.rate) AS total
    FROM Employee
        INNER JOIN TimeEntryDetail ON Employee.EmployeeID =
TimeEntryDetail.EmployeeID
        GROUP BY employee.firstname+' '+employee.lastname
        Order By Sum(timeentrydetail.hours*timeentrydetail.rate) Desc
```

Figure 9.11 illustrates the resultset of this query.

FIGURE 9.11

This resultset
totals hours ×
rate and sum-
marizes by
employee.

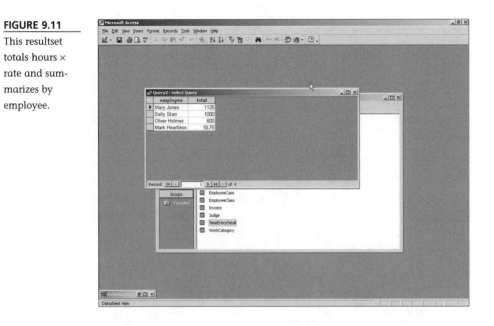

How about summaries based on work category? Work category exists in two contexts. First, it exists in its own right. Second, work category exists in the context of an
employee. In other words, you can summarize data based solely on work category or
on work category and employee. The following code summarizes the work data
based on work category:

```
SELECT WorkCategory.Description AS workcategory,
       Sum(timeentrydetail.hours*timeentrydetail.rate) AS total
   FROM WorkCategory
      INNER JOIN TimeEntryDetail ON WorkCategory.WorkCategoryID =
TimeEntryDetail.WorkCategory
      GROUP BY WorkCategory.Description
      ORDER BY Sum(timeentrydetail.hours*timeentrydetail.rate) Desc
```

Figure 9.12 illustrates the output of this query.

Figures 9.11 and 9.12 provide two viewpoints of the same data. Figure 9.11 shows
the data summarized by employee and Figure 9.12 shows the data summarized by
work category. Being able to slice, dice, and summarize data in this manner is how
the combination of SQL and a database provides value to an organization. What
about the combination of these two queries—a summary of work by work category
by employee? This requests two levels of grouping. As previously mentioned, as more
detail is provided, the more tables your query will require. The following code supports this more detailed query:

FIGURE 9.12

This resultset totals hours × rate and summarizes by work category.

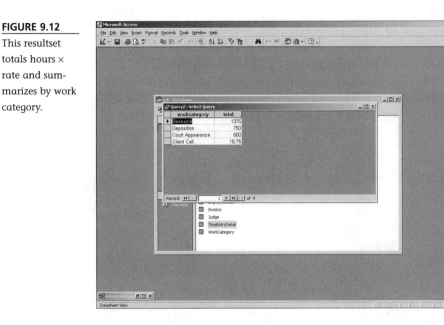

```
SELECT  WorkCategory.Description AS workcategory,
            employee.firstname+' '+employee.lastname AS employee,
            Sum (timeentrydetail.hours*timeentrydetail.rate) AS total
        FROM WorkCategory
            INNER JOIN (Employee INNER JOIN TimeEntryDetail ON
Employee.EmployeeID =
            TimeEntryDetail.EmployeeID)
            ON WorkCategory.WorkCategoryID = TimeEntryDetail.WorkCategory
            Group By workcategory.description,employee.firstname+'
'+employee.lastname
            Order By workcategory.Description,Sum
(timeentrydetail.hours*timeentrydetail.rate) Desc
```

Figure 9.13 illustrates the results of this query.

Let's take a moment to dissect part of the data. Figure 9.12 shows that research-related tasks generated $1,375 of fees. Figure 9.13 shows that Sally Starr generated $1,000 and Mary Jones generated $375 of the research-related income. Referring to Figure 9.11, Mary Jones generated a total of $1,125 of income. How was the distribution of the additional $750 Mary earned? Figure 9.13 tells you that deposition-related tasks accounted for the additional income.

FIGURE 9.13

This resultset totals hours × rate and summarizes by work category by employee.

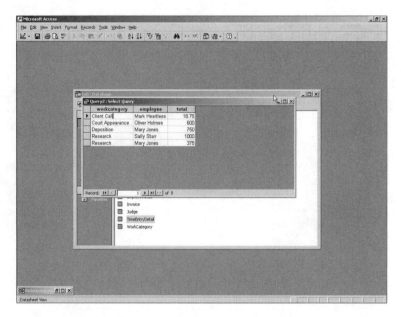

By now, you should be seeing a repeatable pattern. The level of detail you need is directly related to the number of tables you need, the number of fields that are in the resultset, and the contents of the Group By clause. Just to solidify the point, consider a resultset that summarizes by case. The following code is very similar to the previous code that summarizes by work category and the code that summarizes by employee:

```
SELECT Case.Title ,
        Sum(timeentrydetail.hours*timeentrydetail.rate) AS total
    FROM Case
      INNER JOIN TimeEntryDetail ON Case.CaseID = TimeEntryDetail.Caseid
      GROUP BY Case.Title
      ORDER BY Sum(timeentrydetail.hours*timeentrydetail.rate) Desc
```

Figure 9.14 illustrates the output of this query.

Now, does it seem complicated to further summarize this query by employee or work category? The process is no more complicated than adding the appropriate table and join to the query, adding the additional fields to the select list, and finally, adding the fields to the Order By and Group By clauses.

What if all you want is a grand total of income generated? Because there is a lack of detail, you would expect the SQL statement to be very simple. The following is the code—you be the judge!

FIGURE 9.14

This resultset totals hours × rate and summarizes by case.

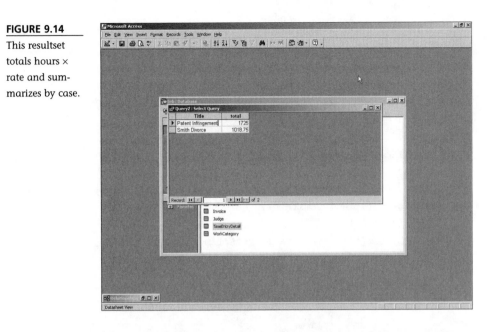

```
SELECT    Sum(timeentrydetail.hours*timeentrydetail.rate) AS total
   FROM TimeEntryDetail
```

Figure 9.15 illustrates the output of this query.

FIGURE 9.15

This resultset provides a grand total of hours × rate.

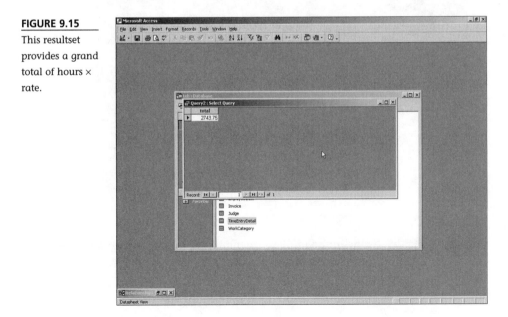

Because the entire table is summarized, there is no need for an Order By or Group By clause.

Finally, what if you were concerned with summary data for only a specific case employee, work category, or so on? Simply add the Where clause to filter the data returned in the resultset. The following code retrieves the summary data for the Smith Divorce Case:

```
SELECT Case.Title ,
      Sum(timeentrydetail.hours*timeentrydetail.rate) AS total
    FROM Case
      INNER JOIN TimeEntryDetail ON Case.CaseID = TimeEntryDetail.Caseid
      WHERE case.title = "Smith Divorce"
      GROUP BY Case.Title
      ORDER BY Sum(timeentrydetail.hours*timeentrydetail.rate) Desc
```

Figure 9.16 illustrates the output of this query.

FIGURE 9.16

This resultset provides a total of income earned on a specific case through the use of the Where clause.

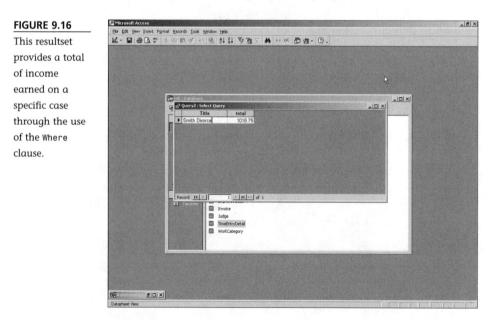

The Avg() Function

The Avg() function, as the name implies, calculates an average based on the expression contained within the function. The following code is a simple example of how to use the Avg() function:

```
SELECT Avg(defaultrate) As AverageRate
    From Employeeclass
```

Figure 9.17 illustrates the output of this query.

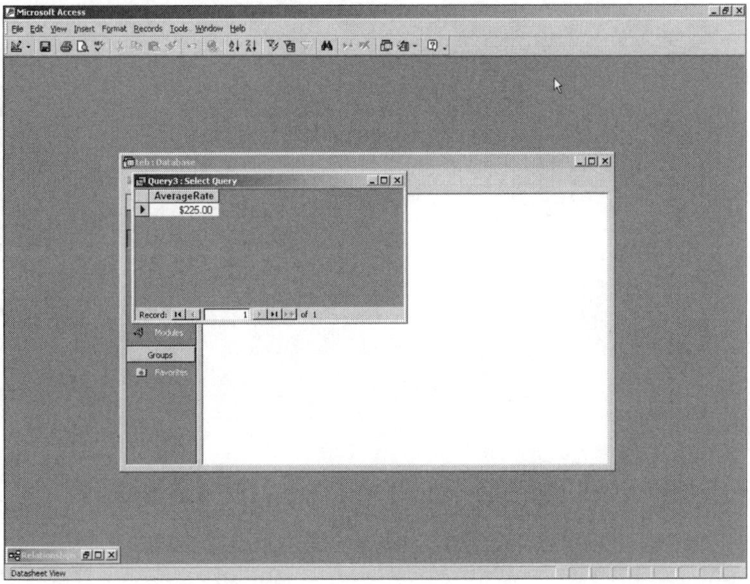

FIGURE 9.17

The Avg() function calculates the average of a passed expression.

Figure 9.17 illustrates the average billing rate among the employee classes in the firm.

The Min() and Max() Functions

What if your goal is to find the minimum or maximum value of a specific field in a table? This is where the Min() and Max() aggregate functions come into play. The following code illustrates how these functions work:

```
Select Min(defaultrate) As minrate,
    Max(defaultrate) As maxrate
  from employeeclass
```

Figure 9.18 illustrates the output of this query.

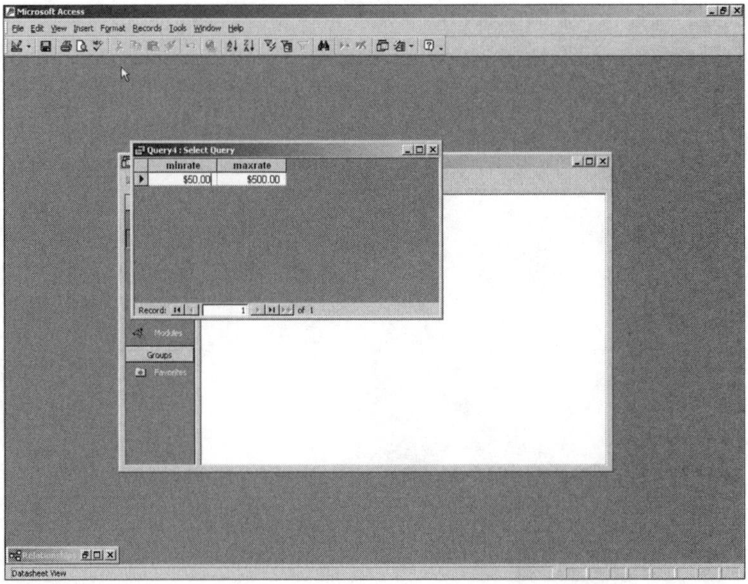

FIGURE 9.18

The Min() and
Max() functions
return the mini-
mum and maxi-
mum values for
a passed expres-
sion.

Filter Results II: Use the Having Clause

Often, you will need to filter the result based on aggregate data. For example, you
may want to view only records where an employee has generated more than $1,000.
The following code employs the Having clause to achieve the desired results:

```
SELECT employee.firstname+' '+employee.lastname AS employee,
        Sum(timeentrydetail.hours*timeentrydetail.rate) AS total
    FROM Employee
        INNER JOIN TimeEntryDetail ON Employee.EmployeeID =
TimeEntryDetail.EmployeeID
        GROUP BY employee.firstname+' '+employee.lastname
        Having Sum(timeentrydetail.hours*timeentrydetail.rate) > 1000
        Order By Sum(timeentrydetail.hours*timeentrydetail.rate) Desc
```

Figure 9.19 illustrates the output of this query.

The Having clause works after the data has been aggregated. If you tried to use the
Where clause, SQL would generate an error. On the other hand, if you had a Where
clause, such as Where timeentrydetail.hours * timeentrydetail.rate > 1000, the criteria
would have been applied to each TimeEntryDetail record. Any record that did not
pass the $1,000 threshold would have been ignored. In this case, you want to aggre-
gate all the time records first and then apply the filter criteria.

FIGURE 9.19

The Having
clause allows
you to filter the
resultset based
on the aggregate
data.

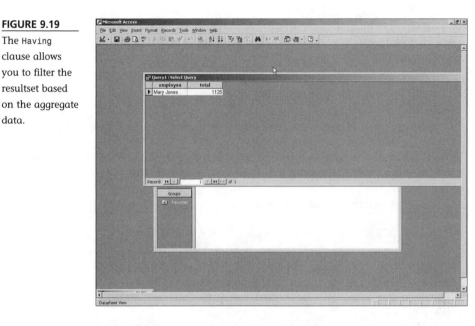

FIGURE 9.19

The Having
clause allows
you to filter the
resultset based
on the aggregate
data.

When you want the criteria to be applied to each source record, use the Where clause.
When you want the filter criteria to be applied to the results of aggregation, use the
Having clause.

Filter Results III: Create Parameterized SQL Statements

In a previous example, the SQL Statement was hardcoded to return summary data
for only the Smith Divorce Case. Often, you will want to let the user specify the case.
This issue strays into two important areas of database application development.
Obviously, it is an issue for the database. It is a user-interface development issue as
well. Issues regarding user interface are addressed in Part V, "Putting Your Database
to Work—Building a Simple Access Database Application," of this book. The issues
regarding how the database deals with these "dynamic" SQL statements will be
addressed now.

SQL statements that require immediate user input are known as parameterized
queries. The SQL Statement definition contains a placeholder instead of a static
value. To illustrate, consider the following code:

```
SELECT Case.Title ,
       Sum(timeentrydetail.hours*timeentrydetail.rate) AS total
FROM Case
    INNER JOIN TimeEntryDetail ON Case.CaseID = TimeEntryDetail.Caseid
    WHERE case.title = [Please enter a case title]
    GROUP BY Case.Title
    ORDER BY Sum(timeentrydetail.hours*timeentrydetail.rate) Desc
```

Figure 9.20 illustrates what happens when this query is executed. At runtime, you will be presented a dialog box that enables you to specify a case title.

FIGURE 9.20

Parameterized queries allow the user to specify criteria at runtime.

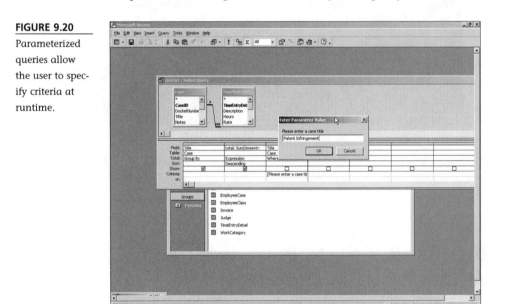

Figure 9.21 illustrates the results of the query after the user provides a value.

In the last chapter, you were introduced to the * wildcard character used in Access. Parameterized queries can implement wildcards as well. The only difference is that instead of the = operator, you need to use the Like operator. Figure 9.22 illustrates a parameterized query that implements a wildcard search and Figure 9.23 illustrates the output.

FIGURE 9.21

This resultset was generated from a parameterized query.

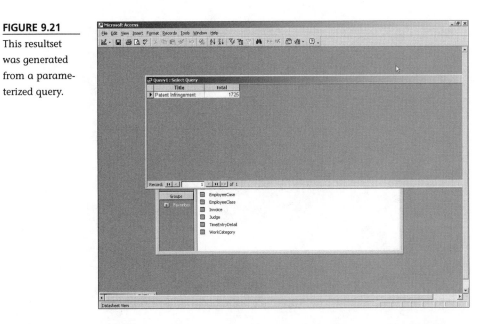

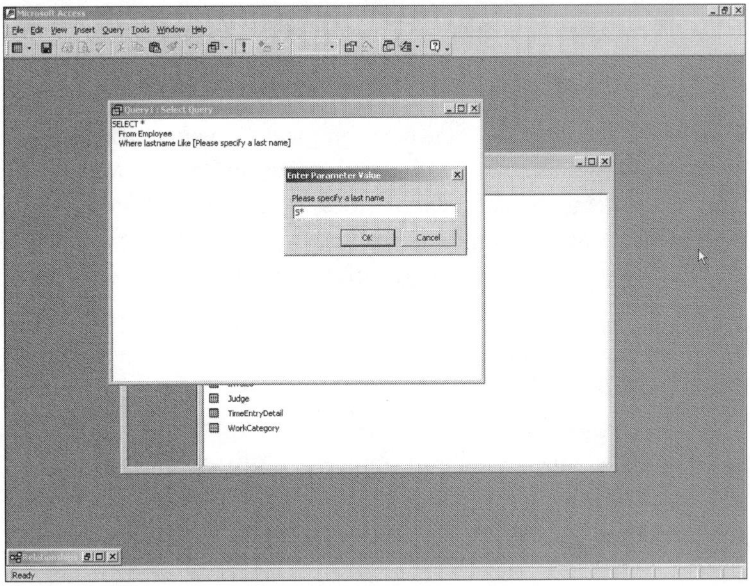

FIGURE 9.22

The Like operator and wildcard matches can be used in conjunction with parameterized queries.

FIGURE 9.23

Parameterized
query results
using a wildcard
match on last-
name such
as S*.

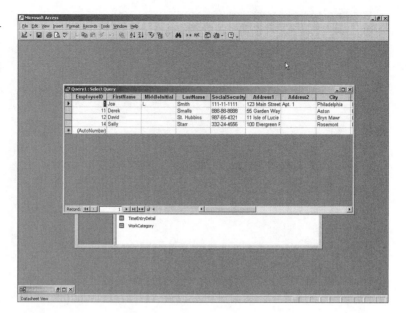

Modify Data with the `Insert`, `Update`, and `Delete` Statements

Your introduction to SQL is nearly complete. The only elements left are the portions of the Data Definition Language that allow you to Add, Modify, and Delete data. The SQL statements that facilitate these operations are the `Insert`, `Update`, and `Delete` statements. This section provides a brief introduction to these SQL DML components. As you will see, the `Insert`, `Update`, and `Delete` statements are very simple and easy to understand.

The `Insert` Statement

The `Insert` statement consists of three parts. The first part designates the table you want to affect. The second part is a listing of fields. The third part is a listing of the actual data. The following code illustrates how an `Insert` statement would look for the Department table:

```
Insert Into Department
    (Description)
    Values ("Criminal Law")
```

Figure 9.24 illustrates how to execute this query in Access.

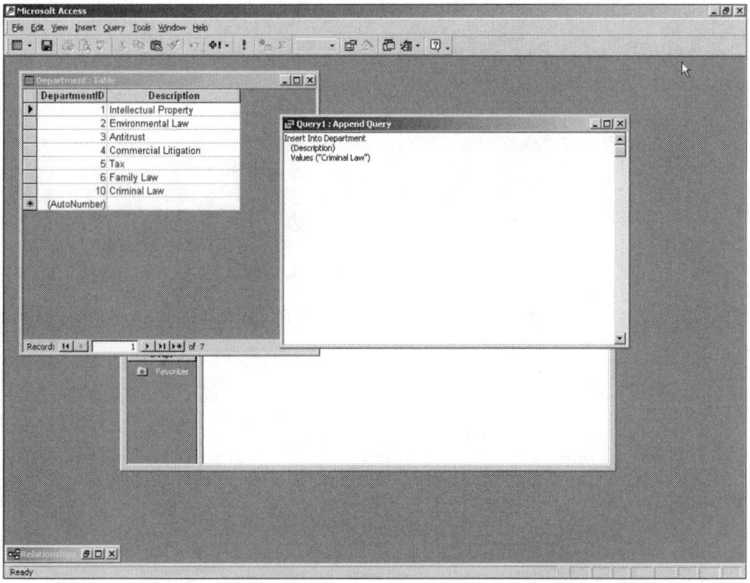

FIGURE 9.24

The Criminal Law Department was added by executing the SQL Insert statement.

Note

Some databases would accept the following statement:

```
Insert Into Department
    Values ("Criminal Law")
```

In other words, some databases will allow you to forgo an explicit listing of fields. Access, however, requires a field listing. Even if you can omit the field listing, it is not a good idea. By omitting the field list, you are making the assumption that the underlying table structure has not changed. If the underlying structure has changed, it is very possible that your SQL code will result in an error. By explicitly listing the fields, your code is more readable and maintainable. And, if your table makes use of default values, you have to list only those fields that have to be provided a value.

Clue

After you have inserted a new value into a table, how can you go about determining its primary key value? Remember, the system generates key value. Because you can be assured the last primary key value is the largest value in the table, the Max() function will do the trick:

```
Select Max(departmentid) As lastkey
        From department
```

Figure 9.25 illustrates a case where multiple fields are inserted into a table. It is simply a matter of listing all the fields you need to affect as well as the corresponding values that go into those fields.

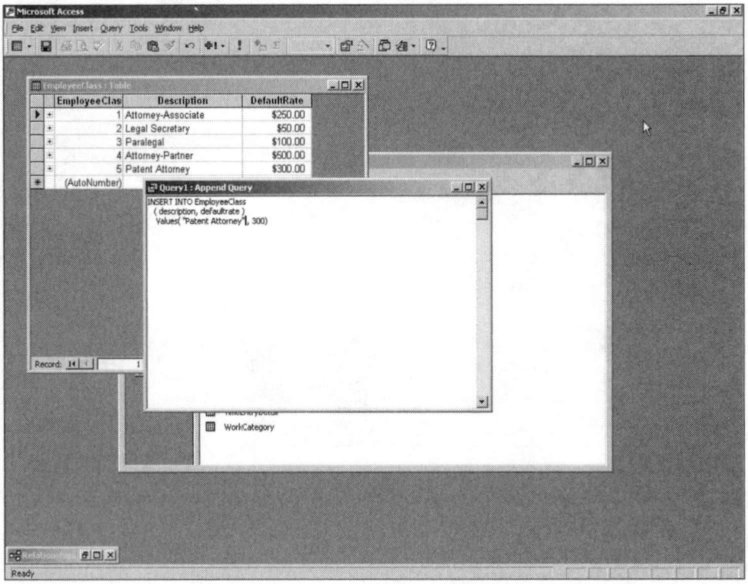

FIGURE 9.25

This SQL Insert statement inserts multiple values into the new EmployeeClass row.

The Update Statement

The Update statement contains two basic parts. The first part designates the table you want to affect. The second part is a listing of fields and the new values that need to be written to those fields. The following code increases the default rate values in the EmployeeClass table by 10%:

```
Update Employeeclass
    Set DefaultRate = DefaultRate * 1.10
```

Figure 9.26 illustrates how to execute this query in Access.

The Update statement can be scoped with a Where clause. For example, if you wanted to increase only those rates by 10% that were above $500, you would issue code like this:

```
Update Employeeclass
    Set DefaultRate = DefaultRate * 1.10
    Where DefaultRate > 500
```

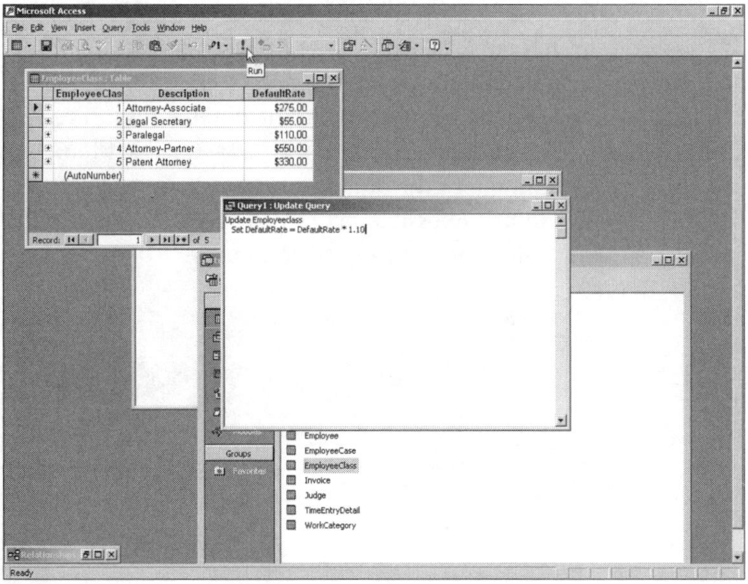

FIGURE 9.26

The default rate
fields were modi-
fied with the
SQL Update
statement.

FIGURE 9.26

The default rate
fields were modi-
fied with the
SQL Update
statement.

If multiple fields needed to be updated, you simply separate the field listings and
assignments with a comma. The following prototype call illustrates how this task
would be accomplished:

```
Update <<tablename>>
   Set <<fieldx>> = <<new value>>,
       <<fieldy>> = <<new value>>,
       <<fieldz>> = <<new value>>
   Where <<field>> = <<some value>>
```

The Delete Statement

The Delete statement has two basic parts. The first, like the Insert and Update statements, is the table you want to affect. The second is the Where clause to properly
scope which rows of data will be deleted. The following code would attempt to delete
every record in the Case table:

```
Delete
   From case
```

Because there is no Where clause to scope the range of data that should be deleted,
SQL will assume that your intent is to delete everything. This is consistent with the
Update statement. In the case of updates, if you do not properly scope the range of
data that should be affected, SQL will assume you want to affect all the data.

Fortunately, there is a built-in mechanism to avoid compromising database integrity. If you recall in Chapter 7, "The Basics of Referential Integrity," you were introduced to the concept of referential integrity. Appendix B, "TEB Referential Integrity Rules," contains a listing of each relationship in the database. With regard to the Case table, a one-to-many relationship exists with the TimeEntryDetail table. Because restricted deletes are used throughout the database and because TimeEntryDetail records exist for each case, it will be impossible to delete a case. Figure 9.27 illustrates what happens if you try to delete records from the Case table.

FIGURE 9.27

Referential integrity rules will prevent you from deleting data and, in turn, compromising database integrity.

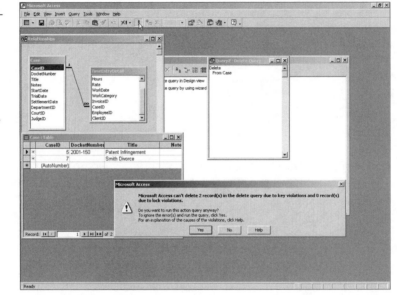

Even though the dialog box shown in Figure 9.27 asks whether you want to continue with the operation, the records will still not be deleted. The referential integrity rules you set up for a database are immutable.

The following code provides one final illustration that incorporates the Where clause with the Delete statement:

```
Delete
    From EmployeeClass
    Where EmployeeClassID = 5
```

As long as no employees are assigned to the employee class you want to delete, the delete operation will succeed because in this case, referential integrity is not being violated.

What You Have Learned

In this chapter, you expanded on the SQL concepts you learned in Chapter 8, "SQL Basics." This chapter focused on some of the advanced uses of SQL. Very often, you will need to aggregate data through the use of the Sum(), Count(), and Avg() SQL aggregate functions. Depending on the granularity of detail you need, you will also need to incorporate the use of the Group By clause. In addition, the Min() and Max() functions provide a simple way to pull minimum and maximum values from a table for a given field.

After you aggregate data, it is very likely you will want to filter the resultset based on the calculated results. As you learned, the Where clause will not help you in this task. Rather, you need to make use of the Having clause. The Where clause acts on the source data when the query is running. The Having clause acts on the resultset after the query has completed execution. Finally, you learned about parameterized queries and the other commands in the SQL Data Manipulation sublanguage: Insert, Update, and Delete.

Now that you have a basic understanding of the core parts of SQL, you are ready to make use of the graphical query tools in Access. The goal of this and the previous chapter was to give you an understanding of SQL as a language, independent of a particular implementation. After you have an understanding of the language, the adoption of graphical tools that buffer you from the complexity of SQL becomes much easier. Also, as you progress down the path of database application development, very often, you will need to resort to embedding SQL in your program code. Simply put, if you are going to be a database application developer or somebody who is going to work as a database administrator, you need to know the SQL language and how to use it!

MAKING SQL QUERIES A PART OF YOUR DATABASE

CHAPTER HIGHLIGHTS:

- An Overview of the Access Query Designer
- Create Advanced Queries
- What You Have Learned

In the previous two chapters, you have learned about the basic and advanced features of the Structured Query Language (SQL). In this chapter, you will learn how to store queries in your database. There are many advantages to storing queries in a database. One advantage is that you achieve something known as *program/data independence*. Program/data independence means that changes in your program code do not necessarily entail changes to the database and vice versa. Good design involves the separation of program code and the specific ways you access and manipulate data.

The focus of this book is on the data side of the equation. That is not to say there has been no attention paid to a programming language. SQL, when you break it down, is just like any other language. The previous two chapters have shown you how to use the SQL language itself, independent of any particular database implementation. As you get more involved in the world of database application development, you will find that it is possible to embed SQL code directly into your application logic. In this chapter, you will learn how to store the SQL code directly in a database. Whereas the former violates program/data independence, the latter encourages it.

Storing queries in a database strays into areas that are specific to a database implementation. In this chapter, you will learn how Access enables you to store queries. Other database products such as SQL Server and Oracle have their methodologies.

An Overview of the Access Query Designer

Believe it or not, you have already been working with the Access Query Designer! Since Chapter 8, "SQL Basics," you have been working in the SQL View of the designer. When you select Queries from the list of database objects, two options appear in the right pane of the main database window. When you choose to create a query in Design View, in addition to the Access Query Designer, a dialog box prompting you to select tables to add to the query appears. Figure 10.1 illustrates the Show Table dialog box.

> The listbox in the Show Table dialog box works like any other listbox in Windows. If you hold the Control (Ctrl) key down while selecting items, all the items Ctrl-clicked will be selected. If you select an item and then hold down the Shift key when selecting another item, every item between the two clicked will be selected.

After you have selected a table, the table will appear in the upper pane of the Query Designer. To illustrate, let's use the Client table as an example. After the Client table is selected, it will appear in the upper pane of the Query Designer. The Client table is depicted in Figure 10.2.

FIGURE 10.1

The Access
Query Designer.

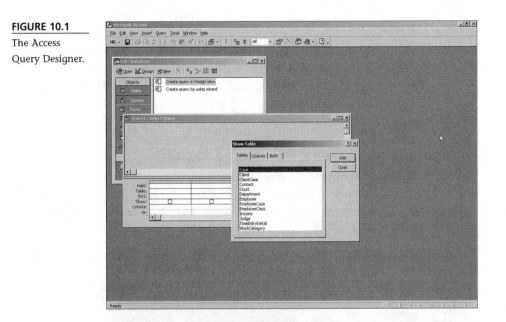

FIGURE 10.2

The Access
Query Designer
in Design View.

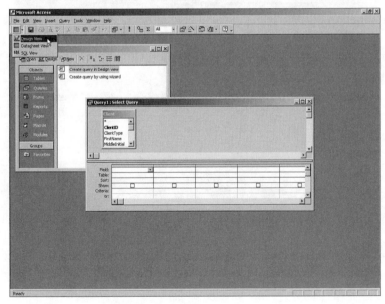

Adding Select Fields

After the table has been added to the Query Designer, you are ready to select fields that will be included in a resultset. To select a field, simply double-click the item in the field list. Alternatively, you can drag items from the table field list in the upper pane and drop them into columns in the lower pane of the designer. A third alternative involves simply selecting an empty column and selecting a field from the drop-down list. Figure 10.3 illustrates how the ClientID, ClientType, and OrganizationName fields will appear after they are selected.

As you build your query in the graphical designer, you can always toggle between the design view and the SQL View. You should already be familiar with the SQL View because that is the part of the Query Designer you have been working with in Chapters 8 and 9. Figure 10.4 illustrates the SQL View of the query.

FIGURE 10.3

The ClientID, ClientType, and Organization-Name fields are selected for this query.

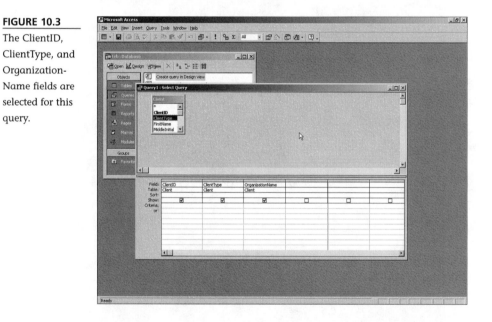

After you have selected fields, you can run the query and view the resultset. The current results of this query are illustrated in Figure 10.5.

FIGURE 10.4

Toggling to the SQL View will allow you to view the SQL Code.

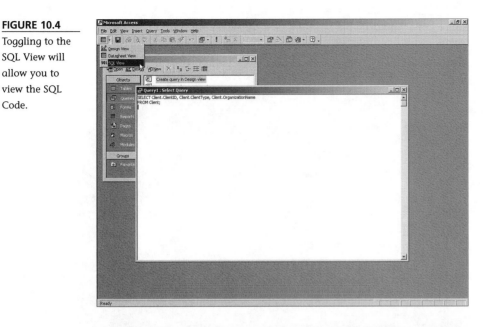

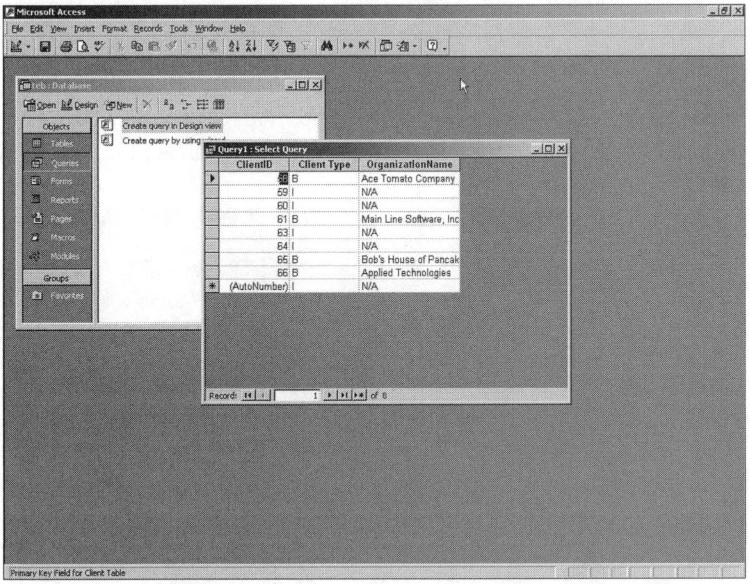

FIGURE 10.5

You can interactively run the query in the designer to view the contents of the resultset.

Adding Selection Criteria

After you have selected your fields, you can now filter the resultset with selection criteria. Looking back to Figure 10.5, it is clear that the individual client records are irrelevant. Figure 10.6 illustrates how the selection criteria appear in the graphical designer.

FIGURE 10.6

Selection criteria have been added to only return records with ClientType = "B."

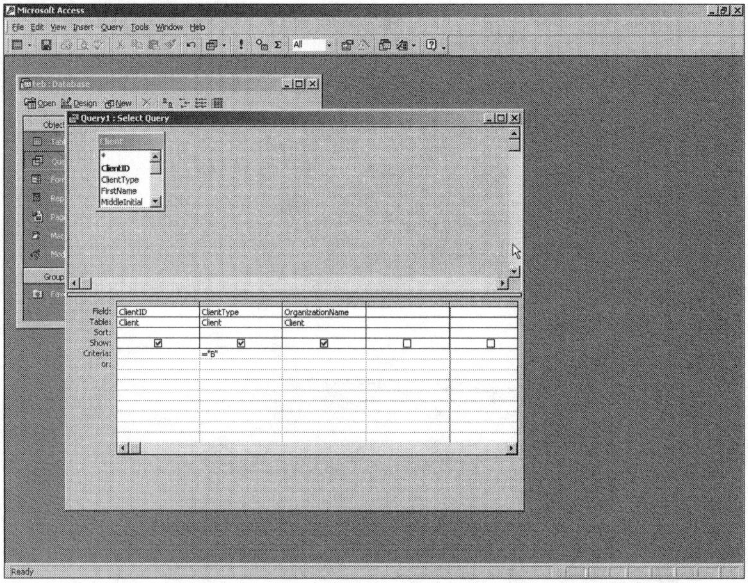

As in the previous example, you can interactively run the query to see the results. The results reflecting the selection criteria are illustrated in Figure 10.7.

FIGURE 10.7

This resultset reflects the addition of the selection criteria.

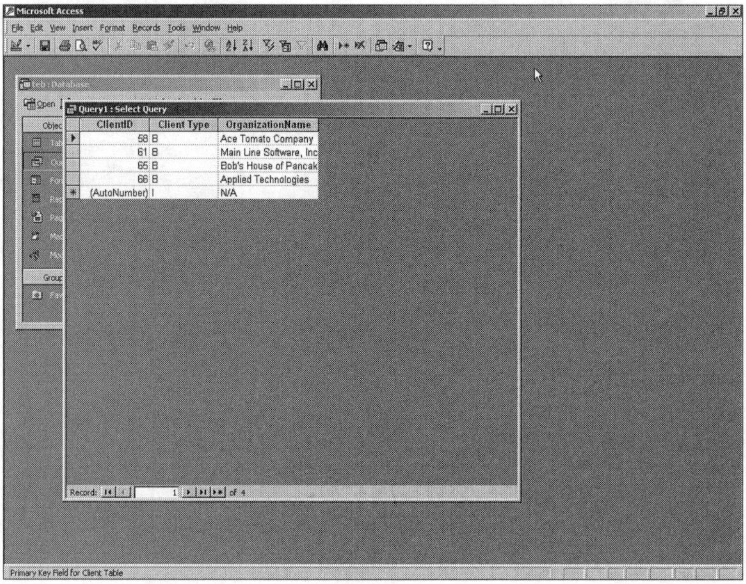

Finally, switching to the SQL View, you can see the underlying SQL Code. The SQL Code for this query is illustrated in Figure 10.8.

FIGURE 10.8

Adding selection criteria in the graphical designer adds the Where clause to the SQL Code.

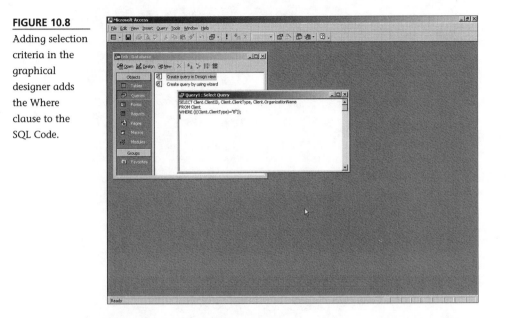

Suppressing Columns

The only purpose of the ClientType field is to filter the resultset. There is no need to output that column. Between the Sort and Criteria portions of the lower pane of the query designer, you will find a check box that will toggle whether the column is returned in the resultset. Figure 10.9 illustrates how to suppress the ClientType field from the resultset. Figure 10.10 illustrates how the resultset is modified.

Figure 10.11 illustrates the SQL code for the query. As you can see, suppressing a column is simply a matter of removing the field from the select list.

FIGURE 10.9

You can toggle whether a column should appear in the resultset.

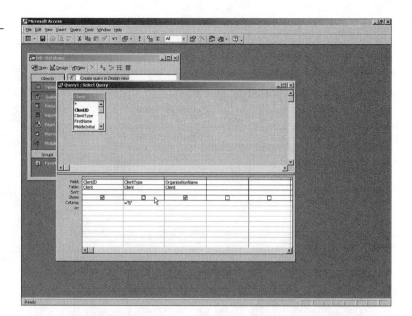

FIGURE 10.10

This resultset reflects the removal of the ClientType field.

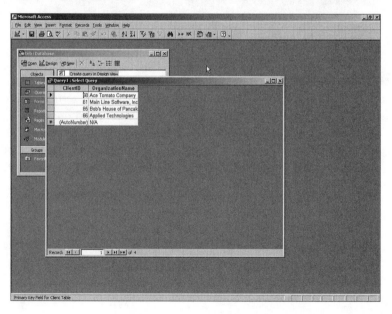

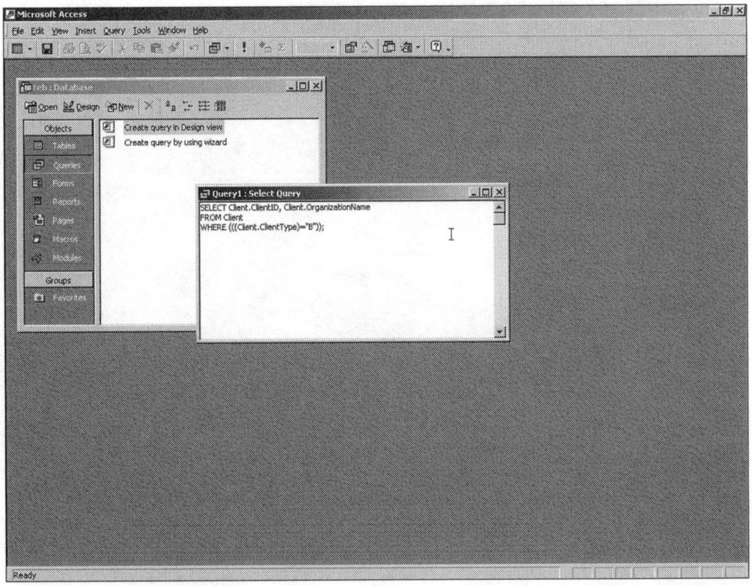

FIGURE 10.11
Suppressing a column from the resultset is simply a matter of removing the field from the select list.

Adding a Sort Order

The only major task left is to supply a sort order. Figure 10.12 illustrates how easy it is to apply a sort order on the OrganizationName field. Figure 10.13 illustrates the resultset and Figure 10.14 illustrates how the SQL code will appear.

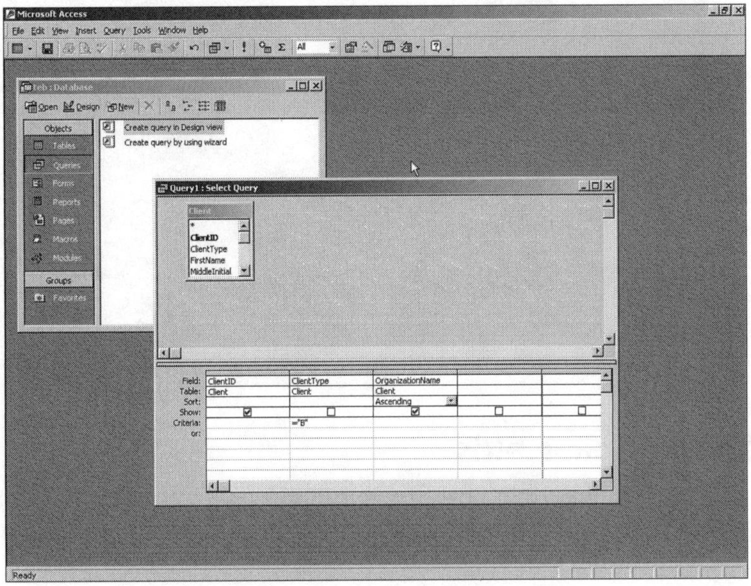

FIGURE 10.12
You can specify an ascending or descending sort order for any field.

FIGURE 10.13

This resultset reflects an ascending sort order on the Organization-Name field.

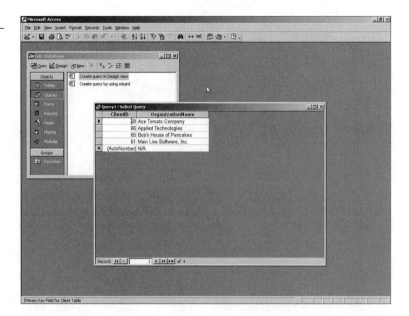

FIGURE 10.14

Specifying a sort order in the graphical designer adds the Order By clause to the SQL code.

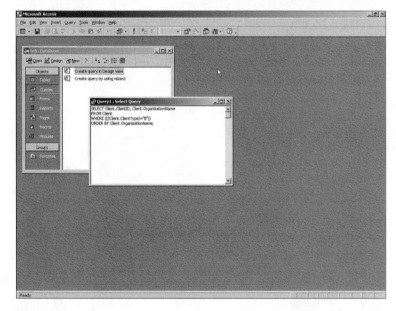

Sorting on Multiple Fields

Figure 10.15 illustrates how easy it is to sort on multiple fields. It is simply a matter of specifying whether the field should be sorted ascending or descending. The order of sort precedence will work from left to right. In this scenario, the resultset will first be sorted by state and then by organization name. To support this additional sort, the state field has been added to the query.

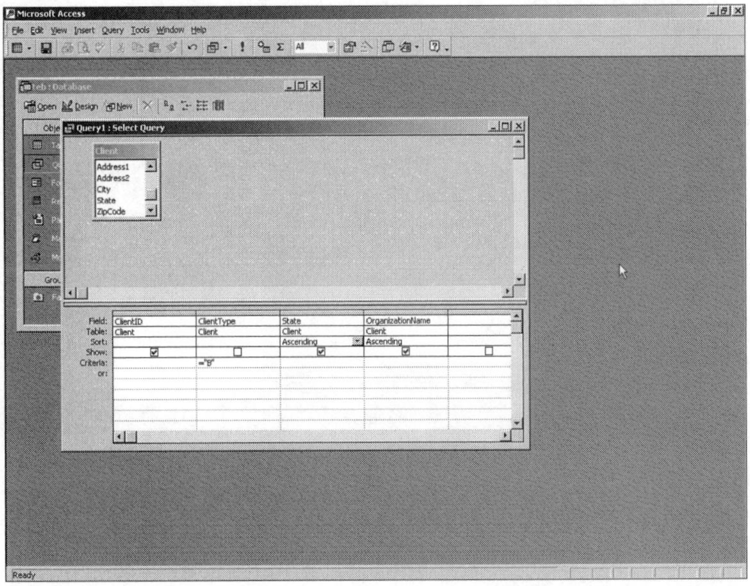

FIGURE 10.15

This resultset is sorted first by state and then by organization name.

Saving Your Query

Saving your query is easy. Simply click the Save button on the toolbar. Figure 10.16 illustrates a prompt that provides you with the ability to specify a name. After the query is saved, double-clicking the query in the main database window will execute the query.

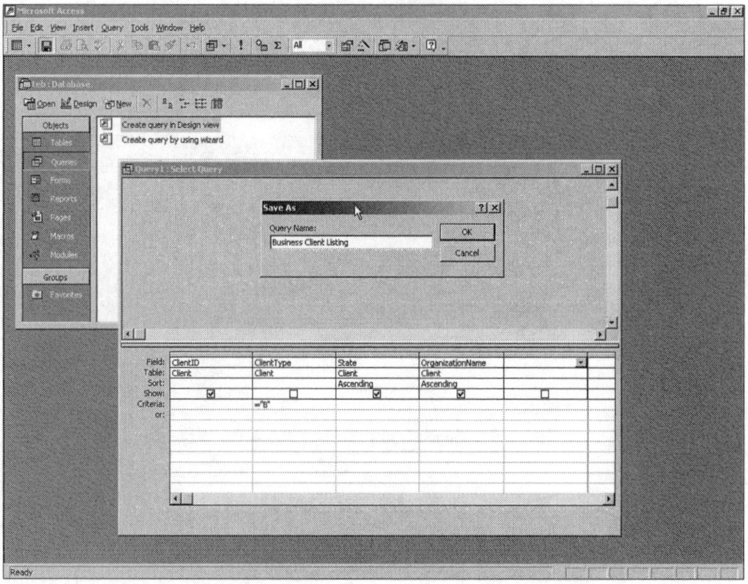

FIGURE 10.16

The Save As dialog box allows you to specify a name for your query.

Create Advanced Queries

At this point, you have seen the basic features of the Access Query Designer. Creating advanced queries with the designer is almost as simple as creating basic queries. Consider a simple employee listing that outputs the EmployeeID, employee classification, firstname, and lastname fields. As you already know, the employee classification description field is contained in the Employee Class table. This means the query will require two tables and a join statement. Because the relationship is stored in the database, you don't have to remember the details of the join. When you create the query and add the Employee and Employee Class tables, the join will automatically appear. Figure 10.17 illustrates how this query will appear in the designer. Figure 10.18 illustrates how the resultset will appear.

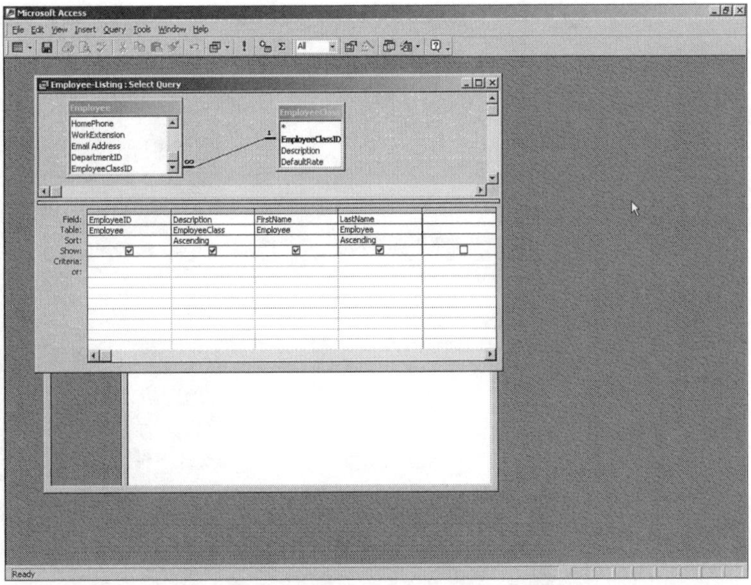

FIGURE 10.17

Joins are automatically created when adding related tables to a query.

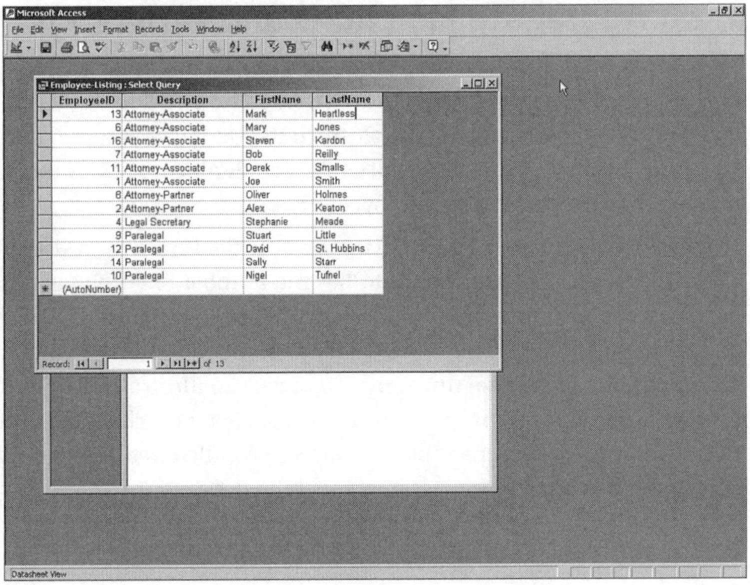

FIGURE 10.18

This resultset contains data from the Employee and Employee Class tables.

Figure 10.19 illustrates the SQL code for the Employee-Listing query.

FIGURE 10.19

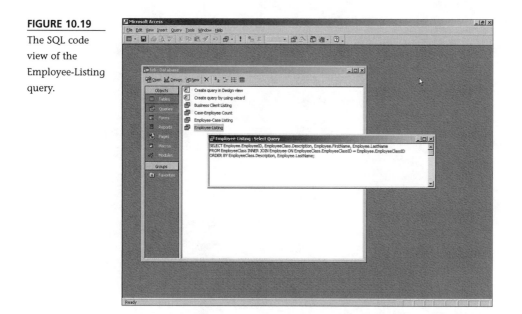

Implementing Aggregate Functions and Groupings

The last area to tackle involves aggregate functions and groupings. To illustrate, let's say you need to create a query that lists each case and the number of employees associated with each case. Right off the bat, you know you are going to need the Case and EmployeeCase tables. Because you don't care about the specific employee names, you don't need the Employee table.

From these two tables, you will need the Title field from the Case table and the Count() Aggregate function that tallies the number of employees associated with each case. To facilitate the count, you will need to establish a "group by" function on the Title field. By default, the Query Designer does not provide the ability to add groupings and aggregate functions. Figure 10.20 illustrates two things. First, it shows you the Totals button on the main toolbar. When you click this button, the lower pane of the query designer gets a new section called *totals*. Second, Figure 10.20 shows you how this query will appear in the designer.

FIGURE 10.20

FIGURE 10.20

This query
implements the
SQL Group By
and Count()
Aggregate func-
tions.

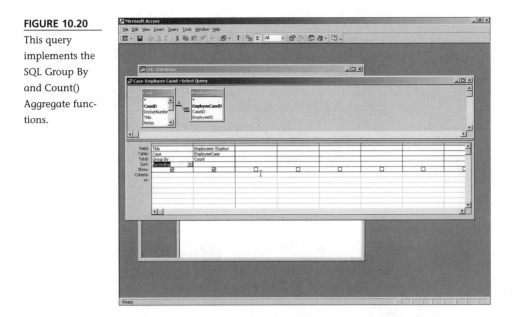

In the Total section of the Query Designer, you can pick the specific aggregate function you want to implement. Figure 10.21 illustrates the resultset and Figure 10.22
illustrates the SQL code view.

FIGURE 10.21

The resultset of
the Case-
Employee Count
query.

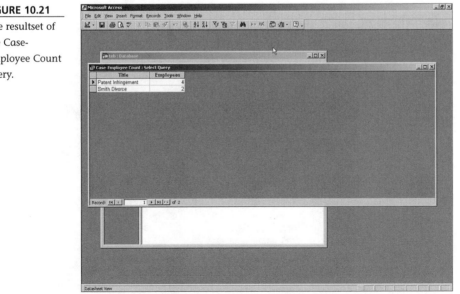

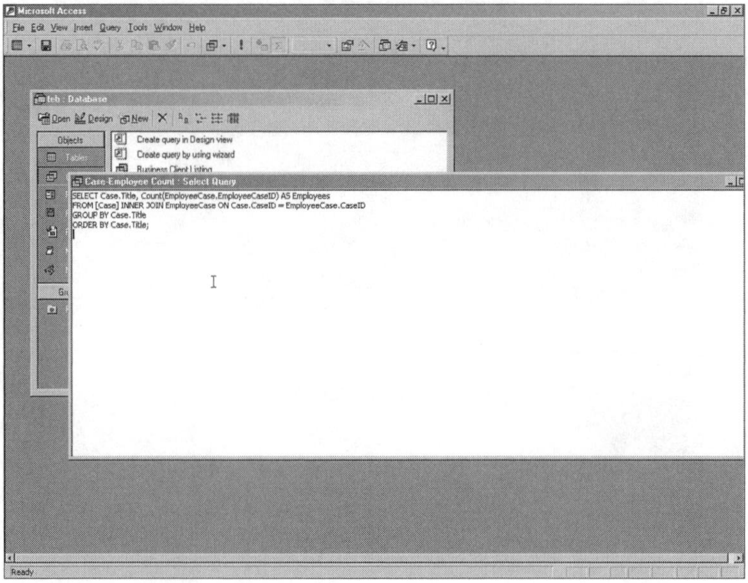

FIGURE 10.22

The SQL code view of the Case-Employee Count query.

Parameterized Queries

Parameterized queries are easy to implement as well. To illustrate, let's say you want to create a listing of business clients. The key difference is that when the query is run, the user will be prompted to enter a state. Figure 10.23 illustrates how this query will appear in the designer.

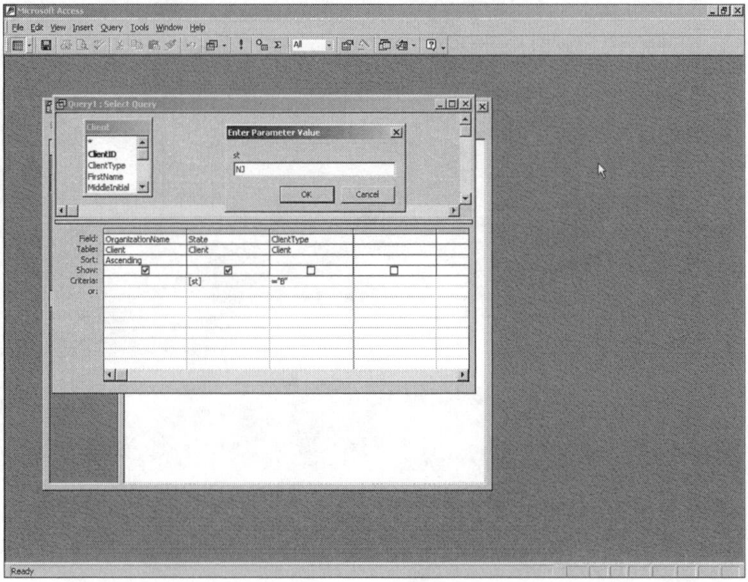

FIGURE 10.23

When this query is executed, the user will be prompted for a value to compare to the State field.

Figure 10.24 illustrates how the user will be prompted for the parameter and Figure 10.25 illustrates the results of the query.

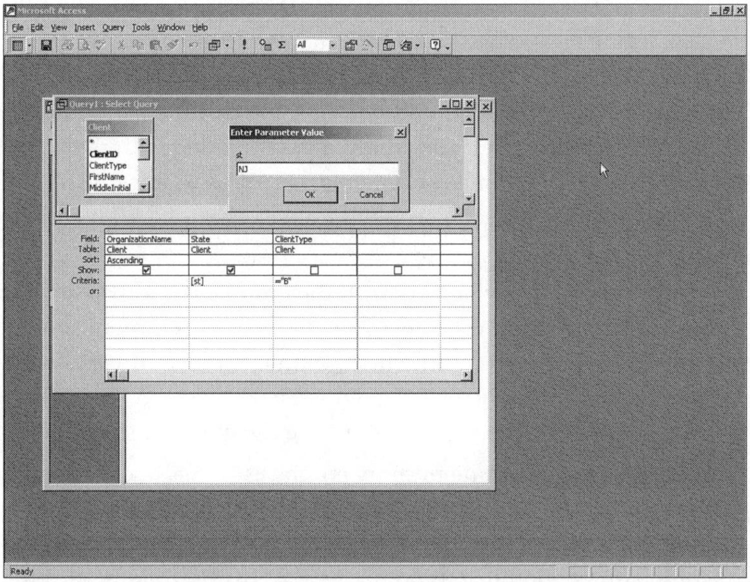

FIGURE 10.24

When a para-
meterized query
is executed, the
user is prompted
to specify a
value for each
parameter.

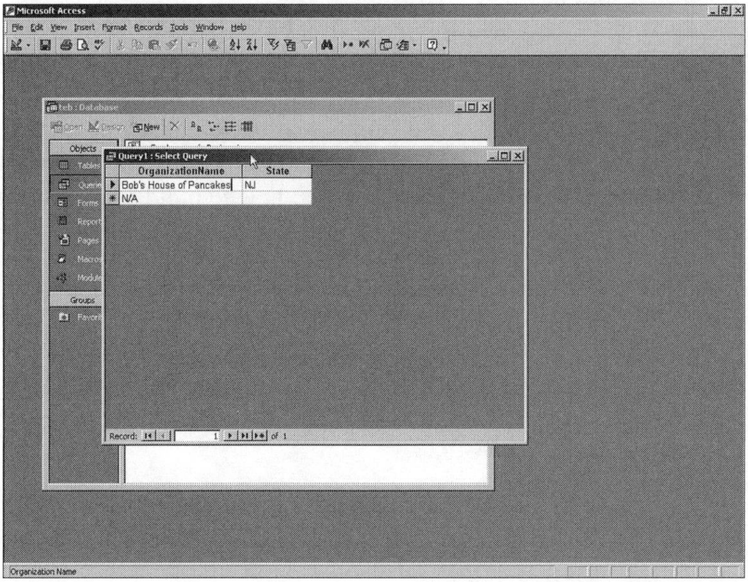

FIGURE 10.25

This resultset
shows the list of
business clients
in the state of
New Jersey.

What You Have Learned

Hopefully, you have learned that the graphical designer is nothing more than an extension of the SQL language you already know. You may find that working with the code directly is easier and more productive than working with the graphical designer. Alternatively, you may find that working with the graphical designers is easier. More likely, you will find that in some cases, the graphical designer will work better and in other cases, you will find that working with the code is better. What is important is that you understand the code first and how the graphical query designer works second. That is why Chapters 8, 9, and 10 have been structured in this manner.

Regardless of whether you work with the graphical query designer or the code, in all cases, you are working with the query designer. It is important to note that graphical and code views are nothing more than two different views of the same query. Because you are working in the designer, regardless of whether you work with the graphical tools or code, you can still store the query in the database.

This chapter concludes the primary emphasis of this book. To review, Part I, "Database Basics," introduced you to the basics of database theory. Part II, "Designing and Building Your First Database," took you through the process of designing and building your database. Part III, "Maintaining Your Database—An Introduction to Database Integrity," showed you the mechanics of maintaining your database. Part IV, "Using Your Database to Provide Information—An Introduction to SQL," introduced you to the SQL language that you will use to provide information from your database. The next and last part of the book, Part V, "Putting Your Database to Work—Building a Simple Access Database Application," will show you how you can build simple user interfaces to enter and maintain data in your database. In addition, you will also be shown how to build simple reports. In the report discussion, you will see how the queries you have just built will be put to work.

PUTTING YOUR DATABASE TO WORK— BUILDING A SIMPLE ACCESS DATABASE APPLICATION

BUILDING THE USER INTERFACE COMPONENTS

CHAPTER HIGHLIGHTS:

- ■ Overview of the Access Form Designer
- ■ Create Forms for the TEB Application
- ■ Create a Main Menu Form
- ■ What You Have Learned

For some, this chapter might represent the fun part of building a database application. Building user interfaces, more commonly referred to as *forms* in Access, is an incredibly easy task. If you are not familiar with how to write programming code, don't worry! You can accomplish 99% of what you need to do without writing a single line of code. Where you will have to write some code, don't worry! What you have to write and where you have to write it will be clearly explained in this chapter.

This chapter will bring together several concepts that have already been presented in this book. Specifically, you will revisit some field attributes and query definitions stored in the database. At the conclusion of this chapter, you will have a good understanding of how a database and form components can be combined to offer a comprehensive solution.

Overview of the Access Form Designer

Long ago in Chapter 2, "The Anatomy of a Real Database," you were briefly introduced to the Access Form Designer. At that time, all you were told was that the designer existed and that later on, the Form Designer would be covered in detail. This chapter fulfills that promise. Figure 11.1 illustrates a form called IndividualClients.

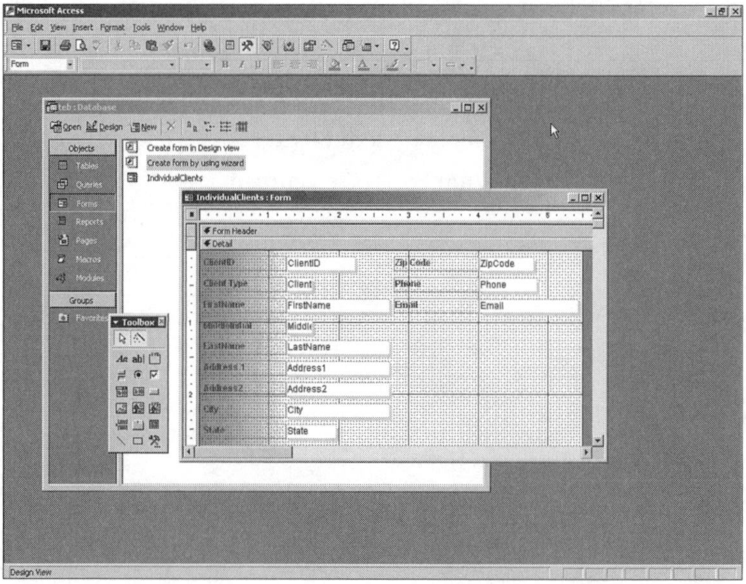

FIGURE 11.1

Forms like everything else in Access are stored in the database itself.

The Access Form Designer consists of two main components: the design surface and the toolbox. Fortunately, most of the work in creating interfaces in Access can be accomplished with wizards. For good reasons, the use of wizards has been avoided. When it comes to working with the core database components and understanding how databases work in general, you need to understand what is going on behind the scenes. When you stray into the area of forms, wizards help you get started by taking care of the tedious work for you. In many cases, you will go in after the fact to adjust for your specific implementation.

As you build forms, you will find the procedure to be constant. In other words, you will always follow the same basic steps, which are as follows:

1. Start the Form Wizard.
2. Pick a table or query the form is to be based upon.
3. Pick fields to display on the form.
4. Choose a layout and style.
5. Save the form.
6. Go to New Form Definition and make minor adjustments.

Create Forms for the TEB Application

The following sections will take you through the process of building forms to maintain clients and employees. In addition, you will also create a main menu form that will be used to launch the other forms. There will be two client forms: one for business and another for individual clients. To build the client forms, two queries will have to be created. As far as the employee form is concerned, that form will make use of two lookups. If you recall, an employee belongs to a department and is assigned a classification. You may also recall that various field attributes were set up to facilitate the production of forms. Don't worry about flipping back through the book, as the whole process will be reviewed in this chapter!

Client

You may recall that two types of clients exist: individual and business. Each type is differentiated by the ClientType field. Individual clients use the first- and lastname field as well as the middle initial field. Business clients use the OrganizationName field. When providing users a way to enter data, you want to make it as easy for them as possible. In this case, it would make sense to have two separate interfaces.

The easiest way to build two separate interfaces is to define two queries: one for individual and one for business clients. Because you already know how to build queries manually and with the designer, this chapter will show you how to use the Query Wizard to quickly define these queries.

IndividualClient Query

Figure 11.2 illustrates where you launch the Query Wizard. The reason for using queries in this case is that one table serves two purposes. To support these two purposes, it makes sense to logically divide the table between individual and business clients.

FIGURE 11.2

The Query Wizard can be launched from the main database window.

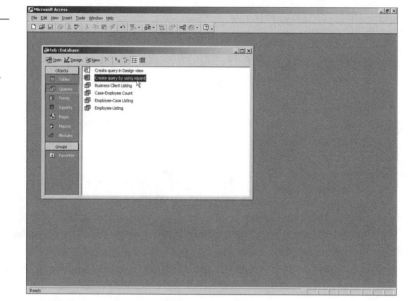

Figure 11.3 illustrates the first step in defining the query, which involves picking a table or another query. In this case, the Client table is used. Because this query will involve only individual clients, there is no need to return the OrganizationName field in the resultset. Therefore, the OrganizationName field has been omitted.

Figure 11.4 illustrates the second step of the Query Wizard, providing a name and specifying whether the query will be run or modified upon saving the query definition.

FIGURE 11.3

Step one of the
Query Wizard
enables you to
define which
fields will be
included in the
resultset.

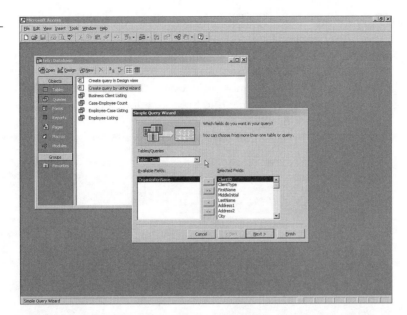

FIGURE 11.4

Step two of the
Query Wizard
enables you to
provide a name
for the query
and to specify
whether the
query is exe-
cuted or open
for modification
upon saving.

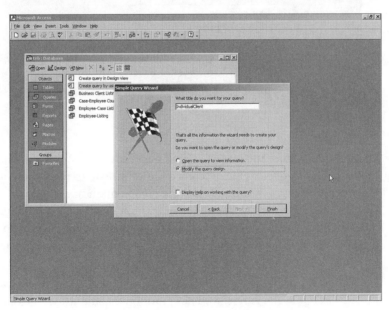

After you have clicked the Finish button, the query will be saved and a new instance of the Query Designer will be opened. There are two additional steps that must be completed before the IndividualClient query will be finished. First, the query must be sorted by last name in ascending order. Second, criteria must be added to the ClientType field to return only those records that have a ClientType = "I." Figure 11.5 illustrates the Query Designer and these additional modifications.

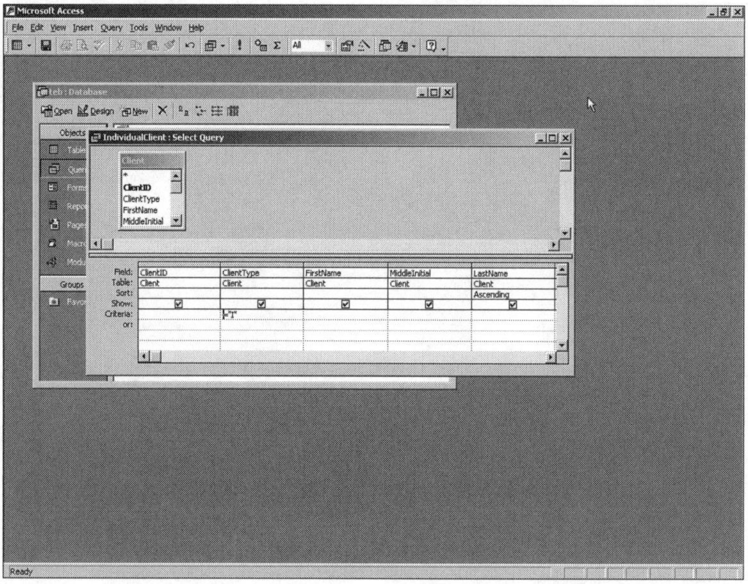

FIGURE 11.5

A sort order and criteria have been added to the IndividualClient query produced by the Query Wizard.

BusinessClient Query

The steps to produce the BusinessClient query are almost the same as the IndividualClient query. One difference is that instead of including the first name, middle initial, and last name fields, the organization name field is included. Further, the sort order on the organization name field is in ascending order. The other difference relates to the criteria. For the BusinessClient query, only records with a ClientType = "B" will be returned in the resultset. Figure 11.6 illustrates how the BusinessClient query will appear in the designer.

Figure 11.7 illustrates both individual and business client queries in action. With the queries out of the way, the work of putting together the individual and business client forms can begin.

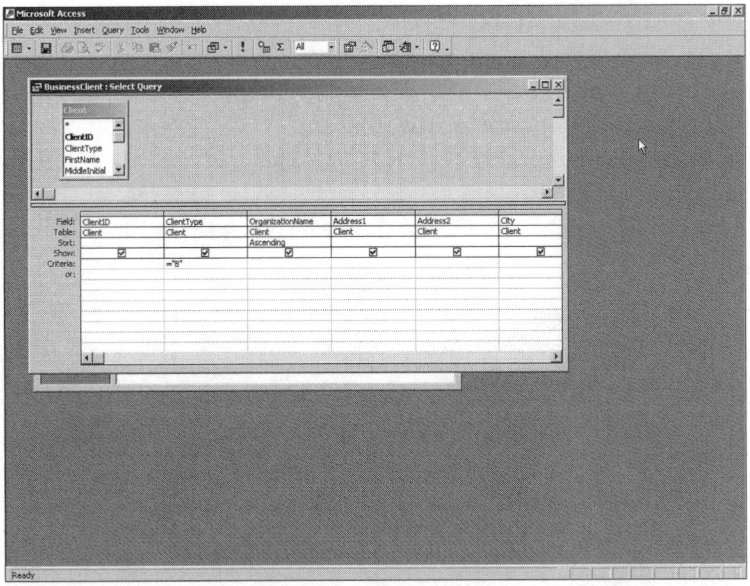

FIGURE 11.6

The BusinessClient query complete with additional sorting and criteria attributes in the Query Designer.

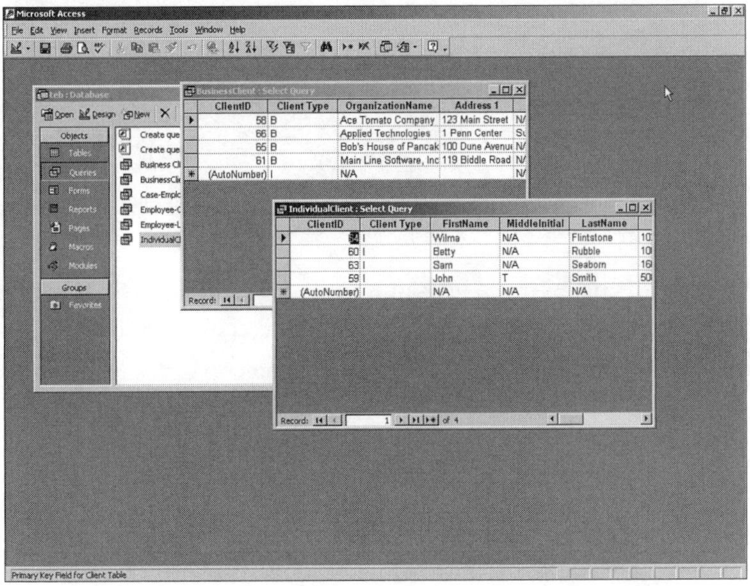

FIGURE 11.7

The individual and business client queries provide two views of the Client table.

IndividualClient Form

If you did not have wizards to assist with the tedious parts of putting forms together, the task would consume a lot of time. Although you could rely on what the wizard provides alone, for a more fully functional and user-friendly interface you will want to modify the forms after their creation. The good news is that for many of the post-creation tasks you will undertake, wizards exist for those tasks as well! Figure 11.8 illustrates the first step in using the Form Wizard.

FIGURE 11.8

Step 1 of the Form Wizard enables you to pick a table or query and associated fields to base the form upon.

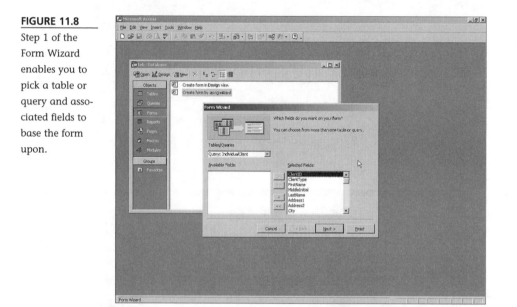

In this case, the IndividualClient query will serve as the basis of the IndividualClient form. For this and all forms, you will elect to choose all fields.

Figure 11.9 illustrates step 2. In this step, you can choose a layout for your form. In this case, the default choice of columnar will be selected.

In step 3, illustrated in Figure 11.10, you can choose a style. Access ships with several layout styles. The Blends style will be used in these examples.

FIGURE 11.9

Step 2 of the Form Wizard enables you to pick a layout for the form.

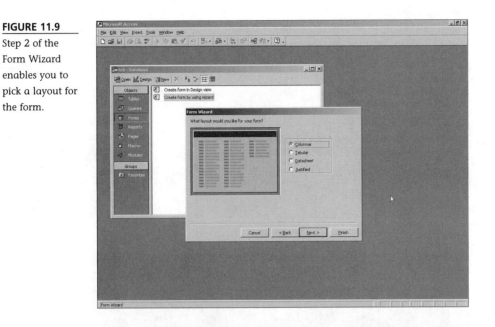

FIGURE 11.10

Step 3 of the Form Wizard enables you to pick a style for the form.

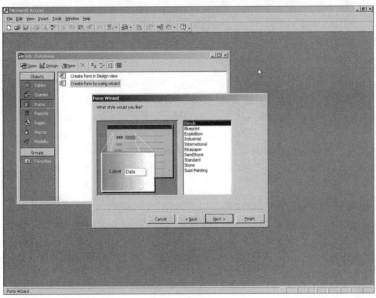

In the last step, illustrated in Figure 11.11, as in the Query Wizard, you can choose a name for the form as well as specify whether the form will be run or modified upon saving.

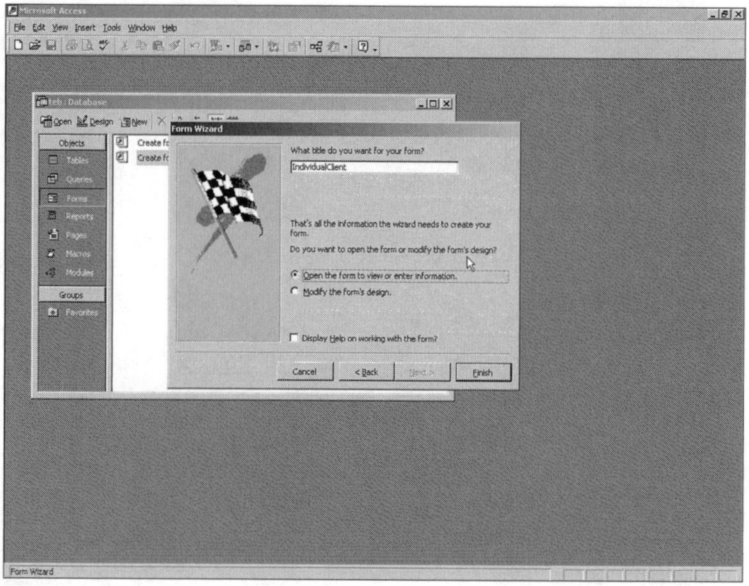

FIGURE 11.11

The final step of the Form Wizard enables you to specify a name for the form as well as specify whether the form is executed or modified upon saving.

Figure 11.12 illustrates the finished product. Using the toolbar at the bottom of the form, you can navigate to the top, previous, next, or last record. In addition, you can add new records. What is missing is the ability to delete and cancel changes. This is why you will need to go in after the creation process to add a set of buttons that provides more complete functionality. Details regarding the process of adding custom command buttons will be discussed later in this section.

BusinessClient Form

The steps required to create the BusinessClient form are nearly the same as those required to create the IndividualClient form. The only exception is that, in this case, you will base the form on the BusinessClient query. Figure 11.13 illustrates the BusinessClient form.

FIGURE 11.12

The form produced by the wizard has the capability both to navigate through and to create new records.

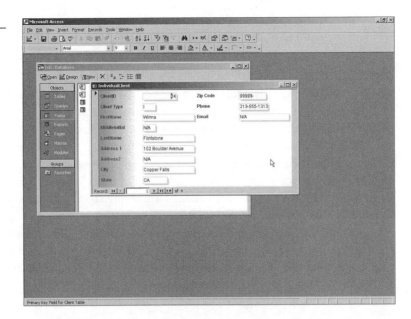

FIGURE 11.13

The BusinessClient form is based on the BusinessClient query.

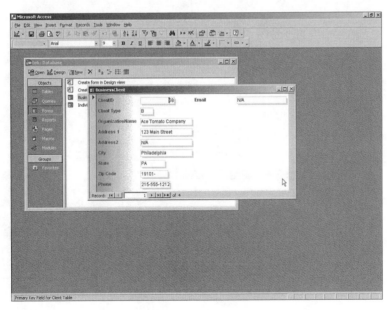

Now that you have created two forms, it is time to modify the layout and add a few custom command buttons to round out the functionality of the forms.

Modifying the Layout

Although the wizard does a lot of work for you, it cannot do 100% of the job. Figure 11.14 illustrates the modified layout of the IndividualClient form. The modified layout has a more balanced and professional look. There are changes other than just the position. First, the client id field has been removed. There is no need for the user to see this field because it is in place for the database to use. Second, the Client Type field has been moved to the bottom of the form and the Visible property has been set to No. Remember that for each client form, every client will have the same client type value. Therefore, there is no need for the user to see it. Still, the field does provide a valuable service for new records. You will see why the field is important in the next section. Finally, some of the text labels used to describe input fields have either been changed or removed entirely. To remove an item, simply select it with the mouse and press the Delete key. To modify the text of a label, click the item to select it and modify the Caption property in the property box that is illustrated in Figure 11.14.

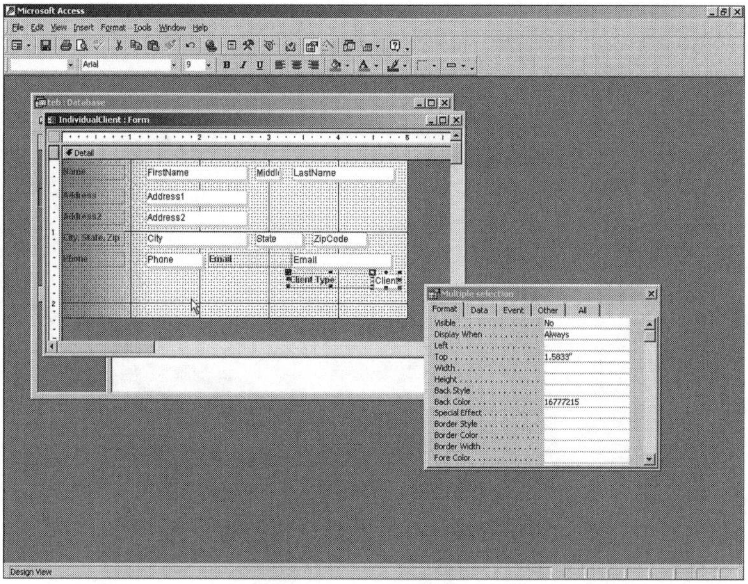

FIGURE 11.14

The modified version of the IndividualClient form has a more balanced and professional look.

Figure 11.15 illustrates the same changes that were applied to the BusinessClient form.

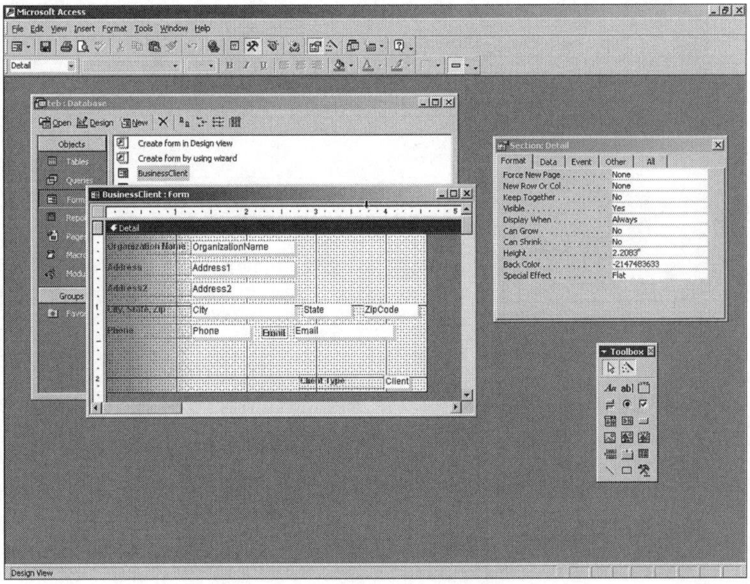

FIGURE 11.15

The modified version of the BusinessClient form has a more balanced and professional look.

Adding Record Navigational Command Buttons

The two client forms are almost complete. The last step involves adding custom buttons that facilitate record navigation, adding, and deleting. In addition, functionality to save and cancel changes as well as functionality to find records based on search criteria will be added. Fortunately, there are wizards to handle these tasks and virtually no code is required. As you will see, one line of code will be required in the Add button.

Figure 11.16 illustrates the IndividualClient form in design mode. The Form Design toolbox, also shown in Figure 11.16, contains a variety of controls that can be added to the form. The Form Wizard used these same controls when the original versions of the forms were produced.

To add a button to the form, simply click the command button icon in the toolbox. Figure 11.17 illustrates how the mouse pointer changes in appearance.

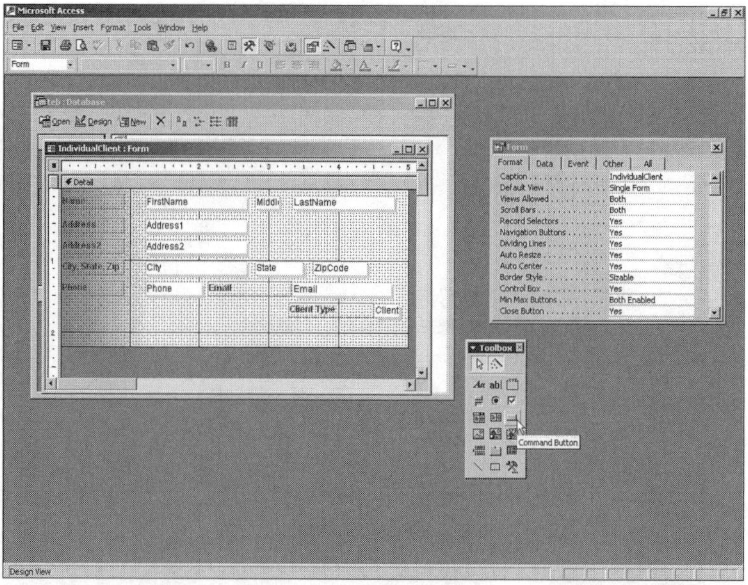

FIGURE 11.16

The toolbox in the form designer contains a variety of controls that can be added to a form.

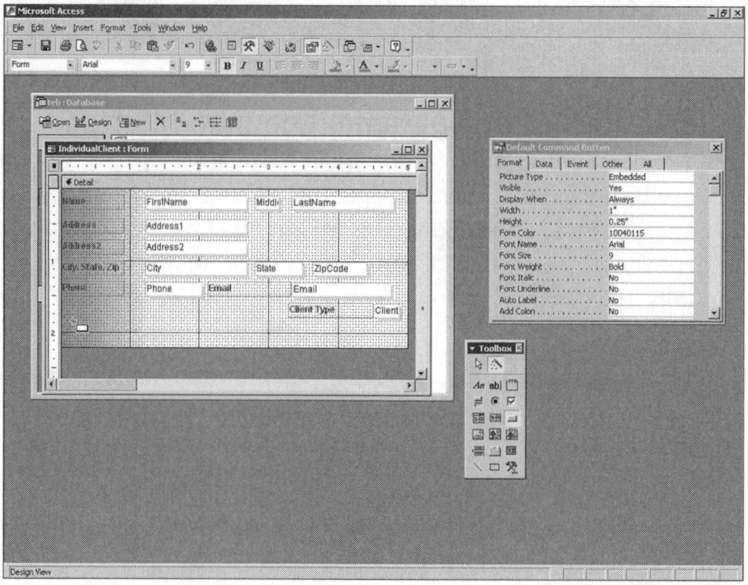

FIGURE 11.17

When you click an item in the toolbox, the mouse pointer changes appearance, helping you to place the object on the form design surface.

After you have selected a place on the form where you want the object to appear, click the mouse. Figure 11.18 illustrates the first step of the Command Button Wizard that appears when the object is dropped onto the form.

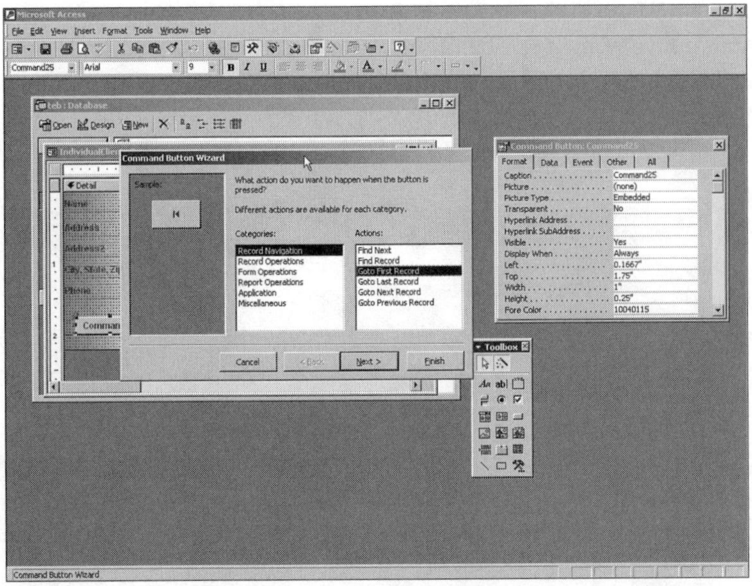

FIGURE 11.18

Step one of the
Command
Button Wizard
prompts you to
select the type
of operation
that is to be
performed when
the button is
clicked.

After you select an operation, the second step, illustrated in Figure 11.19, prompts
you to select how the button will appear.

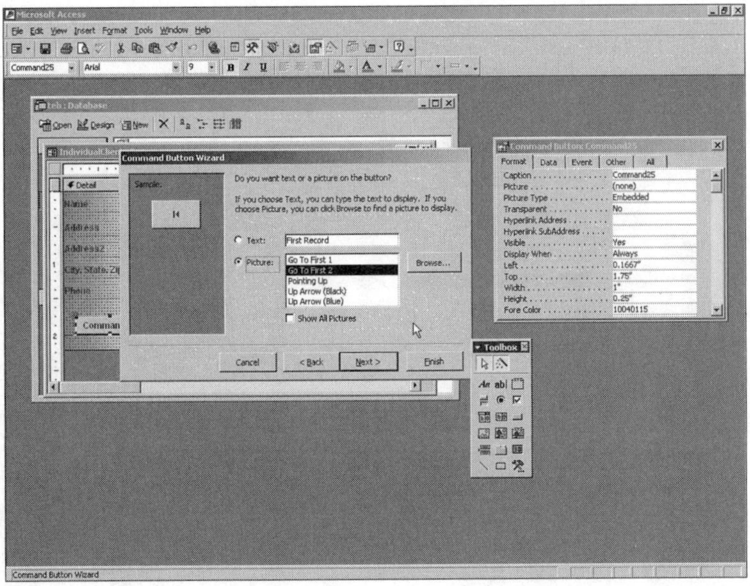

FIGURE 11.19

Step two of the
Command
Button Wizard
prompts you to
select how the
button will
appear.

The final step of the wizard, illustrated in Figure 11.20, prompts you to specify a descriptive name for the button. When it comes time to add additional code to the Add button, you will see just how important it is to specify a name for a button.

FIGURE 11.20
Step three of the Command Button Wizard prompts you to select a descriptive name for the command button object.

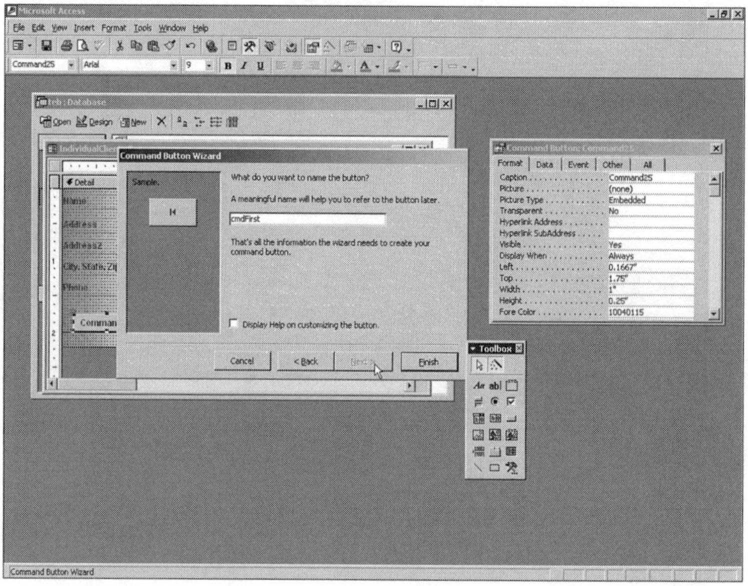

Figure 11.21 illustrates how the IndividualClient form appears after the remaining navigational buttons have been added.

FIGURE 11.21
The IndividualClient form with custom record navigational buttons.

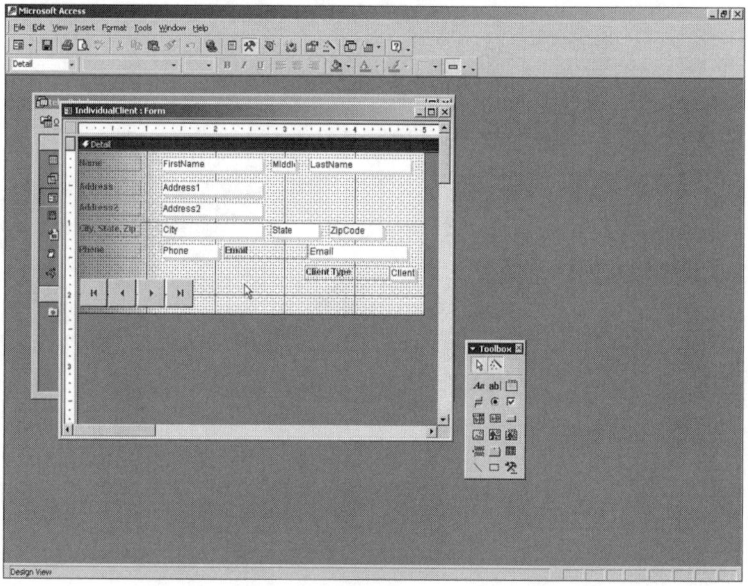

After the record navigational buttons have been created, the next step involves adding functionality that allows the user to create and delete records, save and cancel changes to records, and finally search for a specific record based on search criteria.

Adding Additional Functionality to the IndividualClient Form

Adding functionality to support the creation and deletion of records, and the saving and canceling of changes to records, as well as search capability, is just as easy as adding any other type of command button. The search capability can be found in the Record Navigation section of the Command Button Wizard. The additional functionality in this section can be found in the Record Operations section. Figure 11.22 illustrates the first step in adding a button that adds a new record.

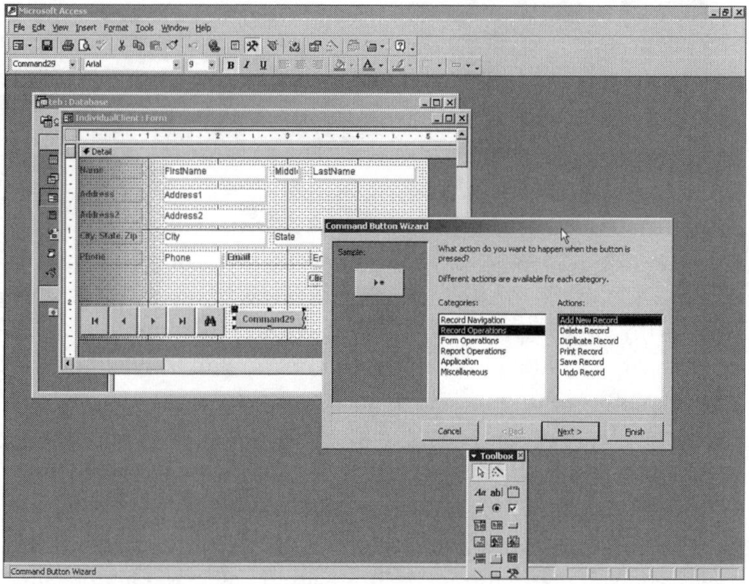

FIGURE 11.22

The Record Operations section of the wizard provides the capability to create add, delete, save, and cancel functionality to a form.

Figure 11.23 illustrates the IndividualClient form with all the additional functionality that a typical data entry form requires.

With all the buttons added, there is one more element of customization required. If you recall, although the promise was made that almost no code was required, one line of code would need to be added to the Add button. This task is covered in the next section.

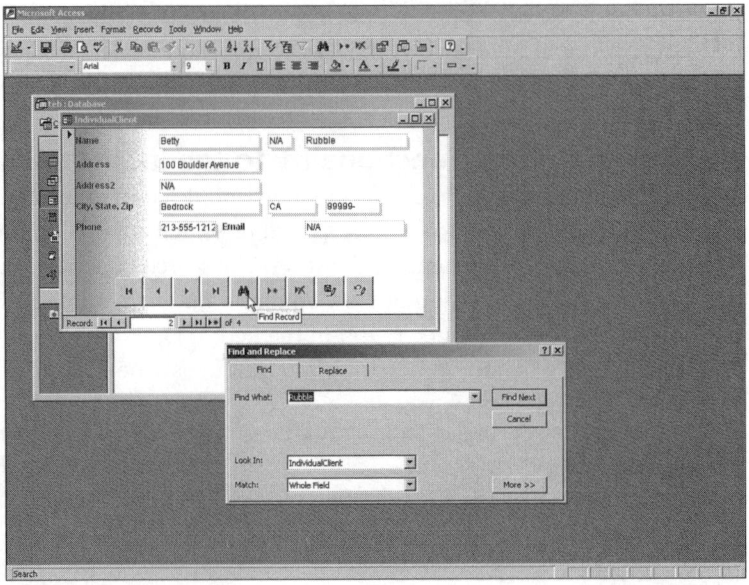

FIGURE 11.23

The
IndividualClient
form complete
with the func-
tionality that a
typical data
entry form
requires.

Adding Custom Code to the Add Button

Form controls respond to a variety of events. Typical events include clicking and
double-clicking the mouse and pressing a key, to name a few. When a button is
clicked, the On Click event fires. Event-driven programming is based on attaching
code to various system events. The Command Button Wizard takes care of most of
the program code for you. There are a few cases when you will have to go in after
the fact to augment the functionality. In this case, the additional code performs the
task of setting the ClientType field to the appropriate value. Figure 11.24 illustrates
how to access the On Click event procedure from the Property window.

Next to the On Click event procedure in the Property window illustrated in Figure
11.24, you will notice a small button with an ellipsis. Making sure the Add button is
selected, when you click the button with the ellipsis, a Visual Basic Code Editing window will appear. The code-editing window along with the additional code that must
be added is illustrated in Figure 11.25.

FIGURE 11.24

Event proce-
dures for each
control can be
accessed from
the Event tab
of the Property
window.

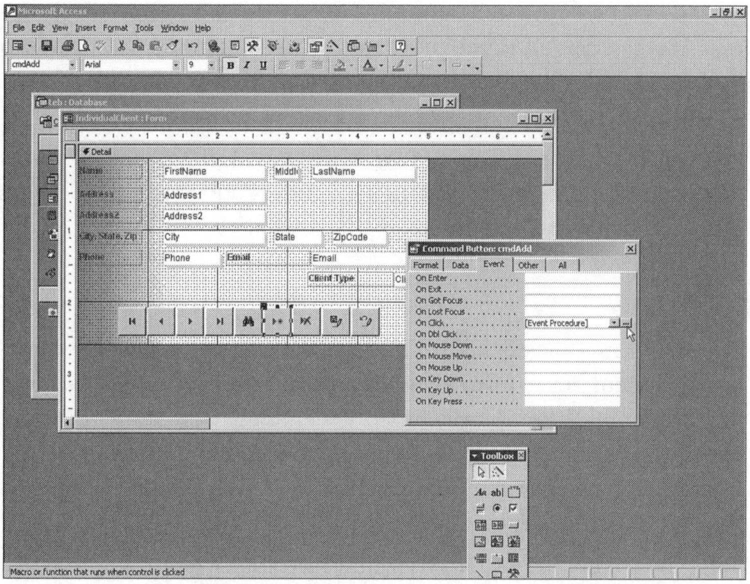

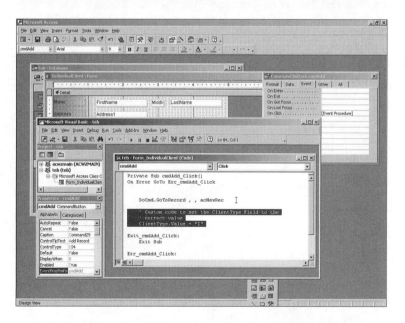

FIGURE 11.25

The additional
code added
with the
cmdAdd_Click()
procedure
assigns the
appropriate
value to the
ClientType field.

Now do you see why it is important to give each button a descriptive name? If you relied on the default name provided by the Command Button Wizard, you would have a difficult time differentiating among the various code procedures.

At this point, the IndividualClient form is complete. As for the BusinessClient form, you would follow precisely the same steps used to prepare the IndividualClient form, with the exception of the custom code that is added to the Add button. In the BusinessClient case, the ClientType field would be set to "B."

Employee Form

The last form discussed in this chapter maintains employee records. Unlike the client forms, the employee form does not require a query. Rather, the employee form will act directly on the employee table. The interesting feature of the employee form is not in its complexity because, actually, the employee form is very simple. Rather, the interesting feature of the form lies in how it derives some of its characteristics from the employee table metadata.

You may recall that various user interface characteristics and lookup metadata can be stored in the Access database. Figure 11.26 illustrates the lookup metadata for the DepartmentID field.

FIGURE 11.26

Display control and lookup metadata can be stored in the field metadata.

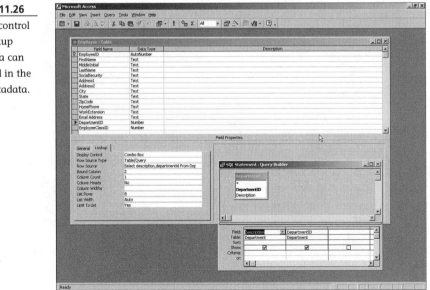

Figure 11.26 shows that a drop-down combo box display control is used to display the lookup data from the Department table. The data from the Department table is found in the RowSource property in the Lookup tab. You may recall that a one-to-many relationship exists between the Department and Employee tables. The DepartmentID foreign key field carried in the Employee table corresponds to the primary key of the Department table. This is how items in the combo box are properly synchronized with the Employee table records. The Form Wizard uses the metadata information when it constructs the Employee form. Figure 11.27 illustrates the Employee form complete with custom command buttons.

FIGURE 11.27

Many of the characteristics of a form and related controls can be derived from the database metadata.

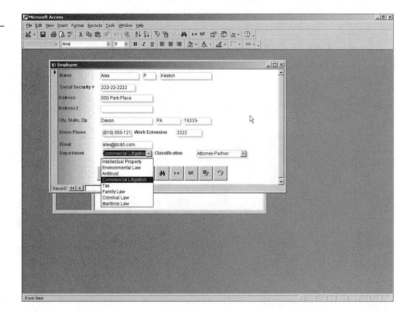

After you have created a few data-bound forms, you begin to see a lot of commonality in the process. In other words, after you build a few, they all begin to look alike! The only type of form not covered so far is one that maintains data from two or more tables at the same time. These types of forms present a level of complexity that is beyond the scope of this book. For a sample of such a form, you can refer to the sample Northwind Traders Database that is included with Access.

The next section discusses how to build a non–data-bound form. Specifically, you will be shown how to build a main menu form. In addition, you will be introduced to how to manipulate various form properties that you will want to use for both data and non–data-bound forms.

Create a Main Menu Form

Figure 11.28 illustrates a form design session initiated by going directly into the design view, not the wizard. Because this is a non–data-bound form, the record navigation bar that normally appears at the bottom of a form is not required. There are other form attributes that you may want to manipulate such as whether the min/max button is enabled, the type of border style, and the form caption, to name a few.

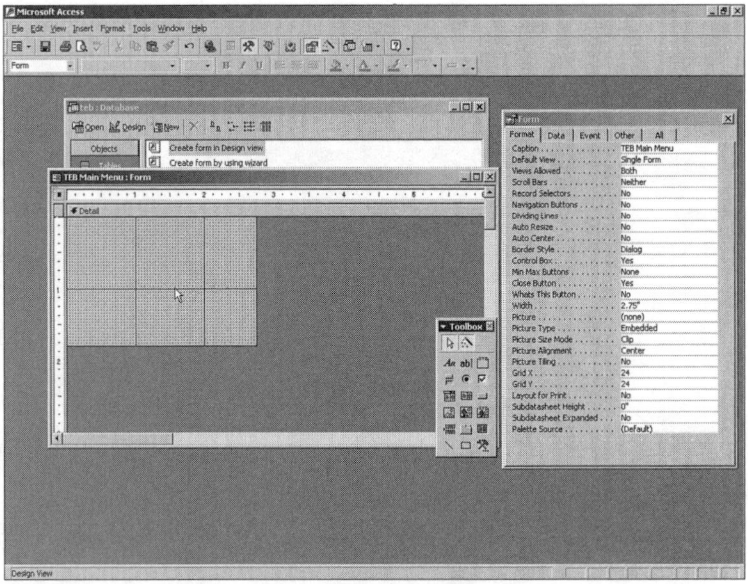

FIGURE 11.28

The form property sheet enables you to manipulate various attributes of the form.

After you have set up the form, you are ready to add command buttons that will launch the forms created in this chapter. The good news is that the Command Button Wizard does most of the work for you. Figure 11.29 illustrates the first step in adding a button that launches a form.

Figure 11.30 illustrates the second step in the wizard that prompts for the name of the form that is to be launched.

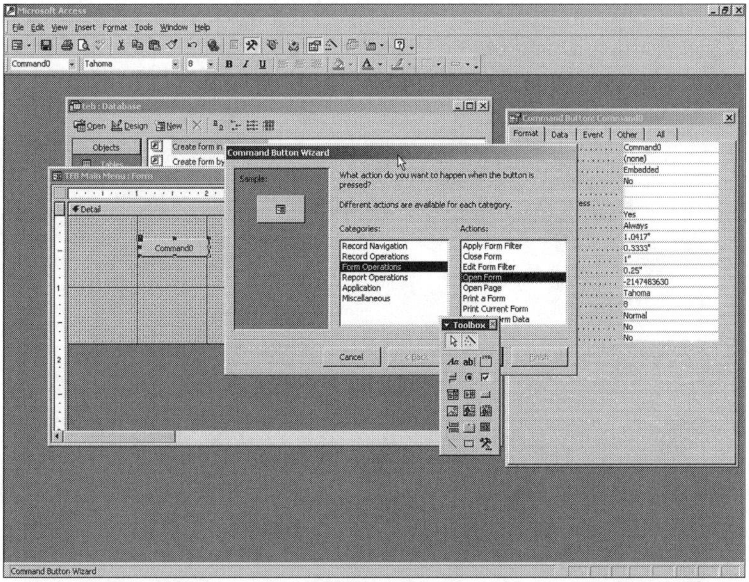

FIGURE 11.29

The process of adding buttons to launch a form uses the Command Button Wizard.

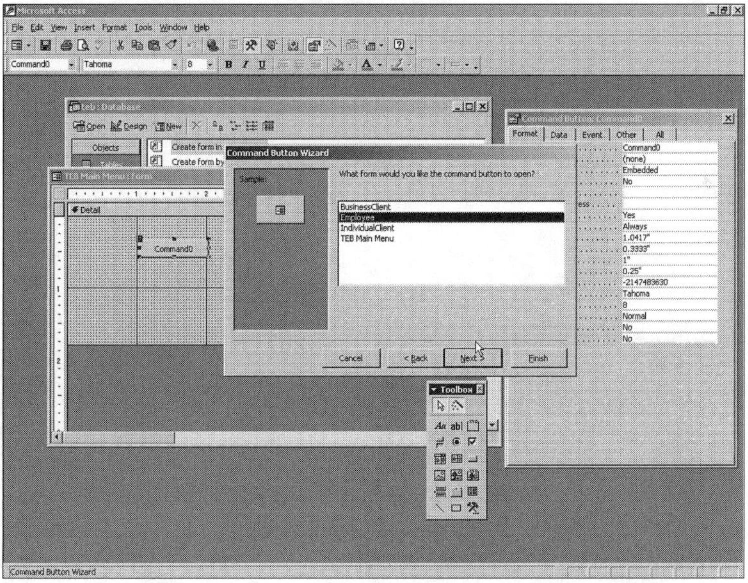

FIGURE 11.30

The second step of the wizard prompts the user for the name of the form that is to be launched.

Figure 11.31 illustrates the third step of the wizard, which provides the option of whether the form should be opened to find a specific record or whether the form should be opened to display all records.

FIGURE 11.31

The third step
of the wizard
specifies how
the form is
to be opened.

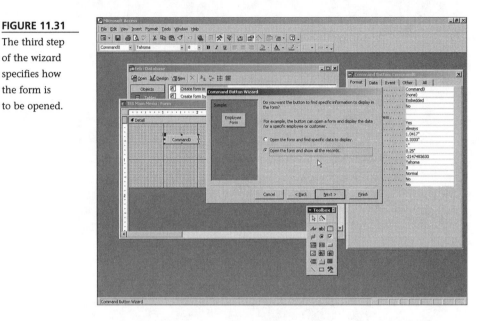

Figure 11.32 illustrates the fourth step of the wizard, which provides the capability to specify whether the button will contain text or a picture.

FIGURE 11.32

The fourth step
of the wizard
specifies the
appearance of
the button.

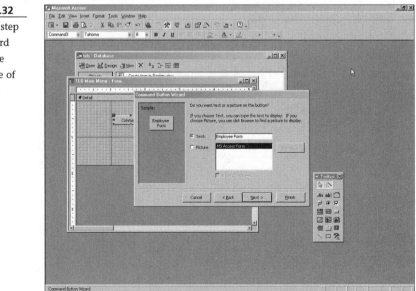

Figure 11.33 illustrates the fifth step of the wizard, which provides the capability to add a descriptive name to the button.

FIGURE 11.33

The fifth step of the wizard provides the ability to specify a descriptive name for the button.

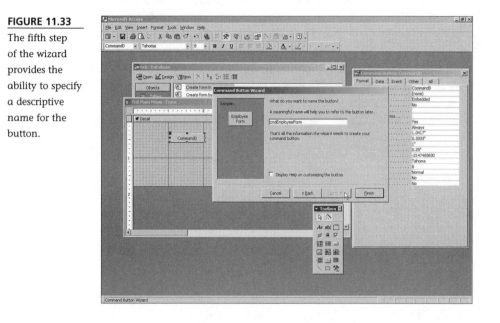

Figure 11.34 shows the completed menu form as well as the three forms created in this chapter.

FIGURE 11.34

The completed main menu form and the three forms created in this chapter.

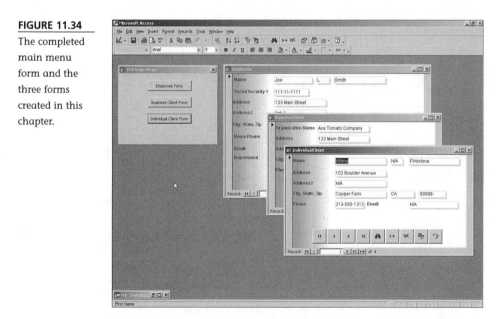

What You Have Learned

Hopefully, in this chapter, you have seen how simple it is to build forms in Access. Because wizards can do most of the work, you don't need to be proficient in a programming language to build a database application. In fact, it should be apparent that you are well on your way to developing a database application! The last step on this initial journey is to provide the ability for the user to extract information by way of reports. That topic of reports is covered in the next chapter.

PROVIDING USEFUL OUTPUT: AN INTRODUCTION TO CREATING AND DESIGNING REPORTS

CHAPTER HIGHLIGHTS:

- Overview of the Access Report Designer
- Create Reports for the TEB Application
- Add Report Items to the Main Menu Form
- What You Have Learned

Early in this book, the following proposition was made: "The value of a database is only as good as the quality of data it contains and the information that it can provide." For the most part, you have dealt with individual data elements and records. The exception to this occurred when you were introduced to queries and the Structured Query Language (SQL). Using queries, you can gather and aggregate data. The process of running queries is often referred to as the process of turning data into information. The issue of how to present the information to the user still remains. That issue is addressed by providing reporting capabilities in your application. Reports may very well be the most important feature of an application, second only to the quality of the database and the data itself. In this chapter, you will be introduced to the Access Report Designer and the basic techniques you need to understand in order to create simple reports in Access.

Overview of the Access Report Designer

Like forms, long ago in Chapter 2, "The Anatomy of a Real Database," you were briefly introduced to the Access Report Designer. This chapter fulfills the promise of showing you how to use the Report Designer. Figure 12.1 illustrates a new instance of the Access Report Designer.

FIGURE 12.1

The Access Report Designer.

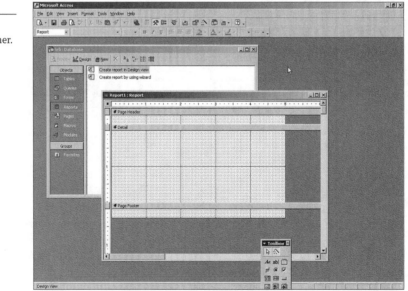

All report designers work in the same basic manner. Most take a "banded" design approach. In other words, when designing a report, you typically have page header and footer bands as well as detail bands. Figure 12.1 illustrates these three bands. The names of the bands accurately reflect the contents of the band. The page header typically contains a report title and labels that describe the content of the report. The page footer typically contains page number and data elements. The detail band, as the name implies, contains the detail of the report. As you will see, the detail band can be subdivided into additional bands of detail. The level to which a detail band is subdivided depends on how your data is grouped. The details on how a report can be grouped will be discussed later in this chapter. Figure 12.1 also illustrates the control toolbox, which is the same toolbox you work with when designing and building forms. Fortunately, because Access is replete with wizards, for the most part, you will not have to get into the messy details of creating reports from scratch. The Report Wizard is used extensively in this chapter.

Create Reports for the TEB Application

This chapter will take you through the process of creating a client listing report. Like forms, reports can be created with wizards. If needed, you can go into the designer and make minor adjustments. As you will quickly learn, after you create a report with the wizard, you have all the knowledge to create most reports. Complex reports exist and there is little doubt that at some point, you will need to create them. For examples of more complex reports, please refer to the sample Northwind Traders Database that ships with Access, as a detailed discussion of complex reports is outside the scope of this book.

It is important to note that the real work lies in the query design. A report is nothing more than a delivery mechanism. Well-designed reports do one thing: provide the formatting to display data effectively.

Client Listing

Before the client listing report can be created, you will need a query to support the report. In Chapter 8, "SQL Basics," you were introduced to how to build a union query. A union query combines two SQL statements for the purpose of creating one resultset. Because clients are categorized as business or individual and because different fields are used to store the names of the clients depending on the categorization, a union query is required. Figure 12.2 illustrates the Query Designer with the ClientListing query definition.

FIGURE 12.2

Because the
ClientListing
query uses the
union clause,
the query can
only be created
using the SQL
View.

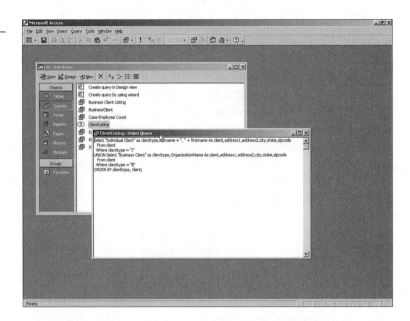

Figure 12.3 illustrates the ClientListing resultset. You may be wondering why the words "Individual Client" and "Business Client" are returned to the resultset instead of the client type codes. To a user, a simple code of "I" or "B" may not be as intuitive as the actual words themselves. Remember, the purpose of a report is to provide information. The user should not have to guess what something means.

FIGURE 12.3

The ClientListing
Query resultset.

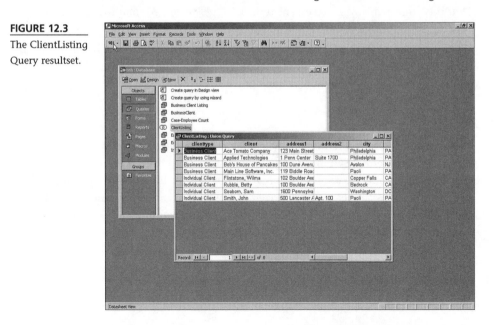

Figure 12.4 illustrates the first step in the Report Wizard. Like the Form Wizard, the first step prompts the user for a query or table definition to base the report on. In step one, you can pick the fields you want to display.

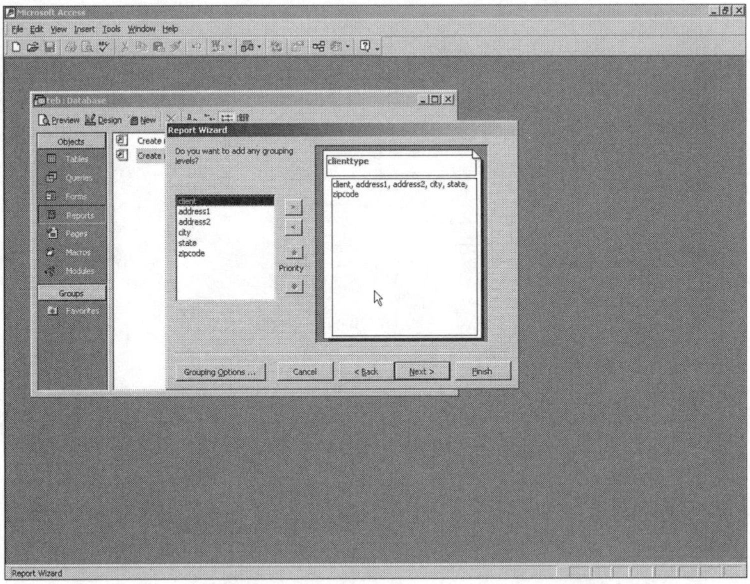

FIGURE 12.4

Step one of the Report Wizard prompts the user for a query or table definition to base the report on.

After you have selected your fields, you can proceed to step 2. In step 2, you specify how the report is to be grouped (see Figure 12.5). By default, a report does not contain groups. In the client listing scenario, the report will be grouped by client type. If you recall, the query must be designed with groupings in mind. This is why the ClientListing query is first ordered by client type.

Step 3, illustrated in Figure 12.6, prompts the user to specify how the report is to be sorted. If you designed your query correctly, there is no need to specify an alternative sort order.

FIGURE 12.5

Step two of the
Report Wizard
prompts the user
to specify how
the report is to
be grouped.

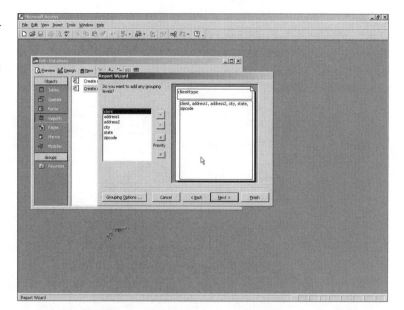

FIGURE 12.6

Step three of the
Report Wizard
prompts the user
to specify how
the report is to
be sorted.

Step 4 of the wizard prompts the user to specify how the data is to appear in the report as well as the page orientation (see Figure 12.7).

FIGURE 12.7

Step four of the Report Wizard prompts the user to specify the appearance and page orientation of the report.

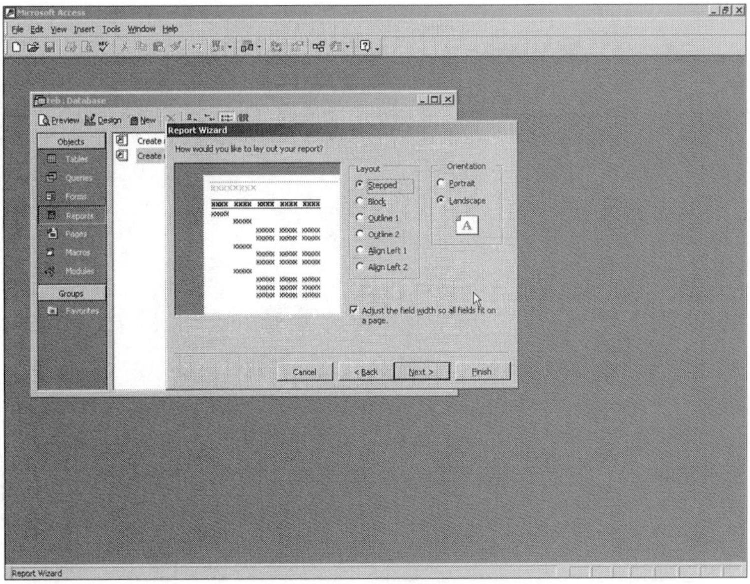

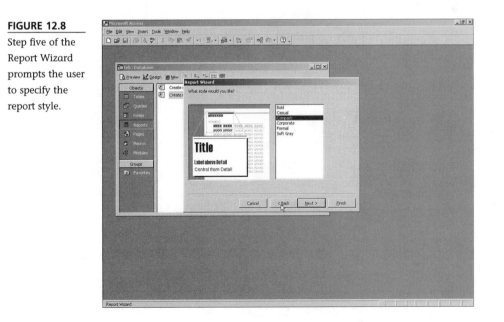

Figure 12.8 illustrates step 5, which prompts the user to specify a report style. Access ships with a number of predefined report styles.

FIGURE 12.8

Step five of the Report Wizard prompts the user to specify the report style.

The final step of the Report Wizard prompts the user for a report name and whether the report is to be previewed or opened in the Report Designer (see Figure 12.9).

FIGURE 12.9

The final step of the Report Wizard prompts the user to specify a report name and whether the report is to be previewed or modified.

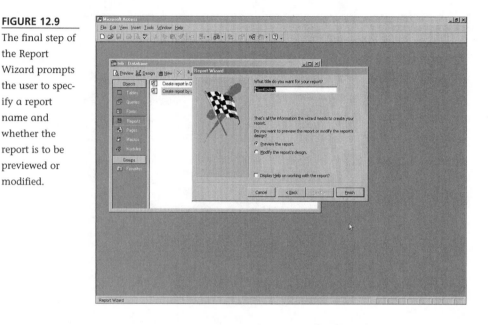

Figure 12.10 illustrates the first cut of the report. As you can see, some of the data is truncated. The next section shows you how to modify the report design.

FIGURE 12.10

The ClientListing report produced by the Report Wizard.

Modifying the ClientListing Report in the Report Designer

Modifying reports is done in the same manner as modifying forms. As you click each item in the report designer, various attributes of the item can be manipulated in the Property window. Alternatively, you can work with the object directly to change the size and/or location. Figure 12.11 illustrates the modified report in the designer.

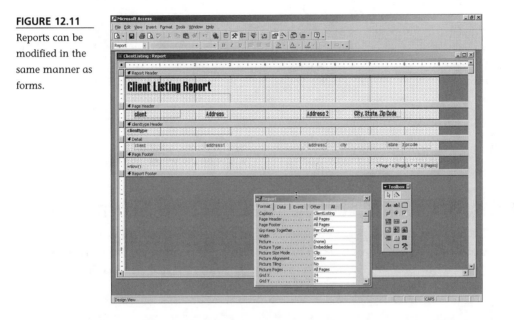

Figure 12.12 illustrates how the modified ClientListing report appears in print preview mode.

FIGURE 12.12
The modified
ClientListing
report in print
preview mode.

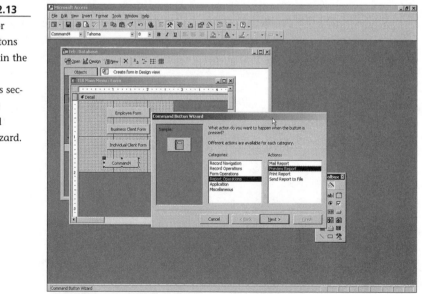

Add Report Items to the Main Menu Form

After you create a report, you need to give your users a way to run the report. In this context, you can provide access to the report in the main menu form that was created in the previous chapter. Figure 12.13 illustrates the first step in adding a report button to the main menu form.

FIGURE 12.13
Options for
report buttons
are found in the
Report
Operations sec-
tion of the
Command
Button Wizard.

Step 2 prompts for the name of the report the button is to launch (see Figure 12.14).

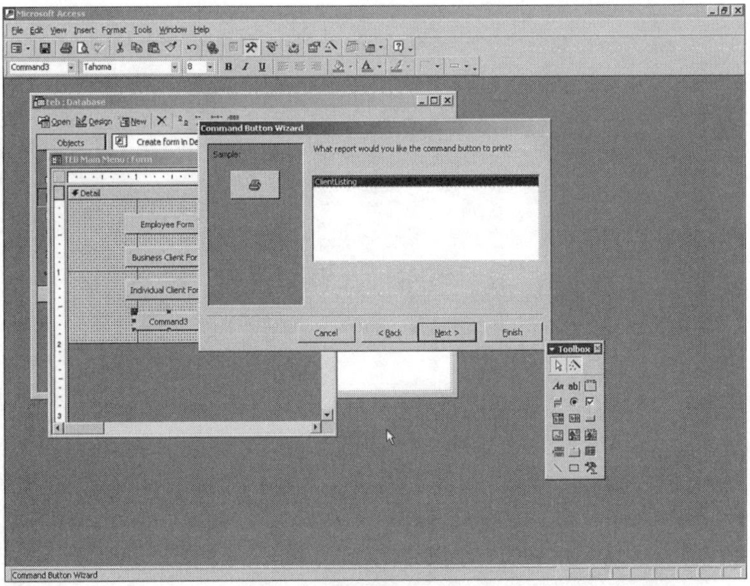

FIGURE 12.14

Step two of the Command Button Wizard prompts for the name of the report to launch.

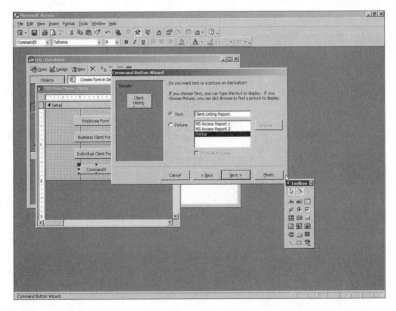

Step 3, shown in Figure 12.15, prompts for whether text or a graphic is to appear on the button.

FIGURE 12.15

Step three prompts for whether the button is to have a text or graphical appearance.

The final step of the wizard prompts the user for a descriptive name for the button (see Figure 12.16).

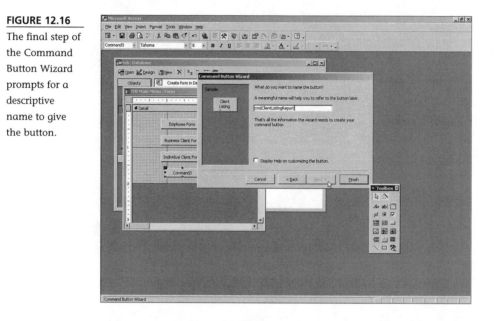

Putting it all together, Figure 12.17 shows the modified main menu form launching the ClientListing report in preview mode. Running the Command Button wizard again, it would be a very simple task to add a button that would direct the report output to the printer.

FIGURE 12.17
The Main Menu form now has the added capability of launching the ClientListing Report in Print Preview mode.

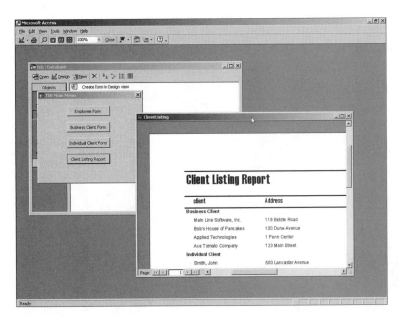

What You Have Learned

Creating reports, like forms, is a simple task in Access. With the wizards, you don't need to know how to write program code in order to produce valuable and useful output. With this in mind, there is no question that knowing how to write program code greatly enhances your ability to create more flexible and sophisticated application components. Now that you have finished this book, exploring more of the features in Access and learning how to program in Visual Basic is the next logical step. Regardless of the next step you take, remember that it all has to start with a database. Good luck!

THE STRUCTURE OF THE TEB DATABASE

Case

Field Name	Data Type	Description
Caseid	AutoNumber	Primary Key
DocketNumber	Text	Court-assigned Docket #
Notes	Memo	Freeform note field
StartDate	Date/Time	Date when work begins
TrialDate	Date/Time	Assigned Trial Date
SettlementDate	Date/Time	Date case settled
DepartmentID	Number	Department Table Foreign Key
CourtID	Number	Court Table Foreign Key
JudgeID	Number	Judge Table Foreign Key

Client

Field Name	Data Type	Description
ClientID	AutoNumber	Primary Key
ClientType	Text	Client Type (B or I)
FirstName	Text	First Name (If ClientType = I)
LastName	Text	Last Name (If ClientType = I)
MiddleInitial	Text	MI (If ClientType = I)
OrganizationName	Text	Org Name (If ClientType = B)
Address1	Text	Address Line 1
Address2	Text	Address Line 2
City	Text	City
State	Text	State
ZipCode	Text	Zip Code
Phone	Text	Phone Number
Email	Text	Email Address

ClientCase

Field Name	Data Type	Description
ClientCaseID	AutoNumber	Primary Key
ClientID	Number	Client Table Foreign Key
CaseID	Number	Case Table Foreign Key

Contact

Field Name	Data Type	Description
ContactID	AutoNumber	Primary Key
FirstName	Text	First Name
MiddleInitial	Text	Middle Initial
LastName	Text	Last Name
Title	Text	Job Title
Phone	Text	Phone Number
Extension	Text	Extension
Email	Text	Email Address
ClientID	Number	Client Table Foreign Key

Court

Field Name	Data Type	Description
CourtID	AutoNumber	Primary Key
Description	Text	Court Name

Department

Field Name	Data Type	Description
DepartmentID	AutoNumber	Primary Key
Description	Text	Department Name

Employee

Field Name	Data Type	Description
EmployeeID	AutoNumber	Primary Key
FirstName	Text	First Name
MiddleInitial	Text	Middle Initial
LastName	Text	Last Name
SocialSecurity	Text	Social Security #
Address1	Text	Address Line 1
Address2	Text	Address Line 2

Field Name	Data Type	Description
City	Text	City
State	Text	State
ZipCode	Text	Zip Code
HomePhone	Text	Home Phone #
WorkExtension	Text	Work Phone Extension
Email	Text	Email Address
DepartmentID	Number	Department Table Foreign Key
EmployeeClassID	Number	EmployeeClass Table FK

EmployeeCase

Field Name	Data Type	Description
EmployeeCaseID	AutoNumber	Primary Key
CaseID	Number	Case Table Foreign Key
EmployeeID	Number	Employee Table Foreign Key

EmployeeClass

Field Name	Data Type	Description
EmployeeClassID	AutoNumber	Primary Key
Description	Text	Employee Class Name
DefaultRate	Currency	Default Rate

Invoice

Field Name	Data Type	Description
InvoiceID	AutoNumber	Primary Key
InvoiceNumber	Text	Invoice #
InvoiceDate	Date/Time	Invoice Date
ClientID	Number	Client Table Foreign Key

Judge

Field Name	Data Type	Description
JudgeID	AutoNumber	Primary Key
FirstName	Text	First Name
MiddleInitial	Text	Middle Initial
LastName	Text	Last Name
Notes	Memo	User-defined notes
CourtID	Number	Court Table Foreign Key

TimeEntryDetail

Field Name	Data Type	Description
TimeEntryDetailID	AutoNumber	Primary Key
Description	Text	Work Description
Hours	Number	Hours Worked
Rate	Currency	Hourly Rate
WorkDate	Date/Time	Date of Work
WorkCategory	Number	Work Category Table FK
InvoiceID	Number	Invoice Table Foreign Key
CaseID	Number	Case Table Foreign Key
EmployeeID	Number	Employee Table Foreign Key
ClientID	Number	Client Table Foreign Key

WorkCategory

Field Name	Data Type	Description
WorkCategoryID	AutoNumber	Primary Key
Description	Text	Work Category Description
DefaultRate	Currency	Default Hourly Rate

TEB REFERENTIAL
INTEGRITY RULES

All relationships implement restricted deletes and restricted inserts. Restricted updates are not applicable because surrogate primary keys are used. The following sections outline each parent table and their respective related child tables.

Case (PK: `caseid`)

Employee: many to many (using EmployeeCase link table)

Client: many to many (using the ClientCase link table)

TimeEntryDetail: one to many

Client (PK: `clientid`)

ClientCase: one to many (facilitates Case many-to-many relation)

Contact: one to many

Invoice: one to many

TimeEntryDetail: one to many

Court (PK: `CourtID`)

Case: one to many

Judge: one to many

Department (PK: `departmentid`)

Case: one to many

Employee: one to many

Employee (PK: `employeeid`)

EmployeeCase: one to many (facilitates Case many-to-many relation)

TimeEntryDetail: one to many

EmployeeClass

Employee: one to many

Invoice (PK: `InvoiceID`)

TimeEntryDetail: one to many

GLOSSARY

Aggregate Function

SQL aggregate functions such as `Count()`, `Sum()`, `Avg()`, `Min()`, and `Max()` provide the capability to summarize data when performing a query.

Alias

An alias is a name variation of a table in a SQL query. For example, the following query uses an alias name of `c` in place of the actual name of the customers table:

```
SELECT C.CompanyName, *
    FROM Customers c;
```

Attribute

- A field/column of a table.
- A property of a field such as a caption, data type, size, and so forth.

Boyce-Codd Normal Form (BCNF)

BCNF is an extension of the Third Normal Form. A table is in the Boyce-Codd Normal Form when the dependency of each data item in a table can be traced to a candidate key. To illustrate, consider the following structure: Student, Advisor, and Major. Advisor depends on the major but the advisor is not a key. To get into the BCNF, the structure would need to be split into the following two structures: Student, Advisor and Advisor, Major.

Candidate Key

A field or a group of fields that can uniquely identify a record.

Child

The target of a relation. For example, in a relation between orders and order line items, order line items is the child because it is the target of a relation with the orders table.

Compound Key

A type of primary key that is composed of two or more fields in a table.

Conceptual Database Design

A logical database model that is independent of a specific database implementation.

Concurrency

Simultaneous access to the same data element by different users.

Contention

Resource contention occurs when two or more users try to update the same data element at the same time.

Data

The facts contained in a database. Data elements in a database can be extracted, grouped, and summarized to produce information.

Data Definition Language (DDL)

A DDL sublanguage enables users to create, modify, and delete various database elements including tables, columns, and views.

Data Dictionary

The data that describes the data structures in a database; also referred to as *metadata*—data that describes data. For example, the data type and size are metadata that describe a specific field of data. The collection of these attributes comprises the data dictionary of a database.

Data Independence

A separation between the way data is stored and the way data is accessed and manipulated.

Data Manipulation (DML)

A DML sublanguage enables users to create, update, delete, and query data elements in a database.

Database

A collection of data managed and organized by a database management system.

Database Administrator (DBA)

A DBA is responsible for managing and organizing a Database Management System (DBMS).

Database Design

The process of identifying real-world entities and relationships and translating those items into a database model.

Database Management System (DBMS)

Software that is capable of defining and managing databases. Popular DBMSs include SQL Server, Oracle, and DB2.

Deadlock

A scenario when two or more processes are not able to continue because the same resource is required. Also known as a *deadly embrace*.

Denormalization

The reverse process of normalization.

Domain

The set of all possible values a data item can contain. For example, a field representing a day of the month would have a domain range of 1 to 31.

Domain Restriction

Constraints placed on a data element to ensure only those values in the domain range can be stored. Also known as *column/field validation rules*.

Entity

A database object that is capable of storing data; also known as a *table*. A database object that stores data about a person, place, thing, or concept that is organized into rows (records) and columns (fields); also known as a *table*.

Entity Relationship Diagram (ERD)

A specific diagramming technique that is used to illustrate a relational database design.

Field

Fields, also known as columns, are the building blocks of a table. For example, a typical customer table would be composed of first name, last name, city, state, and ZIP Code fields. A field (also known as an *attribute*) is a column of a table and stores an atomic descriptive element about an entity.

Fifth Normal Form (5NF)

The fifth normal form isolates semantically related multiple relationships. Very rarely used.

First Normal Form (1NF)

The first normal form involves the removal of repeating groups.

Foreign Key

A key stored in another table for the purpose of supporting a relationship. For example, the primary key or the orders table is carried as a foreign key in the order line items table.

Fourth Normal Form (4NF)

The fourth normal form isolates independent multiple relationships. Very rarely used.

Hierarchical Database Model

A database model in which data is stored in a hierarchy. To access data, you must start at the top of the hierarchy and drill down to the desired data element. XML is an example of hierarchical data storage.

Index

A database element that is used to optimize a specific way of accessing data. For example, if you need to access customer data based on the city, you would build an index based on the city field.

Join

A SQL operation that combines data from two tables into a single resultset. A join combines only two tables; a query requiring the combination of more than two tables uses multiple joins (each combining two tables).

Key

A field used to access a specific record. Specific types of keys include primary and candidate.

Link Table

An intermediary table that is used to support a many-to-many relationship.

Lock

A control device that is used to provide exclusive access to a particular resource, usually a record.

Logical Record Ordering

An ordering of records based on a specific index.

Many-to-Many Relationship

A relationship between two tables when multiple records in one table can be related to multiple records in the other tables. To facilitate a many-to-many relationship, an intermediary linking table must be used.

Metadata

Data that describes data. Data contained within a Data Dictionary is often referred to as metadata that describes the structure of a database.

Normalization

The process of organizing a database in a manner that eliminates redundant data.

Null Value

Indicates the situation when a user has not assigned a value to a data element. Null is distinct from 0 or an empty string. For example, if a customer record contains a null value for the state field, it means the value for state has yet to be determined. Think of null as the value of "I don't know."

One-to-Many Relationship

A relationship between two tables in which one record from the parent table is related to many records in the child table. For example, a single customer record (parent) can be related to multiple order records (child).

Parent

The source of a relation. For example, in a relation between orders and order line items, the order table is the parent because it is the source of a relation with the orders line items table.

Physical Database Design

The result of implementing the conceptual database design in a particular database management system.

Physical Record Order

The order of records as they are physically stored on disk.

Primary Key

A field or combination of fields that uniquely identifies a row of data. There are two types of primary keys: surrogate and simple.

Query

The process of gathering data from a database based on command syntax the database management system can understand. The most common way of querying data is via the SQL Select command.

Record

A group of fields that are contained within the same table. Records are also referred to as *rows* and *tuples*. A row within a table, a record includes all the fields for a particular instance of an entity.

Redundant Data

Data that is stored in more than one place in a database. The goal of normalization is to remove redundant data.

Referential Integrity

Constraints that enforce relations between tables. For example, in the case of customers and orders, a user would be prevented from deleting a customer record if related order records exist. Further, a user would be prevented from creating an order record for a nonexistent parent.

Relational Database Model

A database model that is composed of two-dimensional tables that are related to each other. Dr. E. F. Codd developed the relational model in 1970.

Repeating Data

A field value that appears multiple times in a table. For example, a customer type description could appear multiple times. The normalization process would move a single instance of each description to a separate table to eliminate the repeating data and associated redundancy.

Row

A group of fields that are contained within the same table. Rows are also referred to as *records* and *tuples*.

Second Normal Form (2NF)

The second normal form isolates and moves redundant data to a separate table.

Self-Join

A join where a table is joined to itself. A common example is a supervisor:employee relationship. All supervisors are employees. Each employee has a SupervisorID field that references another EmployeeID field.

Structured Query Language (SQL)

SQL is a database independent language that is used to query, update, delete, and modify data.

Surrogate Key

A surrogate key is field that is created for the purpose of uniquely identifying a row of data. Typically, a surrogate key is an auto-incrementing integer data type. The alternative type of primary key (PK) is a compound key, one that is made up of two or more fields. The alternative to a surrogate key is a natural key (one that has meaning other than being the PK). Natural keys are not necessarily compound as in customer number, invoice number, or order number, all of which are natural keys and are simple single-field keys.

Table

A table is a representation of an entity and is composed of rows and columns of data.

Third Normal Form (3NF)

The third normal form ensures that fields in a row are dependent on the primary key.

Transaction

A set of operations that must either entirely succeed or fail. For example, an operation that adds a new customer and a new order must entirely succeed or fail. An integrity violation would occur if the customer were added without the order and/or the order were added without the customer.

Tuple

A group of fields that are contained within the same table. Tuples are also referred to as *rows* and *records*.

Union

A SQL operation that joins two SQL Select statements to produce a single resultset.

View

A database object that represents a collection of data from one or more tables. Also known as a *query*.

Wildcard

A wildcard operator allows the user to match data based on a pattern. For example, comparing a customer name to A* would fetch all customer records that have a name beginning with the letter A.

DATABASE-ORIENTED PERIODICALS

D

The following are popular and informative magazines that either focus on database development or address database development:

- SQL Server Magazine (www.sqlmag.com)
- Oracle Magazine (www.oramag.com)
- DB2 Magazine (www.db2mag.com)
- Sybase Magazine (www.sybase.com/inc/sybmag)
- Access/VB/SQL Advisor (www.advisor.com/AccessVBSQLAdvisor)
- Visual Studio Magazine (www.devx.com)
- Intelligent Enterprise (www.intelligententerprise.com)
- DM Review (www.dmreview.com)
- Inside Microsoft Access (www.elementkjournals.com)
- Smart Access (www.pinpub.com/access)
- Database Administrator Newsletter (www.tdan.com)
- Database Trends (www.databasetrends.com)

WEB-BASED
RESOURCES

The following are popular and informative Web sites that either focus on database development or address database development:

- www.sqlservercentral.com—A community of SQL Server Developers and DBAs.

- www.devx.com—Devx is an informative application development Web site from Fawcette Publications.

- www.msdn.microsoft.com—The online version of the Microsoft Developer Network provides access to the support knowledge base.

- www.msdn.microsoft.com/newsgroups—Access to online newsgroups for peer-to-peer support.

- www.sqlmag.com—Online counterpart to SQL Server Magazine.

- www.microsoft.com/office/access/—Microsoft Access Web site.

- www.microsoft.com/sql—Microsoft SQL Server Web site.

- www.databaseanswers.com—A nice general information site on database analysis, design, and best practices.

Index

C

X–Z

Hey, you've got enough worries.

Don't let IT training be one of them.

Get on the fast track to IT training at InformIT,
your total Information Technology training network.

 | **www.informit.com** |

■ Hundreds of timely articles on dozens of topics ■ Discounts on IT books from all our publishing partners, including Que Publishing ■ Free, unabridged books from the InformIT Free Library ■ "Expert Q&A"—our live, online chat with IT experts ■ Faster, easier certification and training from our Web- or classroom-based training programs ■ Current IT news ■ Software downloads ■ Career-enhancing resources

Special Edition Using

The One Source for Comprehensive Solutions™

The one-stop shop for serious users, *Special Edition Using* offers readers a thorough understanding of software and technologies. Intermediate to advanced users get detailed coverage that is clearly presented and to the point.

Special Edition Using Microsoft Office XP
Ed Bott and Woody Leonhard
0-7897-2513-4
$39.99 US

Other Special Edition Using Titles

Special Edition Using the Internet and the Web
Michael Miller
0-7897-2613-0
$29.99 US

Special Edition Using Oracle 11i
Boss Corporation
0-7897-2670-x
$75.00 US

Special Edition Using XML Schemas
David Gulbransen
0-7897-2607-6
$39.99 US

Special Edition Using Visual Basic.NET
Brian Siler and Jeff Spotts
0-7897-2572-x
$39.99 US

Special Edition Using Microsoft Windows XP Professional
Bob Cowart
0-7897-2628-9
$49.99 US

Special Edition Using Enterprise JavaBeans 2.0
Chuck Cavaness and Brian Keeton
0-7897-2567-3
$39.99 US

Special Edition Using MS-DOS 6.22, Third Edition
Jim Cooper
0-7897-2573-8
$49.99 US

Special Edition Using Microsoft Access 2002
Roger Jennings
0-7897-2510-x
$49.99 US

Other Related Titles

Visit our Web site at
www.quepublishing.com

- New releases

- Links to deep discounts

- Full catalog of hot computer books

- Source code

- Author links and Web sites

- Customer support